Ilse Weber with a lute, 1928

DANCING
on a
POWDER KEG

ILSE WEBER

Translated from the German, and Foreword,
by Michal Schwartz

Afterword by Ulrike Migdal
Essay on Theresienstadt by Ruth Bondy

Dancing on a Powder Keg, letters and poems by Ilse Herlinger Weber (1903–44), translated from the German by Michal Schwartz, with Afterword by Ulrike Migdal, and Theresienstadt essay by Ruth Bondy

2016 © Bunim & Bannigan Ltd, Yad Vashem, Michal Schwartz
Translation and Foreword © 2016 Michal Schwartz
© 2008 Carl Hanser Verlag München
Afterword © 2008 Ulrike Migdal

Published by: Bunim & Bannigan Ltd.
P.O. Box 636, Charlottetown, PE, C1A 7L3 Canada
Yad Vashem, P.O.B. 3477, Jerusalem 9103401 Israel

With exception of Foreword by Michal Schwartz, essay by Ruth Bondy, and additional footnotes by Michal Schwartz, this book was originally published in German, as *Wann wohl das Leid ein Ende hat. Briefe und Gedichte aus Theresienstadt Herausgegeben Von Ulrike Migdal*, in 2008 by Carl Hanser Verlag GmbH & Co.KG, Kolbergerstrasse 22, 81679 München, Germany. This English translation is published by arrangement with them.

Printed in Canada

Design by Jean Carbain

Library of Congress Control Number 201693788

ISBN 978-1-933480-39-8
1-933480-39-4
1. Holocaust, Czechoslovakia 1933-1944, social life outside and inside ghetto

www.bunimandbannigan.com

www.yadvashem.org

In memory of Tomáš Weber, 1934-1944

CONTENTS

Table of Contents   vii

Foreword by Michal Schwartz:
Ilse Weber and Her Cultural Milieu   xi

Acknowledgements and Translator's Note   xxiii

The Letters, 1933-1944   1

The World of Theresienstadt by Ruth Bondy   175

The Poems from Theresienstadt, 1942-1944   181

Afterword by Ulrike Migdal: Against Forgetting   263

The Drawings   313

My dear son, it is three years today
since you traveled, all alone, far away.
I can still see you in the Prague station, on that train,
in the compartment, shy and tear-stained,
your curly-haired head leaning toward me,
how you begged, "Let me stay with you, Mommy."
That we sent you away seemed to you cruel,
you were eight years old, small and frail,
and as we walk home without you, each step I take
is harder, it feels as if my heart will break. . . .

The full text of "Letter to My Child" appears on pages 203-4

FOREWORD: ILSE WEBER AND HER CULTURAL MILIEU

by Michal Schwartz

On May 6, 1939, Ilse Weber, writing to her sister-in-law, Zofiah Mareni, noted, *You will probably be happy to know how do we live here now? Well, at least we're not pestered by boredom. It's like dancing on a powder keg. The air is impregnated with insane rumors, which we no longer believe.*

With the exception of this letter and a few others, Ilse's letters, starting in 1933, were to her Swedish friend Lilian von Löwenadler, in England. It is in these that we see recorded the lives of her small family during a time of increasing danger, when Europe descended from peace to the chaos of war and genocide.

Ilse Weber's letters were found accidentally in an attic in London in 1976. It was only in 1977, that Hanuš, her older son, received them. More than ten years would pass before he was able to revisit his painful childhood and read them.[1]

We shall never know how many letters Ilse wrote in those years; we only have these found in the house in which her friend Lilian once lived. These begin on February 6, 1933, when Ilse was living in Vítkovice, Moravia, continue from Prague, and end with her last letter from Theresienstadt, dated September 29, 1944. They provide vivid testimony of Jewish daily life in a Czechoslovakia increasingly corrupted by Nazi ideology.

A born writer, Ilse describes with unsparing precision the effects of the Nazi's ingenious sadism. Her at times ironic tone, with startling immediacy, painfully accompanies her relentless honesty and humanity.

The letters present a poignant record of the realities of Jewish life in Czechoslovakia in the years of persecution and extermination. Conveying personal experience, the letters complement the impersonal nature of "historical objectivity." Ilse writes to her friend Lilian about her daily struggles, intellectual milieu, fears, hopes, family life and relations with the surrounding world. This individual perspective brings history alive.

Ilse felt at home in the German language. Like many secular Jews, and as a successful writer of books and radio scripts for children, she considered herself a part of German culture. Her letters reveal a cultural life shaped by the political, literary and intellectual figures that embodied the multifaceted exchange between Jews and their surroundings.

Ilse's letters mirror the German-Jewish encounter and its contribution to German culture. When Hitler came to power, Jews formed 0.8 percent of the total German population, and 2.6 percent in Czechoslovakia. This minority produced an astounding variety of entrepreneurs, artists, writers, scholars and radical political activists. The persecution and eradication of what had been the vibrant Jewish-German confluence is a distinct element in the history of the Holocaust. The writers, newspapers and books Ilse mentions evoke events and activities, a cultural richness that the Nazis considered "racial pollution." Ironically, many Jews in the German-speaking world believed their passionate devotion and achievements would counter the Nazi threat. Up to 1933, the surging of Nazism was coupled with growing assimilation and Jewish prominence in almost every field of Weimar culture that preceded Hitler's rise.

Ilse lived and worked most of her life outside the metropolitan cultures of Berlin, Prague,[2] or Vienna; but was well versed in contemporary literature and political thought. Her list of reading includes books and magazines of liberal and left orientation that recognized the danger of fascism and criticized the situation in Germany. The names Ilse brings up lead to a net of intellectual, literary and artistic interrelations that demonstrates the extent to which

Jews were immersed in German culture. One such example is the weekly magazine *Die Weltbühne* (The World Stage). Ilse was a reader of the magazine and mentions it in an early letter, dated September 5, 1933. The story of the *Weltbühne* reflects the context of Ilse's cultural milieu.

Founded in 1905 in Berlin as a theatrical weekly, the magazine evolved into one of the Weimar Republic's most influential journals. A magazine of art, politics and economics, its orientation was humane, tolerant and left liberal. Siegfried Jacobson, its founder and a colorful pugnacious figure, was born in 1881 to a Jewish family in Berlin. In 1926, the magazine was taken over by Kurt Tucholsky, the brilliant Jewish satirist and one of the most important journalists of the Weimar Republic. A fervent opponent of nationalism, Tucholsky was a regular contributor (under seven pseudonyms). In 1933, the Nazis banned his works. He committed suicide in 1935. From June 1932, under the leadership of Carl von Ossietzky (who won the Nobel Peace Prize in 1935), the *Weltbühne* featured two adjoining columns, one reporting social progress during the former week, the other regression. The latter column was long, while the one reporting progress was often declared as annulled.[3] Banned by the Nazis in 1933, the magazine continued in exile.

The first of Ilse's letters, dated February 6, 1933, was written the week after Hitler became chancellor of Germany. In April 1933, the Deutsche Studentenschaft (German Students' Association) declared its "cultural" war on non-Aryan culture. Posters everywhere in Germany listed the ways they intended to "cleanse" German language and literature. On May 10, 1933, university students across Germany burnt books to "cleanse un-German" spirit from German culture. In Berlin, a large crowd gathered in front of the Opernplatz to chant against the banned writers, watch books thrown into the pyre and listen to Goebbels, the Reich's propaganda minister, who announced the end of "Jewish intellectualism." As the *Jüdische Rundschau* newspaper commented, the actions against un-German culture were a war declaration on Jews, "a condemnation of the idea of 'Jew' as such."[4]

Many of the writers Ilse read and mentioned in her letters were of Jewish origin and chose to go into exile. The writer Anna Seghers, for instance, established an anti-fascist club in Mexico. Her 1939 novel *The Seventh Cross*, published in the USA in 1942 and made into a movie in 1944, gave a rare depiction of Nazi concentration camps. Another writer, Alice Berend, was less fortunate. After her popular books were put on the unwanted literature list, she emigrated to Italy, where, in 1938, she died penniless and forgotten. Others, such as Hermann Kesten and Otto Zarek, left Germany in 1933 and remained active, writing and publishing works against the Nazis.

In 1933, Ilse had no illusions regarding the ominous nature of events in Germany. In a letter of September 5, 1933, she laments the murder of Theodor Lessing, a German-Jewish philosopher and one of the most famous political writers of the Weimar Republic. His 1925 visionary article on the fatal consequences of the presidency of the conservative nationalist Paul von Hindenburg, [5] had earned him the hatred of nationalists and conservatives. In March 1933 Lessing fled from Germany and settled in Marienbad in Czechoslovakia. Different Nazi-oriented newspapers announced a price on his head. On the night of August 30, he was shot by two Nazi sympathizers. The murder was carried out on order from Joseph Goebbels. [6]

Ilse's letters record the gradual process that trapped her and many others. Commenting on the Reichstag fire [7] and the show trial that ensued, Ilse wrote on October 18, 1933: *Reality is ever more interesting and more atrocious than all the inventions of poetic imagination. I spare myself any mendacious reading by listening to the German news broadcast on the radio, which I do with a certain grim pleasure.* The political situation became increasingly ominous. On June 14, 1938, Ilse wrote: *Being Jewish means being without rights, defenseless, a scapegoat for everybody. What have we here in the Republic, for which we are willing, with trembling fear, to sacrifice our lives? The German plague infects everybody and the Czechs have never loved us, just as other nations have not.*

The situation of Jews worsened. They were caught between three cultures: German, Czech, and Jewish. Ilse found it harder to define her identity. She humorously expressed her confusion in a letter of June 1936, describing her difficulty answering her little son, Hanuš' inquiry about what kind of Jews they were, German or Czech? In a letter of May 23, 1938, she chronicled with desperation the quandary of Jewish identity: *We Jews are naturally hit the hardest again. Our children are all Czech, but we adults have always spoken German between ourselves, which is our mother tongue after all. Now the Czechs declare: "How can you use this language when the Germans inflict on you so much injustice?" But on the other hand, when we make the effort to speak Czech, they scornfully say: "Look at the Jews! They know how to readily adapt!"* On October 15, 1938, German troops occupied Ilse's Vítkovice. It was located in what the Germans called the Sudetenland, a part of Czechoslovakia inhabited by over 3 million Sudeten Germans, ceded to Hitler in the infamous Munich Agreement. The Czech government resigned. On March 15, 1939, the Nazis took the rest of Czechoslovakia. With her keen sense of realism and self-observation Ilse painfully admitted her reluctance to accept her predicament: *I simply can't grasp that I have to leave everything I love. I have never done anything wrong therefore I don't need to fear the Gestapo. On the contrary, behind all the swastikas that lavishly adorn many windows now, there are likely very few people who have worked as enthusiastically for German culture as I have, a Jew, who loves and respects the Czechs.* (March 24, 1939).

Ilse's cultural landscape had changed. The newspapers and magazines she read had been long banned. With the ongoing "de-Jewification," traces of Jewish history and culture had been erased from works of art, music and literature, while bold anti-Jewish movies gained popularity and rave reviews. The Nazi propaganda film *Jud Süss* for example, was presented at the Golden Lion Venice Film Festival and highly praised by no less than the director Michelangelo Antonioni.[8]

The only German newspaper Ilse now mentioned was the *Die Stürmer* (The Attacker), an antisemitic weekly Nazi tabloid. To her son Hanuš, whom the Webers sent from Prague with the Winton Kindertransport to England in the spring of 1939, she sends the

Czech children's magazine the *Mladý hlasatel* (Young Announcer).
It, too, will be banned by the Nazis in 1941. In occupied Czechoslovakia she no longer possessed the peace of mind for reading, let
alone writing books. She mentioned literature only when visiting
the grave of the Czech poet Božena Němcová. But Ilse could not
escape her mother tongue. German was the language in which she
expressed herself best in her letters to her son and her friend Lilian.
She was caught between her hatred for the Nazis and their regime
and love for German language and literature, as were so many other
Jewish writers and poets. For Ilse and the other Jews who identified so strongly with the German language and culture, this conflict
meant a loss of identity. Nevertheless, for his third birthday away
from her, Ilse sent Hanuš a book of German folk and art songs.

In February 1942 Ilse, her husband Willi, and younger son
Tommy, were deported to Theresienstadt.[9] Ilse sent a few letters
from Theresienstadt. To meet the censor's restrictions, the letters
were short and reported how well the three of them were doing.
Ilse's true experience and emotions are recorded in the more than
sixty poems she wrote there between 1942 and 1944. Such informal
artistic creativity was illegal. Just before deportation to Auschwitz in
1944, Ilse's husband, Willi, presciently hid the poems in the garden
shed to which he had access as a ghetto gardener. He retrieved them
after the war. They remained mostly unknown until published in
Munich in 2008.[10]

Ilse's poems belong to modern concentration camp and ghetto
poems in German, which occupy a peculiar position in the literary
culture of that period. Yet, as Andrés Nader points out in his recent
study, this poetry has been largely ignored by historians of literature
as well as by critics and Holocaust studies scholars.[11] Only recently
has this poetry gained a larger public.[12] As a matter of fact, in the
years following the Holocaust, the very possibility of representing
the concentration camp and ghetto in literature and especially poetry, was debated by historians and philosophers. Assembling camp
and ghetto horrors into any aesthetic form was suspected by some as
an act of sacrilege that might trivialize the unspeakable.[13]

Poets, who survived the ghettos, concentration camps and Nazi persecution, struggled with the prospect of creating a form to represent the universe of the concentration camp, of overcoming the difficulties of finding language that would convey the extent of catastrophe and distortions of human experience. The dissidence between representing such experience and the necessity to give it a voice haunts the works of Nelly Sachs, Dan Pagis, Paul Celan and others.

In contrast, Ilse found refuge and consolation in language. Camp poetry and literature were not avant-garde aesthetic experiments, but acts of resistance. For Ilse, writing and citing poetry provided a pragmatic, albeit illegal and dangerous, means of coping with and bearing witness to the universe of the Nazi concentration camp and ghetto.

The National Socialist concentration camp and ghetto epitomized Nazi terror and persecution. It was a place of abuse and de-humanization, a singularity where moral and ethical norms approached meaninglessness. Writing poetry in the language of her tormentors was a way of insisting on her own origin and culture. Ilse's poetry directly confronts Nazi efforts to erase Jewry from German culture. She mastered German no less, in fact more, than many "Aryans," and her literary success was not confined to the Jewish world. Her references to traditional German children's rhymes and tales, as in her "Theresienstadt Nursery Rhyme" or "The Magdeburg Barracks," are a statement of her owning the German language and culture, of her resistance against the Nazi corruption of this language[14]. At the same time, Ilse transformed these traditional poetic forms and themes into a macabre rendering of her experience, thereby using the culture of the perpetrators to describe the suffering of their victims. Ilse's cultural references helped her retain continuity with the past while responding to the rupture with its values.

Ilse's play with words and rhymes stands in sharp contrast to the poems' depressing content. This discrepancy creates a tension that corresponds to the ghetto's daily friction between the normal and the extreme. The "scandalous" use of rhyme and meter that often reminds one of nursery rhymes or cabaret songs, employs familiar forms to represent radical situations, conveying brutal truths with painful clarity. Thus a rhythmic nursery rhyme[15] renders the macabre routine of children harnessed to the dead wagon:

> *Rira, riraearse,*
> we're riding in the hearse,
> *rira, riraearse*
> we're riding in the hearse.
> We stand there, we stand here,
> riding fast, cold corpses near,
> *riraearse*
> we're riding in the hearse
>   from "Theresienstadt Nursery Rhyme"

The incongruity between playful form and agonizing content echoes the paradoxes inherent in the camp and ghetto's life, where elementary forms of human activity gain new meaning in extremity; where helping the weak, taken for granted in normal times, is an exception that verges on the heroic, and where children playing with corpses is an everyday sight.

The Nazi concentration camp or ghetto was a universe ruled by malice and chance. Any act of salvation was unexpected and human encounter was difficult to make sense of.[16] The fundamental paradox of this inverted world was the life-in-death reality. Jean Améry, who survived Auschwitz and Buchenwald, wrote that one had to preserve the principle of life through accepting death. Whoever wanted to survive had to renounce the illusion of survival, had to be prepared to perish.[17] In this illogical reality, rhyme and rhythm might have offered a sense of order, momentarily transcending the chaos. The very process of writing rhymes may have provided an otherwise impossible but needed therapeutic escape from one's immediate surroundings. Ilse professed in some poems how citing or writing poetry provided a form of coping with the camp's radical situations:[18]

Ah, we may be tortured,
threatened with Polandtransport,
but our starving souls are nurtured
with a poet's eternal words.
              from "Barren of Earthly Possessions"

Ilse's poems record the co-existence of the everyday and the extreme without seeking any unifying, redemptive meaning. Her observations are sharp and unrelenting, whether she describes common feelings such as longing for home, greedy survival, or extreme situations as betrayal or acts of defiance. She is as painfully ruthless in criticizing her own behavior, as she is in evaluating others.

Writing, composing and singing with her illegal guitar was Ilse's way of cheering the children she attended at the sick bay, her way of trying to comfort while participating in the legal official cultural activities in Theresienstadt. Her musical activity, as recounted in "Musica Prohibita," was a life-threatening engagement. Indeed, such writing was an act of political defiance and in some cases dangerously so, as when she referred to current events in "The Sheep from Lidice," obliquely referring to the ruthless retaliation for the assassination in 1942 of Reinhard Heydrich, head of the RSHA (Reich Main Security Office), in charge of implementing the "Final Solution" in all German occupied territories. (In July 1941, as reward for his actions against Jews, he was appointed "Reich Protector of Bohemia and Moravia."[19])

Jean Améry noted that the camp was the realization of Sartre's all too famous dictum "Hell, that is the others."[20] Ilse's poems capture this predicament. Depicting young and old inmates' reactions to loneliness and suffering, the poems record cruelty and grief from different perspectives. At times ridiculing and criticizing, at times consoling and encouraging, the poems almost always, in one way or another, insist on compassion. This is mostly manifested in poems such as "Died During Transport," that addresses a nameless corpse, or "A Satchel Speaks," narrated from the perspective of a deserted suitcase. Both are grounded in Ilse's sense of responsibility for the weak and voiceless. She called for kindness and love while acknowledging the basic loneliness of the human predicament:

> Can any friendship reach that far?
> Unconditional love from a friend?
> You might like to give your all,
> but you cannot expect
> love to be reciprocated.
>   from "This Already Happened"

Ilse and her younger son Tommy were gassed in Auschwitz in 1944.

MICHAL SCHWARTZ studied in Frankfurt and Jerusalem literature and philosophy, received her PhD in German-Jewish philosophy from the Hebrew University Jerusalem and completed a Master of Studies in Law at the University of Toronto. She held research positions and lectured in Jerusalem, Bonn and Toronto, and translated and published essays in English and German. Her book, *Metapher und Offenbarung. Zur Sparche von Franz Rosenzweigs Stern der Erlösung*, was published in Berlin, 2003.

ACKNOWLEDGMENTS

Thanks to David Helwig and Elizabeth Denison for advice on rendering Ilse's poems into English, to Ann Winslow for her editorial acumen, to Ruth and Hans Fisher whose resurrection of their favorite childhood book, *Mendel Rosenbusch,* and their identification of its author, Ilse Herlinger, led us to Hanuš Weber, and to his mother's letters and poems; to Ulrike Migdal, editor of the Hanser edition, whose knowledge proved invaluable; to the editorial team at Yad Vashem: Ella Florsheim, Yasmine Garval, Ayala Peretz, Idit Zaken, Enno Raschke; and to Gideon Biger of Tel Aviv University, who recognized Ilse Weber's uniqueness. Special thanks to Dina Porat, Chief Historian of Yad Vashem, for her support.

TRANSLATOR'S NOTE

Translation follows Ilse Weber's inconsistencies: for instance, the two renderings of her home town: Vítkovice (Czech) and Witkowitz (German); and variations in date notations as well as of some individuals' names and her uses of italics. Footnotes are by Ulrike Migdal. Those added by translator are marked MS.

Ilse (right with dog) with Lilian and Willi

THE LETTERS, 1933-44

Witkowitz, February 6, 1933

Dearest Lilian!

I had to take a break again. Hannerle caught a cold; Willi and I joined him. Then we wanted to travel to Ostrawitz,[1] and you do know how reluctant one is to write before travelling. One thinks: well, once there, I will have *so* much time for writing! (Then one doesn't do it after all!)

But we didn't go because our plans literally turned into water. It rains and rains and the flu germs are having orgies. And if I must be sitting in a room, then better without having to pay a lot of money, and with a proper WC.

I'm glad that you finally feel better again. The good advice that I have for you I leave in storage, since anyway you do what *you* want. But I hope, for my own sake, it will be the right thing!

While I'm writing, our Herr son occupies himself in his own way. Rummaging through the bookcases, he appears to have inherited the burden of my love of books. He's taking the cover off my typewriter, going "on tip-toes." And now he's standing next to me asking, "Mutti what *else* have you got for Hannele?" lkmj[2] *That's* his greeting to you. He's so funny, the little guy. And fresh! Not long ago, when he was visiting us in bed, he told Willi, "Vatti, you're *such* a rascal!" He doesn't know yet that he's not allowed to repeat everything one says. Now he's getting the small room furnished, which isn't at all so simple considering the tininess of the space. But I want to solve the problem as follows:

I replaced the hanging lamp with an inherited ceiling light, had
the whole room painted in bright yellow, hung airy white cur-
tains on the windows. The small bed goes against the one wall,
on the other the closet that was reshaped for him, under the free
window a small folding table. Finished, that'll do. More doesn't
fit in. After all, he plays the whole day on his mattress in the
kitchen.

He was torturing me now for so long that in order to have
some peace I sat him by the piano. There he's now plunking away.
He always asks me to tell him what he's "playing." "Mutti, what is
that then?" and woe is me if I don't guess right!

Do you know his repertoire covers almost 25 songs? He recog-
nizes them without fail, regardless whether one plays, sings or whis-
tles. I cannot claim though that he himself sings them quite in tune.

Lilian, I have to tell you something anyway, and not indirectly
but straight out. I don't want to "annoy" you and also won't. Please
do not alienate yourself completely from your mother.[3] To prevent
false assumptions; *I'm* not in touch with her. But there must be a
way through all the misunderstandings and inhibitions, to heal the
rift between mother and child.

I do not say: try to gain her trust, her understanding. Perhaps
there is really an unbridgeable gulf between you. But you must
hold on to that spot in her heart (and you don't doubt her love for
you?) regardless of everything and everybody. You cannot expect
her to follow you into the sphere of your ideas. I do not fool myself in this regard. For years I have preached my views to Mama
and all of a sudden, when I think she's become a perfect socialist, a
small remark makes me realize that she didn't understand me at all.
But in spite of that, I love her just as before. And as much as I admire your friend Lo,[4] and really take her for the person you need,
I fear that in this respect she doesn't encourage you. She'd have to
be an angel to do that, in light of the resistance that she faces. Stay
therefore in touch with Mutti from a distance for the time being
so that she nonetheless realizes she hasn't lost you. And pour your
heart out to me about this issue, will you Lilian?

I want now to try and still work a little and therefore am concluding. Be healthy and happy; this is today my dearest wish.

     Yours,

     Ilse

Witkowitz, May 22, 1933

Dear Lilian,

    I take your birthday greeting to Willi as a welcome occasion
to write to you, to thereby end and explain the unintentional long
break. On my last letter to you, I wrote the address Lo had given
me: Villastad,[5] Furustigen 5. I didn't write "Hässelby" because I
didn't have it. I thought your new stop is simply called "Villastad." Therefore, if you did receive a letter that carried this insufficient address, enclosing a photo taken in Ostrawitz of Hannerle
in Styrian trousers and a simple head cover, it means *your* reply
letter is lost because since then, I haven't received any post from
you. Hanni indeed got your lovely pull-along-wagon, although it
wasn't quite simple to collect. First he received a notification from
the customs he should present himself and "provide a passport
or a certificate of poverty." I packed him up and drove with him
into town, which for him meant a special pleasure, since he all too
readily rides the "seetca" (streetcar). I was happily anticipating the
baffled face of the custom officer when the little one would present
himself as the parcel's receiver; but just imagine: they were hu-
morless enough to insist on the passport or the certificate, though
this time from me. Luckily, after quite a while, during which I was
trying to clarify their demand as ridiculous, a superior came by
accidentally and shouted rather indignantly at this dutiful do-ev-
erything-by-the-book, "Nedělejte komedie!"[6] i.e. "Don't make such
a fuss!" Unfortunately, this good man left too soon. They gave me
the pull-along wagon free of charge, but didn't allow me to take
it. No, it came only in the afternoon mail and the delivery charges
cost a good bit of money. But Hannerle had, despite everything, an
enormous joy, apparently also when he mistook the parcel courier

for "Aunt Lilian." But you shouldn't spend unnecessary money on
the boy, who is swimming in toys. He has so many. I preach that to
all my acquaintances and friends; each understands and yet thinks
that he alone is privileged and allowed to give Hannerle a present.
Only in rare cases can I give those things to others, since I am
always being asked: "Well, does Hanni still play with the thing?"
i.e. "Does he still *have* it?" and I find it too embarrassing to say he
doesn't have it anymore. Well, *your* toy wagon is now "the Swedish pull-along wagon" and, coming from you, occupies a special
place; but Hannerle owns a delightful duck cart (the duck wobbles
its tail and head when cruising), a hen cart (without wheels, the
chicken runs on its feet), a wooden railway with spacious wagons,
two complete iron railways, a truck, an automobile (a fire engine
I nonetheless gave away), and a large menagerie of wheeled animals. I keep those toys meticulously tidy! But he is allowed and
wants to play only with one locomotive or the truck, with which
he transports his utmost favorite sand-shovel, the bucket and the
sand molds. Everything else is put aside. He is now with Mama,
playing in the sandbox. Unfortunately, he is unhealthy again. He
has a new middle-ear and light throat inflammation. The doctor
wants to remove his tonsils in fourteen days. This always wears me
out completely. In addition, Willi is not well either, and a sick man
is always impatient and grumpy. Besides, he once again terminated
our apartment contract and I don't know where we will move to,
since what I want: to live alone in Mama's vicinity, with a garden
for the child, is not easy to find. By chance there are actually two
available family houses nearby, but the one which looks really nice
and has four rooms and a big garden shows, on closer inspection,
wet stains, while the other with five rooms, is too expensive and
neglected. And I'm such an enemy of moving. I would happily stay
here, if the house owner weren't such a pig-head. He will never
again get as much as we are paying.

Would you like to do me a favor? Once more I haven't heard
anything from the Edelsteins. I'm no longer on good terms with
Felix;[7] he has been behaving strangely toward me lately. Please

write one more time to Gre;[8] she will tell you what interests me mostly. But write something completely harmless, preferably just a postcard. It is the dirtiest trick that currently transpires in Germany. I hear with my own ears the plotted fraudulent libels disseminated to the people through the radio.

I have now started something new. Ernst Immerglück[9] recently gave a concert. I cannot describe to you how wonderfully he played. The public was enraptured. It occurred to me on this occasion how musically uneducated I actually was. I thought it would really be very good for me to hear lectures with actual examples on classical and modern music, composers and their work, their characteristics and properties. Ernst is obliged to give lessons after all. In that respect there was no obstacle to fulfilling my wishes. But then I thought Willi could benefit from what *I* wanted as well, and further: why just the two of us? Why not some other serious, interested music lovers who, here in the small town, or due to pecuniary reasons, cannot accomplish something for themselves? I spoke to Ernst, who was very enthusiastic, then carefully put out my feelers and . . . today is the first evening lecture at Ernst's, called "The Joy of Music," with approximately eight to fifteen members. I have no doubt that a few will drop out, but eight, up to ten, will certainly continue, and that is enough. This, I hope, will help Ernst and create for us a nice evening every week. As you know, Ernst is very forgetful when he is playing.

There are great things awaiting my books. But unfortunately everything is so uncertain. Translations are once again planned into Czech, Hebrew and English.

Does Sweden have no need for Jewish children's tales? Ach, I need money so urgently! You know, it's not nobility when I say it's not for me. But the situation here is such that I have a guilty conscience when I compare my clean, satiated child with other children. I ease my conscience, or at least try to, by giving away whatever I don't absolutely need. There is Else Haas, surely you remember her? She was well-married to a Slovakian businessman. I heard that things have been very bad for them lately, but she is too proud and tells nothing. Just on Saturday I accidentally found out that her little boy shares a pair of shoes with her sister's little girl (one can buy a pair of children's shoes for just seven crowns!) so I told her that my little nephew, for whom I keep Hannerle's things, is too fat and can no longer wear them. Wouldn't she like to do me a favor etc. etc. She was very happy, and I too, when her little Joszi received three complete suits, shoes and socks, and even pajamas. Hannerle added a small wagon so at least one child is supplied. Else confessed to me that her husband had to give up his business and is now earning pitiful pocket money as a barker in a shooting gallery three evenings a week. Isn't this terrible? And this is just one case! If Willi also didn't have to struggle with difficulties, I would have known what I would do.

It just rang twelve o'clock. I must pick up Hannerle. Write again soon, so that we're o.k. again, all right?

Kisses, Ilse.

Witkowitz, September 5, 1933

Dearest Lilian!

My dearest Lilian! I do not keep my views to myself and am convinced that we will still very often, figuratively speaking, be at loggerheads. Or, if you prefer, I will very often offer you my opinion, which you will dismiss without pursuing it further: with disdain and the gesture of "Ach, the little one doesn't understand this after all!" Despite my all-too-often proven richness of imagination, I cannot make sense of the vague allusions that you make. I would like to know how come Herbert visited you, if there was still anything between you, if despite all the criticism, you continue to see in him "the" man in your life; and, then again, what does he otherwise do generally, and particularly, in Sweden? I promise you to no more "react fiercely."

I now actually believe you; it is impossible for you to build a harmonious relation with Mutti, and I now believe it is also Mutti's fault, or better said: she shares the blame. When I reflect

on the reasons for my good relationship with my mother, I think
that the main cause is that I am uncritical toward her. Were I to
start and regard Mama's faults as anything but loveable weak-
nesses, I'm sure discord would quickly get in the way of harmony.
But *my way is* to quickly cover each little flaw that reveals itself to
me with a vast number of new endearing virtues, for which I'm
an inexhaustible source. On the other hand, your Mutti should
have confronted you with a little of what my Mama, for example,
brings up against Ernst,[10] with whom I do not want to compare
you, God forbid. But Mama is completely aware that Ernst simply has to be as he is, and *she* is, after all, the one who has to stick
to him whatever happens. His flaws? It is her fault. Papa did not
like him very much, and she didn't try to replace this deficit of
love. Says she. And she addresses, and persuades him of his good
sides, which he has never, not even remotely, possessed. I use
this comparison merely to express one thing: that your mother
doesn't have this motherly imagination with which she would
conceal your curtness and spirit of contradiction, in my opinion
the flaws that provoke her the most. And you do not possess the
self-denial and, above all, the humble love necessary for bearing
with an unjust treatment from a beloved person. Please, refute
me if you think I'm wrong.

I find it really important to discuss this issue with you
seriously. I have no intention to claim to be a know-it-all: it is
just *so*! Look, Wilma Gross[11] is a very simple person. She was
in such awe of her mother that she never discussed intimate
matters with her. There was always an enormous distance between them. Frau Gross was a particularly reserved, unlovable
character. Nevertheless, whenever one needed the other, there
was between them wordless understanding, true love.

I have been reading a lot lately. Been shattered by Anna
Seghers' book *Die Gefährten*,[12] and deeply repelled by Hermann
Kesten's novel *Der Scharlatan*.[13] In addition, I'm reading a good
deal of *Die Weltbühne*,[14] the *Aufruf*,[15] *Neue Wahrheit*,[16] and
Vorwärts.[17] Altogether with the depressing feeling that after all

nothing helps. In Germany, an entire nation brutalizes and God allows for a *human being*, a human being, like Theodor Lessing,[18] to fall victim to such brutes. Not even two months passed since I was deeply stirred and shaken, seeing Theodor Lessing and hearing him speak. I do not like the German Jews in general. I mean, for example, the type which Männe Abraham represented. Do you recall my indignation when I met him and he mistreated me because I too belonged to "those listless Austrians?" The twit!

Curt was one of those all too "brash" Germans. But only a people that sees itself caricatured and lacks the humor to draw the right conclusion can reproach them for having become too similar to their dreamed-of German ideal in their endeavors to assimilate. I can't think of a more revolting physiognomy than Adolf Hitler's. They call this face in Austria "Watchengefries."[19]

Among other "leaders" too, you can hardly find a noble intelligent countenance.

I was absorbed in writing and lost track of time. At four o'clock, Hannerle is going for the first time to the gym. It is a quarter to four and he is still asleep. Just now he has fallen over the guardrails out of his little bed.

Many kisses!
Your Ilse

Witkowitz, October 18, 1933

Dear Lilian!

I feel uneasy knowing you are in a region I have grown to hate, but that is not your fault, and it should not be a new reason for us not to hear from each other for a longer time. Hopefully you do not have to stay away for too long from your much nicer homeland! Regarding the Herbert affair, I am now reassured. As concerns Erich, I like him so much that I have no objection against a friendship with him, should you ask about it, which in fact I do not expect. I look forward to receiving your description of your stay in Hamburg. You have to tell me about all the people I know, all right? The Barthels couple, Walmi and family, and last but not least, Herr von Zwehl, are surely among those few who did not find the changes unpleasant. Right? Did you see Curt and your mother-in-law?[20] I suspect that *Glückliche Menschen* and *Der Scharlatan*[21] are the same. But the book made me sick. How come you're lying in bed with a stomach ache after such good reading as Balzac, France, and L'Isle d'Adam?[22] Perhaps you might find Courths-Mahler[23] a more digestible recommendation?

I read recently the *Braunbuch*.[24] Do you know it? Reality is ever more interesting and more atrocious than all the inventions of poetic imagination. I spare myself any mendacious reading by listening to the German news broadcast on the radio, which I do with a certain grim pleasure. Excuse me if I maybe unsuspectingly touched a sensitive spot, since I completely forget that you may have different leanings than I do.

I can hardly continue to write further because Hannerle noticed I'm writing and came right away with his little wooden cow, which he's pushing persistently against the rubber platen: "Mutti, the little cow really wants to ride the machine just once!" The boy is now so sweet I could eat him up, although he has recently lost quite a lot of his angelic charm. An idiotic hairdresser cut away his pretty curls by mistake, so he is no longer an angel on the outside either. Since Bobby Fuchs has a brother, he also wants one, or a little sister called "Lillan." (Someone who knew about our agreement put this into his head). But I do not think that I would still choose the name Lilian. I like it very much, just as before, but it has been too misused lately. There is an extensive search for names here because nowadays it is no longer trivial how one is named. Friedl's[25] little one, who is very sweet, is called Susel. A boy would have been called Michael. Whatever boy or girl names, they mustn't be Aryan, do you like? Gretel Schott, remember her still? asked my advice. She will soon need some.

In order to make this letter richer in content, I will enclose with it, provided the picture will be finished today, a photo of

Hannerle. Liese Tittor[26] snapped him wearing his first sailor suit inherited from Peter Freud.

Write again real soon.

Yours,[27] Ilse

Witkowitz, March 12, 1934

Dearest Lilian!

It is unbelievable how dependent one is on inert objects: because my typewriter is on strike, I cannot bring myself to write. Then I postponed responding to your last letter and now I don't know any more to what exactly I should answer. Hanni is just reminding me that I promised to allow him "diclale" a letter to you. Therefore:

Deal Aunt Lilian! I thank you vely much for the "pushe" (he doesn't have "r") Aunt Milli from Luthi (Ruth, Milli's[28] baby daughter) also gave me a pushe. It is even bigger, but has no flowels (embellishments). I will give youl pushe to Tommy, all right? Tommy still has no teeth at all. Uncle Karl took Tommy fom me, but I scleamed soo, that he left him with us.

Lots of kissi

Hans Lafael

So, and now he went to Uncle Ernst to shovel sand, and I proceed to explain his "letter" to you in more detail. You'll want to know to which "Tommy" he wants to give your pusher, and on top of that, with my permission. Allow me to introduce you to him: Thomas Weber, born on March 2, 1934 , weighs 3.60 kg, 50 cm long. It should surprise you; I and everybody else were expecting a little girl who should have been called "Lilian Madlen." For Hannerle, she had lived already half a year before. He had put aside everything for the baby sister and had been insanely happy. I howled a lot when they told me, "Jo to kluk!" (It is a boy!), and for several hours kept on looking at the child with dislike only. We had no name for him but it happened to be our president's birthday,[29] and so he received the name Thomas.

Naturally we now love the little one just as the big one. Allegedly he looks like me, which I am unable to take as a compliment. He is ugly like all small children, with a fine lugubrious wrinkled forehead, flat wide little nose and thin dark hair (that, by the way, already starts to fall out and leaves room for a little cover of blond fur). Only his mouth is sweet.

When after ten days I returned from the hospital, the day before yesterday, I could not sort Hannerle out. The boy, you know, is so beautiful; please believe me, I am now objective! He has something so distinguished about him that he does not seem to belong to us at all. He has quite delightful dark blond curls, a high domed forehead, shining dark eyes, a fine little nose, and a mouth that looks especially pretty because the upper lip lets the two upper middle teeth show. He is very clever and highly musical. Sometimes he talks too much; his tongue is loosened like a waterfall. When he was carefully told that a boy had arrived instead of a "girlie," he said bitterly, "When I grow up, I will write God a letter to exchange this child." But in the meantime he has given in to the inevitable.

So now you know about the big change in our house and will indeed forgive me when I conclude for today. Willi sends kind regards. A kiss from me!

    Your Ilse

Witkowitz, August 20, 1934

Dearest Lilian!

    Willi has, do not be horrified at this babbittry! his bowling night and I have been relieved of my regular evening walk. So I can finally once again chat with you, because I have less and less time for myself. Tommi, Hannerle, Willi, the household, the sewing machine and the mending basket are all merciless masters of my time, which I cannot escape even with the greatest resourcefulness. In addition, there's severe rheumatism in my right hand that gives me a lot of trouble: I'm a pitiful human being!

Things must be merry for you if you have guests! How many or how few rooms then does your house have, that you and Mauri

have to sleep in tents? Dear God, for how long I haven't had
guests! But I am not an enticing hostess with my two bambinos.
Hannerl stayed for four weeks in Ostrawitz with Frau Sendler
whom Hannerl, and also we, call just "Nana." Then he became
very sick and I had to bring him home with the doctor by car. The
one kilo he scarcely gained was gone and a second one with it. The
boy is alarmingly delicate. He is gradually thawing again, but has
become so shy and sensitive that it hurts me to look at him. Music
remains his favorite, as well as his model train. He plays best on
his own. Sometimes he becomes boisterous and fresh. He asked
me yesterday, "Mutti, do you know where there are many Russians
(he says Lussians)?" And in response to my nodding: "In Lussia!"
Witty, isn't it? But he says it so mischievously, with such obvious
satisfaction for having hoaxed me, that Willi cracked up. One has
to be so careful with the boy. When Tommy gets a kiss, one must
not forget to give Hannerl one too. All the same, one isn't anymore
as affectionate with such a big boy as with a baby. Especially when
the big boy is sometimes terribly annoying.

Hannerl is definitely jealous, though he also loves his little
brother. Tommy is a perfectly lovable baby. Rosy, plump, always
glowing with cheerfulness (touch wood!!!), he lies in his baby
carriage and whoever throws a glance at him must simply remain
standing. Everybody is proud that the little guy "always smiles at
them"; he is indiscriminately friendly at that. Now he is already
sitting a little, even though still unsteadily, and when I look at him
like that with his proud face (proud that he is sitting), the bright
eyes and the ears that stick out, I could smother him with affection. Allegedly he looks just like me.

Do you still remember my sister-in-law, Erna? That's the blond
with the dark eyes. Her husband died recently, most unexpectedly.
She has one boy who is just about to go to school. It is so sad.

Should I continue to send you magazines? Which ones do you
like? We are reading regularly the *AIZ*,[30] *Simplizius*[31] and the *Aufruf*.
Willi says he definitely wrote "via Gdingen" on the last parcel. I
find it wonderful that Sweden is the first country to introduce

pacifism as a school subject. Every decent human being is dreading Germany.

Please, send Mutti my regards when you write to her. And write me a detailed description of your current life in your next letter that, hopefully, will reach me soon. I send you warmest regards and remain, with a kiss,

Your Ilse

Witkowitz, January 5, 1935

Dearest Lilian,

Lunch is in quarter of an hour so I want to see if I can complete a letter to you by that time. You should not be offended by the belated congratulations. I had and have such worries, that everything else seems unimportant. I also forgot to congratulate Gre. If—with the Lord's help hopefully soon!—things improve, I will catch up on everything.

Meanwhile, as I already wrote to you, I had my radio debut. In fact, the German broadcast performed my children's play, *Servant Rupert's Workshop*. It gave me great joy even when it seemed I would receive no fee. But yesterday I received a retrospective payment of 150 Kč.[32] The school that participated received just as much. Thirty-three children, two teachers and one catechist took part in the play. I myself had to step in at the last moment for the "little angel" who had fallen ill, and as the "sun." As the latter, I had to cry, which I did so naturally that Hans, no longer "Hannerle," who was listening to the radio at home, almost cried along. Surprisingly, the play was well received, allegedly better than all the other Christmas broadcasts. Well yes, no wonder considering my Aryan descent! The main thing is that it gave me pleasure and that I had my share of fun!

The matter with Lo truly grieves me and although I do not know her, I would like to do something for her, if only that were possible! Can't she go to Palestine? Everybody makes a living there, provided she has the traveling money!

Oscar[33] is in Palestine too, and has married there. "She" wrote
to Mama in French, is Russian, has lived in Paris, attended the
Institute of Oriental Languages, and has lived in Palestine for the
last three years. She will surely be fooled by Oscar's good looks and
cajolery. I am not a blinded sister.

I am awfully sorry that you suffer so much and it is nasty you
have no money. I am broke too, since I'm saving my earnings to
buy Willi a suit for his birthday. Will I ever save that much? Well,
otherwise, I will limit my ambition to a few handkerchiefs. Hans'
birthday too, was very modest. Only practical things: just from
Lizzie a beautiful car with electric headlights. By the way, Lizzie[34]
would very much like to write to you. She thinks about you a lot.
Friedl's husband, who was a director at the German theater, has
left for Palestine to work as a cement mixer. It's uncertain when she
will follow him with her little Suse. Olga Meitner already works
down there as an orange packager. Things have changed a great
deal here at home. Less money, modest demands, a lot of misery.
Bruno Ries[35] has lost everything. But his little Eva is a golden little
thing!

Everybody has gathered for lunch. I have to conclude. So a
thousand kisses and just as many regards from Mama and Hans as
well. Nana is leaving. Because of "ill treatment." What do you say
to that? Lilian, I have already been repaid with a lot of ingratitude,
but never as grossly as by Frau Sendler.

Ilse

Witkowitz, April 27, 1935

Dearest Lilian!

It has been a while since I received such a sensible and pleasant letter from you as the last one. However, I am answering only
today. Reason: Hanuš' tonsils were finally removed. Although I
am no hysterical mother and it was I who suggested *it* in the first
place, I was nevertheless preoccupied with it, within and without, especially since, through his continual sickliness, the boy has

become whiny. This was barely over when I was seized with real panic. I had gone to the doctor really to find out the reason for a nasty pain in the right hand and found on this occasion that something is wrong with my lungs. She treated it as very urgent and insisted on an X-ray, so that I was desperately unhappy when I left her. And strangely, although I had been feeling, up to this visit, completely healthy (except for the pain in my hand), after that visit I suddenly discovered I had all the symptoms of respiratory ailments: I sweated, had fever, lost my breath, had sharp pain, and even spat out blood. Until it turned out that apart for some old calcified nodules, my lungs are in good health, touch wood. At least the radiologist assured me so. Now all the symptoms are gone. There only remains the fact that I have become very thin; I weigh 50 kilos and really must go on a fattening diet. To this end, I must go to a sanatorium. I imagine it can be very pleasant to go on a fattening diet, don't you think so too? Only that my family and friends believe I will go without my children, which I naturally have no intention to do. I am taking the oldest one with me.

Tommy is sick again today. I have shaved his head and since he doesn't tolerate a cap, but throws it within two minutes on the floor, he caught a cold. Tell me I need more challenges in my life! On Thursday I had a radio "premiere." The playing group, "Schlesische Bühne,"[36] are a group of pure-blooded Aryans. I derived great pleasure from the way they produced my play. On Mother's Day I am performing again on the radio, with the German School, *Bornemann's Children Celebrate Mother's Day*. That takes up a little time, is indeed fun, but is more trouble. Worst is when honorary students perform. They want to show off, and spoil everything because they always overact. When I correct them a little they make a pitying-superior face, as if to say: "She wants to correct me, when I have nothing but A's!" In June the secondary school will perform something of mine, but I will try to get around that. It is a folksong broadcast for which I have written the framework. The piece is called *A Minstrel Contest in the Bielau Forest*. Do you still think about the Bielau Forest? We were considerably younger and more carefree at the time, when we cycled with the boys outside. It has become, in general, so much more difficult and gloomy. I will make great efforts to give my children a happy, unencumbered adolescence. You know, after all, I cannot save up for Willi's suit. But in the meantime he had his suit from last year changed because it is after all May and "everything, everything must change."[37] (. . .) My older is now recovering gradually and keeps becoming more handsome. He does not get it from me, so this is no self-praise. Tommy is entirely different: rough, wild, a real handful. He tolerates no affection and reacts to kisses by scratching or biting the concerned person. But since he is the little one, we would like to eat him up with love. He remembers melodies very well, sings in tune. Every morning he demands to be taken to the piano. He walks by himself and falls often, but without a lot of crying.

Now he needs his compresses and so my letter to you must end. Lilian don't get angry, but I cannot use the manuscript you sent me. You shall receive it with the same mail. I need something completely different. *What is going on with Elli?*[38] She wanted to come to Prague for Christmas, wrote from Paris, and since then, I have not heard anything from her.

Many Kisses!

Your Ilse

Witkowitz, July 6, 1935

Dearest Lilian!

You are after all a proper Gypsy! It wouldn't surprise me to receive one day a post card from the North Pole. But I am pleased that you are trying to learn this educational subject! I do not know Neil,[39] but would very much like to hear *a lot* about him. Hopefully, when my letter reaches you, you will not have become interested in something else again! But I want to answer your letter in an orderly fashion.

I had a lovely time at Hrebienok. My restlessness didn't allow me to laze around in a deck chair as I was instructed to. I simply

cannot do that. However, I took the most wonderful walks and
even real high altitude hikes in snow and ice, often on my own.
One was, in particular, marvelous. First it went through deep fir
forest, relatively steep uphill. All along, waterfalls roared next to
the path up to the destination. Then they disappeared and gave
place to round Swiss pines. Finally, there were only stones and
sparse meadows with white narcissus; one heard the marmots
whistling, saw very rarely a chamois, and was surrounded by grey,
high walls of rocks with snow troughs and waterfalls. The shelter
hut, small and pathetic at two thousand meters altitude, was next
to five mountain lakes in which big ice blocks were swimming. I
went there all alone. That was during the time Willi was in Hrebienok too. He had brought lumbago with him, and could not even
leave the house. It was too terrible. On that day I finished reading,
Treue, a book by Otto Zarek[40] that had brought me to the verge of
despair. Since I feared a nervous breakdown, I decided to forestall
it and told Willi I planned to wander to Tatra-Lomnitz, a health
resort nearby (two hours descent). Summoning all his strength,
Willi dragged himself out of the hotel and walked a few steps with
me. But when he had to go back, I changed my mind and made
the climb to Terýho Chalet.[41] That was the best I could have done.
I saw once more how much nature can give and help when I am
alone with her. In fact, I have to be entirely alone with her. Not
even Willi, who is after all my best friend, may be with me. After
half an hour, I returned to myself again. On the snowfields, shortly
before the Chalet, I became anxious, so I readily joined the company of a Czech captain. Willi was stunned when he found out
where I had been. But it was marvelous! Nature in the Tatra[42] is
mighty and marvelous. Comparing it with the Beskids is akin to
comparing Beethoven with Mozart. At first, I was depressed by the
magnitude and sublimity, as that of the sea, i.e. the North Sea, because the Adriatic Sea is lovely and peaceful: But the Tatra is even
more beautiful than the sea. I have never before imagined there
could be such vast forests, such uninhabited areas, so much solitude and beauty. There is hardly a more beautiful sight than that

of a mountain lake with sheep grazing on its bank. At one point
we were on the Polish side of the Tatra, in the spa town of Zako-
pane and Morskie Oko. Morskie Oko means "Eye of the sea" and
the name has appealed to me for many years. So I wanted to see it
just once. It is at an elevation of 1400 meters and one can reach it
with the car on a very good mountain road. It was an unfriendly,
grey day and in this light the "Sea Eye," enclosed by grey high
mountain faces, looked gloomy and uncanny. I was feeling uneasy
and sad; moreover, I also suffered a great deal under the downright
hate-filled glances of the Poles who ran across us and recognized
the Czech marque. I suffered the whole day from this impression. I
cannot believe that people hate each other only because they have
different nationalities!

I do not know what is the matter with my lungs. Could not
care less at the moment either. I did not stay there long enough,
but it was impossible to stay longer. Anyway, I gained three kilos
and have also recovered. Whether Zwehl has "become" Nazi? He
truly didn't have to bother since he has been one already. (I've discovered this question just now in your letter!) You must re-consider
the idea of joining the Communist party! You know Willi's and my
own attitude toward Communism, but still we advise you against
it. *Don't* do this! It is another thing to *remain faithful to one's resolution* freely than to be forced. Why provoke new resistances? Why
be at variance with the family, with acquaintances? Your heart
knows what it wants: you already think the right way. One does
not always have to carry a flag. You can be active in the communist
sense even so. Join the Friends of Soviet Russia organization.

Your question, how do I bring up my children, I will answer
separately one day. It requires more space and time. On the 18th
of this month I am reading on the radio "The Trip to Braunsberg."
While I was in Hrebienok I dramatized Grimm's fairy tale "Rum-
pelstilzchen." There is a good chance that it will be performed
on the radio. Lilian, please do read these fairytales again. I must
confess to you that they are causing me quite a headache. There is
so much injustice in them, and they seem to me educationally un-

sound. But this too would provide material for a book and not just a letter.

I received a new radio and am very happy with it.

Too bad the stamp on your last letter was damaged. One corner was missing. You could surely provide me with stamps from the "Silver Jubilee."[43] I have many little and big boys I could make very happy with this. So please think about me! My older one too has started collecting stamps, but for the time being he can't yet tell the difference between a stamp and the little picture on a cheese.

Please write soon. I believe we have so much to tell each other again.

Greeting you most intimately,
Ilse

Christmas Morning, 1935

My Dearest Lilian!

Your kind Christmas greetings yesterday would have made me deeply ashamed had I not sufficiently apologized to myself. But ever since getting the funny card, I think of you even more than usual, and I'm using this free morning hour of the first Christmas day to write to you.

To tell you quickly about the funny fact that your post arrived together with greetings from my unknown admirer from Brazil. (You know, he claims he had shared the compartment with me on my first trip to Hamburg!) Last night I dreamt of Curt. I was somewhere sitting on a beachside terrace, around me there were very high houses with balconies, the people on them were trying to drive me to despair by sitting on the railings or leaning over them (at a sky-scraper height). I played the lute again, but it was almost impossible for my hands are both kaput (which is unfortunately no dream), and so was the lute. Suddenly Curt appeared and we spoke about you. He reckoned that had his mother not bragged so much, you would have long been reunited. I asked if he was married, but he only made a dismissive movement: "That doesn't mean anything!" Then I said that I absolutely did not have the impression you would gladly go back to him. To that he replied, "As if you knew!"

But now back to reality. I live, since December 25, in my new apartment, 18 Švecova (the post building), and have had my hands full with the relocation and furnishing. However, now I do live in a bigger apartment. True, it is on the third floor, but on the other hand, the children's room is big and full of light and so far is occupied only by Hans. He returned home from the hospital just two days ago, while Tommy has been there for nine weeks. Hans had a very light scarlet fever, while Tommy's was a decidedly more serious case. His glands became swollen right at the beginning and he had a middle ear infection on both sides. After some very bad days, he regained his happy disposition, but the pus would not go away and, on the day he should have come home, both his ears were unclogged by inserting a tube, a nasty business for such a little child. Barely did Hans scrape through his light sickness and I hardly had him at home when Tommy's scarlet fever took a sinister turn. I experienced many sad days on the "Bridge of Sighs" in front of the Scarlet-Pavilion (one cannot enter but only look into the room from a sort of a bridge constructed in front of the windows). Three children died from the same sickness (with the addition of meningitis) during that time, one of them lying next to Tommy, and I trembled and worried with his mother. Now a little sweet girl is lying in the same bed after going through the same operation, and yesterday she had fever. You have to realize that in such cases there *must not* be fever. It is a bad sign. We, "the women on the bridge," truly became sisters during these weeks. Initially, the people do not know each other, but the 2 hours they spend daily together in ice and snow on the bridge in front of the scarlet fever pavilion, quickly brings them close. One trembles for a stranger's child as for one's own and I am going there today feeling worried about little Traude and afraid for her. Tommy himself is miserable and thin, but he is becoming gradually joyful again. He is the youngest at the hospital, heartbreaking, with bandaged head and big, astonished eyes, and has settled in quite well. People are very fond of him at the hospital which, for me, is a great consolation. Children, physicians and nurses compete to spoil him. But although almost 3 weeks have passed since the operation, he had a 38.6 fever on Monday. Imagine my fear. But then it turned out it was not his ears but a fistula in his mouth that had caused the fever. I don't know when he's coming home.

8 o'clock in the evening. Only now can I write further. In the meantime, I went twice to Tommy because today, Christmas Day, visits were allowed also in the morning. His temperature was as always, 37.1, and he was truly joyful. Traude had 39.8. Uncanny.

I'm invited this week by the director of the German broadcasting service. We had an especially successful Saint Nicolaus children's performance. I have only skimmed through your article. It is interesting, but I still need something else. One can express oneself only briefly on the radio. I would think one should write first about the situation, the emergence of Summerhill. What you write, for instance, about the paid students' collaboration was interesting and can be used. First, I absolutely don't know if the director has heard of Neil?

Now my "free quarter of an hour" is gone again.

Farewell and be happy and healthy in the new year!

Ilse

Witkowitz, March 17, 1936

My Dearest Lilian!

Outside, the snow swirls so playfully through the air that I'd like to follow the superstition "March snow makes beautiful" and go out a little; but then I remind myself that I owe you *such* an infinitely long answer and stay in. Hanuš, who is still fascinated by the typewriter, decided to likewise back away from the planned visit to his friend Hanne, and so we're sitting most peacefully opposite each other at the kitchen table, I with my machine, he with his marionettes. Tommy went out with the girl.

Meanwhile, the director of German Broadcasting unfortu-

nately sent back your article, or rather your teacher's. And I myself
do not entirely agree with the school. It is, at least for the time
being, overly capitalistic, or could workers' children attend it as
well? Hardly! Nevertheless, it must be very pleasant and interesting
for you to be able to live there and I almost envy you for being
free to make your own decisions. *I* had to sacrifice my freedom
altogether and do not have even one single hour a day for myself.
Indeed, even when I sit down after meals to write something,
thoughts of the mending basket and putting things away force
themselves upon me until I resignedly snap my notebook shut in
order to submerge completely in everyday life's prose. Still I keep
up with my radio commitments and, for the time being, have
"permanent" contracts for April, May and June. Lately I had a
broadcast, *What Children Sing and Say*, my own songs and children's poems, which was a lot of work. I had no special material for
children available and even less time. In addition, I had a miscarriage and was supposed to stay in bed for a longer time, which was
impossible since I simply must not be sick. I have gradually turned
into one of those housewives, enslaved to their homes and children. Maybe it will change someday. For compensation, I have the
love of my husband and boys, and that is something after all.

You are, forgive me, I wanted to write "once again," engaged.
I know nothing of your current future husband except that he's
called James, like the old man in the *Forsyte Saga*, and is about
to divorce. Why does he look like Curt? (God, how dumb! But I
mean something else with my question, hopefully you understand
it.) What is his religion? Do you *love* him? So that you will give up
your entirely superb freedom for his sake? Is he capable of offering
you at least a modest luxury? That you *must* have, for *you* were
not cut out to cook and iron for a man, even if he has the most
interesting profile in the world. Only when you can have at least
that which you have had during your girlhood can your marriage
be good. *I* am happy in my marriage, but we would certainly have
been much happier if Willi were better situated financially and I

could have hired a nanny in order to have more time for him and
me, and not be tired to death when he comes home in the evening.
That is really our sore point. I am so work-worn that all I wish in
bed is to sleep, but a man wants more. If I want to be the only
woman for Willi, as I have been until now, I must practice self-ab-
negation, which is sometimes impossible. You see, this has turned
into a confession letter, which wasn't my intention. I do not know
if I have made it clear to you what really matters.

Lilian, I will always be in touch with you, as often as we should
tangle with each other. We have, nevertheless, a great deal in common and I nonetheless love you very very much, even though I
was so often mad at you.

Yes, but I do not want to write to you more today. Kissing you,
Ilse

Witkowitz, June 24, 1936

Dearest Lilian,

I'm outraged that once again you didn't receive our letter. *To
this end* one lives in the post building: so that one's own letters will
get lost! Hanuš and I wrote *to* you and enclosed pictures, and it is
an odd feeling to imagine that our emotional effusions, these were
truly emotional effusions! should be read by someone other than
you. Where do these "lost" letters end up, actually?

Now I have to inform you over again that the boy was insanely
pleased with the letter, and to this very day knows its content by
heart. He is fighting over the pictures with Tommy, who is a little
good-for-nothing and takes away everything from his brother.
Speaking of Hanuš: you have now, after all, pedagogical experience. Help me with this: he is a very nice, good boy, but asks an
uncomfortable question. I want to quote you a conversation word
for word.

Hanuš: Mutti, are we German or Czech?

(This is pretty much the worst question he can ask me.) I am

raised as German, but since the overthrow in Germany am no
longer "German."

I: (diplomatically) We are Jews.

Hanuš: Yes, but *what kind* of Jews, Czech or German?

I: (Since first I speak insufficient Czech, and second, do not
want to lie to myself): We are Czechoslovakian Jews!!

He is dissatisfied with this answer, but for the time being
cannot argue. Now help me: *What* should I tell him? He is
going to Czech school and speaks flawless Czech (better than
Willi or I). I love the Czechs, but still cannot say, "I am Czech,"
when I attended a German school and write in German. But
this child reflects about it and disagrees with the answer that
he is Jewish. I cannot explain to him the "minorities problem";
he is still too young for that. I can see though, that I will have
to do it. Not so long ago Poldi's boy, Bobby, came over crying
and told us Hanuš insulted him, calling him "Žid peichlatý."[44]
I could not laugh at it because I knew that after all, one of
Hanuš' Christian friends must have given *him* that label and
that he, being innocent, did not understand. Should I ruin his
childhood friendships already and tell him: "Do not play with
the boys; they are Christians and you a Jew!"? I believe recon-
ciliation between people is possible when the adults stop being
vicious examples. But as long as the grown-ups will not stop,
out of malice or stupidity, talking contemptuously about other
nationalities or denominations, there will be no peace in the
world. And Hanuš is so gentle and soft. Tommy perhaps will be
able one day to resist with his fists, but Hannerle, hardly. Many
acquaintances reproach me for loving the bigger one more than
the little. This is obviously nonsense. But the bigger one now
needs me more.

I am really sorry that you do not get to know the children
while they are still handsome and kind. How gladly I would have
you in my summer resort! I am going on July 1 to Einsiedel, a convent at the foot of the Altvater[45] Mountain. It is a recreation home
run by Catholic nuns, and the order is the same as my school sis-

ters of Saint Borromäus. I urgently need rest and no other place is
as inexpensive as it is over there. The convent is very well located,
has high, cool rooms, and a beautiful garden. I will hire a German
maid there for the children because they should, after all, learn
German, although every disaster brought upon us is from Germany. Hanuš knows German more or less, but Tommy speaks only
Czech. He has been speaking since his last illness (they both had
measles in May) but very sweetly and comically. Tommy has never
spoken of himself in third person like other children. He empha-
sizes the "Ja"[46] (I) quite emphatically.

You will already have known that Karl Kraus had died.[47] You
can maybe imagine how sad this made me. I thought of him as the
most truthful and sincere person in the world. No newspaper dares
to write anything unfavorable about him, although he has fought
the "Journaille" most vehemently his entire life. His last words
were "Pfui Teufel!"[48] But his death mask has such a wonderful
transfigured expression, don't you too think?

I'm sending you a booklet of poems I found interesting:
Ragout by Hansi Fuchs. I do not know the writer, who is an
Ostrauer,[49] and is likely no longer young. But if you like them,
I suggest you write to *her*. You are indeed a people-catcher and
I feel *that* would not be a bad catch. Her address should be:
"Hansi Fuchs, c.o. Dr. Fuchs, Mähr. Ostrau"; but better go
through the publisher so that she doesn't suspect an Ostrauer has
lead you to her.

I asked many questions in my lost letter also, about your bridegroom's religion and his name. Do you know how sometimes one
knows nothing about a writer and then suddenly gets one book
after the other by that author? I first received the book *Herren,
Knechte, Frauen* by Jo van Ammers-Küller,[50] and am continually
getting her books. Now I'm reading *Die Frauen der Coornvelts*,[51]
sort of a Dutch *Buddenbrooks* novel, interesting and well written.
Herren, Frauen, Knechte doesn't at all give the impression it is written by a woman. (. . .)

What are your plans for the summer? It is very muggy here.

Our windows face the market square, where the Peter and Paul Fair will take place on the 29th of this month. The carousels and stalls are already being installed. You know, Willi and I have a lot of fun going out with the children and we always spend a fortune. We invite all available nephews and nieces as well.

Many Regards,
Ilse

Ilse Weber with her mother Therese and her sons Hanuš and Tomáš

Witkowitz November 1, 1936

Dearest Lilian!

You're not receiving the letter by the time I planned after all, although I constantly thought about you and about writing it. You won't believe how terribly difficult it is for me to get round to doing anything that does not absolutely belong to my daily routine. But maybe you believe me that whenever my thoughts have a little time, I very often chat with you and Gre in my mind and, so to speak, draft to myself letters, which I then *do not* write. But now I have confined Willi, who's home for Sunday, in the children's room, where he is building houses with Tommy. Hanuš is playing with his friend Jeník, and I can, if nothing unexpected happens, chat with you.

And first let me give you a big kiss and wish you good luck with all my heart. My wish: constant contentment, quiet, and a peaceful home! And that you will always love each other! First, I wanted to congratulate you with a telegram, but that would have been too expensive. And I believe it will be more effective if I my-self put it down. You get also a little present from Willi and me; it is a book by Karel Čapek,[52] *Seltsames England*.[53] You just must wait until it is published. There is a reason why I first announce my present to you. You wrote me that you and James (may I call him that?) are translating Alice Berend[54] into English. Personally, except for *Bruders Bekenntnisse*,[55] I find Alice Berend's writing boring and I think you should translate something that is worthwhile. Čapek is a very important humorous author. I admire him very much, and his works are wonderful. His comments, which he makes quite casually, are deeply touching, or he depicts something in a way you would joyfully agree with and think to yourself: "No, that is exactly how I feel about it, too!"

I know only one short chapter from his new book about En-gland, but it already convinced me that it would be nice if you two could secure the translation rights. The book is published in Ger-man by Bruno Cassirer in Berlin. You will receive it from me, but you would have to try and get the rights. What is actually James' profession?

Hannerle thanks you for the pictures. I could explain to him those without words, the rest I did not understand. He congrat-ulates you on your wedding and sends something that is very dear to him! —three magic pictures, (you have to rub a pencil over them, then the pictures will appear) which, in his view, will very much impress you. You may give to James the duplicate

picture. My older one has been going to school since September.
(. . .) The principal himself teaches the first grade and that way
I am learning Czech from the ground up. Sometimes I have a
guilty conscience for having stolen from my child a carefree year
of childhood pleasures, but he is already going and it is too late.
Lilian, I am such an awful educator! I am so impatient, unsym-
pathetic and quick-tempered, features I would deeply despise
in other women. I lose my temper when he fails to understand
something or makes a mistake. Sometimes I even smack him, and
afterward sit there ashamed of myself. It is actually terrible how
much is poured into today's children! And at school they advance
much faster. They do not learn writing with a slate first, but right
away with the pencil. Hanuš reached "p" and knows the numbers
up to 9. Today he wrote, proudly, "paul" and "ilse." On National
Holiday[56] he got to recite at the school festival, but we only
found out about it from someone else. He does not get yet that
this is an honor. He has problems getting up in the morning. He
is used to lying a bit with me in bed in the morning. When he is
finally happy and ready to step out he gets a tummy ache (from
excitement), and sits so long in the bathroom that he's late. He
cannot eat breakfast, drinks his cup of coffee with great difficulty,
which is no disaster because they now must drink coco or milk
daily at school, and he then eats his croissant with it. Despite
everything, he likes to go to school and gets along very well,
when you consider how much he has to grasp at the age of five:
to read, write and calculate in a foreign language, read Hebrew
and, what's also very difficult, to get accustomed to the tone and
loutishness of the many older boys. He is, anyway, an awkward
child who would definitely interest and attract me if he weren't
accidentally mine. But since he is my boy, I am nasty to him and
impatient. You see that I lack neither self-knowledge nor even
good will, but patience. I have too many things to do. I cannot
allow myself something like "individuality" or "my own life." I
am only allowed to cook, shop, darn, mend, and spend time with
the children. I declare that without being sorry for myself since

I am fully aware that, in comparison with other women, I am still doing marvelously. But stop: Ilse Herlinger is busted! Now I want to tell you also about Tommy. He is cast from a completely different mold than the older: he's what one calls "a real boy": daring, rowdy, and boisterous. Sadly, he hasn't quite recovered from his serious illness. We will try a sunlamp and, if that doesn't help, then a tonsil operation.

¼ 8 o'clock[57] in the evening. Willi went to the theater, the children have eaten, Tommy has his potato compress and lies in bed, and Hanuš will soon get to that point. At the moment I can continue to write. Today I wrote an essay on Božena Němcová, the greatest Czech poet. At the beginning I saw it only as a piece for the radio, but after I studied it more closely I began to feel an emotional connection with the topic, and more than once during my work was on the brink of crying over her sad life story.

Lizzie is expecting a baby. Up to now she wanted none because her family suffered from persecution mania for three generations; besides, they're not doing well financially; but she has spoken with physicians and they didn't advise her against it, so she wants to venture it. Hopefully everything goes well! Nowadays I'm not a hundred percent convinced that one cannot be happy without children. I very much fear the possibility of a war.

Recently it appears as if I have a hidden enemy at the radio who, although my material has been accepted, knows how to prevent it from being broadcast. I really feel that I hardly have any more income opportunities. Antisemitism is shutting all doors on me.

I must now join the children for "evening singing." Usually Willi takes care of that in an eerily beautiful way; today he is not here.

So, dearest girl, a firm handshake and a heartfelt kiss; I wish you both a beautiful, harmonious marriage, in particular, free of financial worries, for they are the worst!

Your Ilse

Sleep, my poppet, go to sleep,
I will keep you warm.
Mother's little child I am,
and you are my own.

Look, how by your bed I sit
and to you I sing.
Just like Mommy sits by me
when the day is fleeing.

Tomorrow we'll be merry
playing, free of care.
Sleep, my poppet, go to sleep,
how sweet to you I am.

December 17, 1936

Dearest Lilian!

I am sitting on my bed, which is already prepared for sleep, keeping the writing pad on my knees; the kitchen is still being cleared, I cannot write in the children's room because of the boys, and it's too cold in the living room. Willi has been away for a few days, and evenings, before I fall asleep, I have a long talk with you and tell you everything that weighs on my heart. Your last letters are again as balanced as they were before; I would be very glad if they remain that way! Have you found now rest and peace, Lilian? I wish you that with all my heart! It is more important than anything.

I am glad your James is interested in me because it proves that you have awakened his interest, even though I do not deserve it. I have gradually become so familiar with myself that I know all my good and bad qualities. I am displeased with a great deal in me!

We celebrated last week the Makkabäerfest (Chanukah). I had ten children at my place and we had a delightful party. We played, sang and danced, then we lit the candles and suddenly our Ernst appeared as the "prophet Eliahu."

Lilian, you had to be there! His costume was dazzling. Such a Servant Rupert, with inverted fur coat, fur cap, covered with Christmas-tree artificial snow, a ski stick in his hand, its knob an electrically illuminated Chinese Lantern. Beard and white hair, thick white eyebrows (which he kept on losing now and then). He had a book (blue-gold) with everything about the children in it. The children were so sweet one could eat them up; they all had faith in its heavenly origin. Eva Ries (Bruno's daughter) was funny: when she had to recite something she stammered, with a trembling voice, a Christmas poem. That is *how* it is with our Jewish children; they do not know where they belong; their poor little heads are a jumble of all religions. On Sunday I had a "premiere" in Oderberg where two of my children's plays were performed for the Chanukah festival as well. I wanted to come "incognito," to view the whole thing for fun, but my little niece Ruth (who lives there and performed as well) had been bribed to immediately report my potential arrival, and the little rascal did it too. Clueless, I took a seat with Hanni and my sister-in-law. After the religious ceremony, a gentleman delivered a speech in Czech and German and welcomed, "in particular, our honored guest, Frau Weber from Witkowitz." I felt so stupid. But it was lovely. Still, almost the entire fee was spent on travelling there. Monday, the seventh, I was on the radio. My next contract, if nothing intervenes, takes place on January 20. It would be nice if you could listen to me! I listen to all the English stations on our radio. I listened also to the Duke of Windsor's farewell speech. Quite frankly, I found it very touching and the voice extremely pleasant. It came to me as a big surprise because I found the whole King Edward fuss disgusting. He totally eclipsed the interest in Spain. What you write about the war is, regrettably, too true. But there's nothing we can do. I have always thought I would raise my children in the spirit of pacifism. I try, too. But the external influences are stronger. Hanuš' favorite toy is a saber.

Just when your letter arrived, they played at the cinema *Svět za let, Things to Come*. I subscribe to your verdict on this movie, although the short scene between the man and the woman lost its lovely meaning in the Czech translation. Did you, by the way, see *The Sinful Women from Bromberg*? It was a delightful movie.

I visited yesterday Wilma Gross, who has been lying in the hospital for the last few days. It is called "swollen glands." But I was beside myself when I saw Wilma. She has constantly high fever from 38.2 up to 38.5 degrees, is terribly depressed, and very miserable. Her mother died of cancer; maybe she fears the same. I fear that as well. After all, "glands" aren't treated with X-rays. Wilma has changed so much; she is pessimistic. I believe she was not otherwise happy either. At the same time, she has no financial worries and two sweet children. I certainly cannot manage a second visit so soon. The sick like to have me around them; I cheer them up with my "joyful and sunny" nature. Oh God, I haven't been happy and sunny for such a long time! But when I visit the sick, I just put on this mask. Behind it there is only pity, nothing else. But I simply cannot go to Wilma if she is really seriously ill. I desperately hope that I am too pessimistic!!!

December 28, 1936

Dearest Lilian,

The congratulations were really fine. It's true I do not understand much, but I like it. I just happen to have a free hour and can write to you. Hanuš is making decals (i.e. he is trying, but he is far too impatient, so they're all totally damaged). Tommy is sleeping, and during the holidays I mended all the torn socks. That is really my loveliest relaxation: torn socks with the radio's accompaniment. You would laugh if I confessed to you that I am still a radio fanatic just as in the past. Still, I've become more selective. But the programs have worsened, especially since the coup.[58] (. . .)

My next radio contract is expected, if it works out! on January 19. In my radio program it is listed under "Mähr.-Ostrau" III kHz-269.5 m-II.2 Kw. I think the middle figure means the wavelength. But you have plenty of time to check out. I am reading on

the German broadcast at 6:10 o'clock (eighteen o'clock ten), but I
do not know the English time.(. . .)

We do not get many English movies here. The next is *Captain
January* with Shirley Temple, which will play here on January 1.
I am taking Hannerle, with two or three of his friends, instead of
having a birthday party. I like that little girl very much.

I have now taken a walk with the big one. He stands in front of
every toy store window and picks out a birthday present for himself.
Last year he still believed in the birthday man. His burning wish is
soldiers with gas masks and tanks. He will never get those atrocious
toys from me. Anyway, he is so naughty that he is getting just practical things: shirts, socks, pajamas. Only Mama is getting him a toy.
Wilma's children are visiting us now. The little one, she is a bit older
than Hannerle, is a sweet little thing with a bewitching, expressive
face with beautiful grey eyes! Plays only with boys' playthings and is
at the same time a typical little woman: cuddly, soft and coquettish.
Hanuš can warm up neither to her nor to Peter, I do not know why.
He only likes the poor workers' children from the neighborhood
of the "Erbrichterei"[59] the dirtier, the more lovable. He appears to
have inherited the burden of our social inclinations. I always have
to wash his favorite friends, "Lojsík" and "Mirek," before they're
allowed in the children's room. Tommy, by contrast, loves all children, everyone. When he is fond of a little girl he cuddles and kisses
her, whether she likes it or not. I have never associated with father's
family, but since Tommy has come into the world, he has brought
us together. He is a real little heart-stealer, dirty and disheveled as he
always looks, because he exhibits such a beaming joy when he meets
an acquaintance; and he is fond of, and greets everyone with his re-
sounding "Ahoj, Ahoj!" which he learned from the bigger boys at the
hospital. He is never shy or embarrassed like the older one, goes with
strangers when they promise him something, or, just as well, when
they don't. He only sings three songs, but lengthily and always with
a new glee. As of New Year I am sending him to the monastery so he
can learn German. You know, later on, an English lady's help would
be fine for us. Do you believe such a thing exists?

When do you think the two of us might meet? I have no one
here except for Lizzie, and I meet her rarely and see her briefly
because she has too many other interests. For now it's the baby.
She is very strong and has lost much of her charm. But perhaps as
a mother she will be handsome again. Gre writes once a year, for
Hannerle's birthday. So there can be no possibility of an "exchange
of ideas." What do you know about Eli? Last time I heard from her
she was in Paris, from where she arranged a rendezvous with me
in Prague. I was looking forward to meeting her, but have heard
nothing further from her. Do you know anything?

My rest hour is now up. Fare really well: may your New Year's
Eve be healthy and happy as well as the whole coming year. Same
holds for your husband. I like best to stay home on New Year's Eve
and remember my most interesting New Year's night, 1931, when
about midnight, just as the bells were beginning to toll, I went into
labor, and I and Willi wandered through the white winter night to
the hospital. I roamed for several hours in the half-dark delivery
room and had a silent chat with my shapeless shadow on the white
tiled wall that walked with me as my only companion. At eight
and a half in the morning my boy screamed for the first time. Can
you understand I no longer want any New Year's Eve celebration?

Well, adieu now. Dearest girl, write again soon, and a lot
    Yours, Ilse

Deal aunt lilian, nany glitings and kissi hanuš

Witkowitz, January 13, 1937

Dearest Lilian!

We, namely Hanuš and I, thank you. We were heartily happy!
Now the "celebrations have died away," the last champagne from
the one bottle we have allowed ourselves, is drained. I struggle
again with financial difficulties, the boys have to go to school, in
short, it is that condition significantly labeled "everyday life."

Before I forget, I am not reading on the 19th, but the 18th of

this month, at six o'clock 25. The reading will not be broadcast from
Prague. I love to read on the radio. You neither see nor hear the au-
ditorium, and you can imagine the size of the audience as you like.
Besides, it's warm and comfortable there, and they treat you with
deep respect, which unfortunately isn't always the case. Last time it
was funny. I had a bit of a cold and had put my handbag with my
handkerchief next to me on the lectern. After the first words I felt
my nose growing runny: I groped, without raising my eyes, for the
handkerchief: nothing. While I go on reading, astonished, I keep
searching: nothing *at all*. A little drop is forming on the tip of my
nose. I possess nothing to wipe it off because the announcer, out of
sheer fear I could make noise with it, had cleared away the handbag.
Without looking around I am making signs for him, which he does
not understand. Eventually I finally found myself forced to revert to
the proven method of our forefathers and dispose of that business
with the hand. But I wasn't too happy about it.

I thank you very much for your invitation. It is tempting, but,
regrettably, out of the question. My children would forget me and
my husband would become unfaithful. But, if you'd still insist, then:
I would very much like in a few years to send Hanuš to you for
three-quarters of a year. I would gladly pay for that, as much as we
can spare, so that he learns English and good manners. I have great
confidence in you in that regard. Well, what do you think? In the
meantime he learns to love you. Since New Year our little one has
been going to the kindergarten at the monastery. He is very brave
and goes there without protest, although anxiety makes bright tears
run from his eyes. On the way he tells himself how lovely it is over
there: "and they have so many toys there, and lots of kids, and a railway, and the dear sister loves me"; and after a while, sniveling, "and
at home I also have toys, and a railway, too, and Mutti and Babele"
(Mama). But he should nevertheless learn German "speak Geman,"
as he already can say, and the old nuns, who have also taught my siblings, Erwin and Herta, treat him really well.

Hanuš plays every free moment with his soldiers. He even sleeps
with them. His dream is soldiers with gas masks. Isn't it horrible

when one sees the children being so unsuspectingly happy with what suddenly can turn into a terrible reality? I no longer ban playing with soldiers, because the forbidden has an even greater lure.

The situation in Spain isn't promising, and now it starts to become turbulent in Palestine as well. Does your husband think it possible the Balfour Declaration[60] could be annulled? Do you believe England will assist the Jews when it will come to an upheaval again? *What* should we Jews do when everywhere people expel us?

Alas, my joy of writing is gone. You'll hear more from me soon. We all send you best wishes, especially Mama and Willi. A kiss from me!

Ilse

March 14, 1937

Dearest Lilian!

The time of opened windows starts again. The sun shines warmly, the sky is blue and one can see the entire chain of the Beskids, still covered with snow. Willi and the children have, as on every Sunday morning, gone out; the poor housewife must stay home, because her maid cannot cook. I find a letter to you is an entirely adequate substitute. It is clear that *your* last influenza letter has been lost. Pity, pity, all the more pity, since it was long. So now you must bear the consequences, for how can I be brief? Now you're celebrating James' debut, and I wish for your sake that he will pass it honorably, although you really couldn't care less. Does he get the jitters? Well, as tax director he probably doesn't suffer from any inferiority complex, besides, your people are so kind it will anyway go well.

In the meantime, Lizzie's little Franz Daniel has arrived; it went surprisingly well, only his stomach is temporarily not quite right, but will be, hopefully, soon. Otto, the "Herr Professor," is a touchingly comical father, Lizzie is once more very lovely and very reasonable. Her address: Lizzie Gross, Mor.-Ostrava, Šeinerová. (In

case you want to congratulate her!) *How* does one travel from England to Sweden? Do describe the trip sometime! We are starting
to make summer plans as well. Willi should, if it's at all possible,
go to Karlsbad again; the children should go to the mountains:
they are both delicate because of the flu. Tommy is evolving into
an astonishing specimen of humor and cheerfulness; he is absolutely the sunshine of the entire house. He is very tender and slob-
bers with kisses the object of his affection to his heart's content. He
abhors nothing, which doesn't always meet my approval. Not long
ago we had a visit from Yehuda Ehrenkranz,[61] who is in Ostrava
again on his lecturing tour. After three minutes the "two men" became such close friends that Tommy found my presence disturbing
and dismissed me with the words, "You go!" After a while he said,
"You, uncle! I can already go to the bathroom by myself: come I'll
show it to you!" and the famous speaker actually went with my
son to be shown "it." By the way, Ehrenkranz has really become
prominent. Your Rabbi Ehrenpreis is said to have heard him in
Vienna and to have offered him an evening lecture in Stockholm.
That would be very good for E., and I wonder if I shouldn't ask
you to refresh Herr Ehrenspreis' memory? Would you do it? I felt
peculiar at the Ostrava recitation evening. Yehuda E. wears for his
lectures a black Russian shirt. His head appears disembodied in
the lamplight, and through the great power of his configuration
he virtually assumes the countenance of the people whose fate he
reproduces. It is overwhelming, even for me, although I'm not
particularly fond of listening to readings. He delivers a piece titled
"The Kabbalists" that is simply wonderful. *That one* you ought to
get to know! Do you still fish for people?

I am expecting an exact description of your trip to Sweden,
especially of Mutti and her daughters-in-law. How is she doing as
a grandmother? Very young, isn't she? What's the baby's name and
how is it? Is the Hungarian-Swedish mixture good? Do Nordic and
hot Hungarian blood mix harmoniously?

Now I don't really know: Have you listened to my piece from

Prague or not? Apparently no, which is no malheur.[62] Irene Harand[63] spoke afterward and I felt, illogically, being personally honored. Do you know her? She has written the book *Sein Kampf*, and many fine words on peace and human rights.

I have a cousin here who many years ago married in Vienna. Two years ago her husband lost his position and, as she was very badly off, she returned with her boy to the aunt who had raised her in order to be relieved at least of existential worries. Last fall the husband committed suicide in Vienna. Now the aunt wants to keep her and the boy, but the boy, he is now 15 years old, will not be admitted to a local school, and cannot apply for an apprentice position because he is a foreigner. He now lives there idly with the two desperate women, is himself already cranky and grumpy, and there's nothing one can do for him. Isn't this extreme injustice?

As Easter greeting you're receiving the newest pictures of my boys. They are my favorite pictures, although Tommy rarely makes such a serious face. But because of that you can see what beautiful eyes he has. Can you truly love my children from a distance? I wish it so much! I had ten little bunnies over for Tommy's birthday party. Among them Friedl Thors' little one. Friedl has finally turned her back on Palestine. Little Suse is the most delightful thing you can imagine and I was really very jealous on that afternoon. This child is the personification of loveliness, has Friedl's charm, and is way more beautiful. Shy, sincere, perfect to love. I once managed to catch her, kissed her, and when she looked at me surprised, with her dark, shy eyes, I said, "Do you know Suse, I had to give you a kiss, because I love you so much. Think it over, whether you want to give me a kiss, too." Then we played and sang the whole afternoon and, when she was already dressed to leave and stood with the other children by the door, she suddenly ran to me and said very coyly and quietly, "I want to!" It was such a happy event. And that is quite rare for me, because since I have been having children myself I am way more reserved toward other children.

Hanuš is always happy with your pictures, Tommy too, but the children are very messy and leave the pictures lying around, which very much annoys me. I threatened the bigger one I would write you how he is handling the pictures and reckoned you would send no more, to which he said angrily, "Then she is getting also nothing from me!"

But now I really have to cook! Enjoy your Easter trip. Regards to Mutti and the "boys" if they're still thinking about me, which I strongly doubt. Willi and Hanuš send you and James their regards. Your plans of coming here we still need to discuss in detail! —and I kiss you heartily!

Ilse

Witkowitz, April 29, 1937

Dear Lilian!

You should be home by now and that is why I'm rushing to write to you. Gosh, you must have had a great time! You have no idea how much I would like to travel! But since I would have nowhere a good time without my boys, and no one invites me with two appendages (nor without), I stay at home cultivating my longings. Is Hitchin, by the way, on the coast? The houses in your pictures gave me that idea. Then you are to be envied! Because my greatest longing of all is for the sea and the beach! You will laugh if I tell you how this longing awakened in me. It happened not long ago, when I was with my boys in the park and they devoted themselves to digging in the sand. It was such a sorry heap of sand, but they had forgotten their surrounding world and played with such complete bliss! Then I remembered our "bandits home" on Wennigstedt, and the superb beach in Grado, and found myself, which happens relatively rarely, wishing passionately not to be such a poor devil!

Nevertheless, I had a very good week. On Monday I won, through a crossword puzzle I sent in by chance, something I never

do, out of laziness or shortage in postage, a pair of fine stilts, for
which I have no use yet. Wednesday I received another contract for
the radio, and Sunday, well, that I must tell you in detail! Two days
after Easter I received from Aunt Weiss an old Easter issue of the
Prager Tagblatt.[64] It featured a competition with the theme, "The
Good Maid." It was just two or three days before the deadline and I
wanted to participate and write something. But then came Mama,
and she always has so many worries that I'm not in the mood for
anything anymore. Same this time. But still wanting to participate,
I sent in a quite short poem from Hannerl's daybook, which I had
written at the time about Frau Sendler. Then I forgot about the
whole thing. When Willi took the children on Sunday for a walk
in the park, a lady congratulated him on my having won the third
prize. (The *first* was a trip to the sea in Yugoslavia. Ach, well!)

My prize (there were three and half thousand submissions)
consisted of cookware worth three hundred crowns, from the finest
shop in Prague. That is superb, although I would have rather won
a voucher for a children's ready-made clothes store as both boys
need coats. That is how we humans are: ungrateful to the bones!
But really, I am very happy and already making plans of helping
my shabby porcelain inventory to gain a new luster. Maybe I
would even fulfill my long-entertained wish for a sandwich server
with onion pattern. Are you laughing at me? Just laugh, I grant
you that pleasure. I laugh very little these days. Mostly only about
Tommy, who is so cheeky and hilarious that I have given up em-
ploying my educational skills on him. There has been here recently
an outbreak of an ocular epidemic, and naturally my scallywags
have joined in. These boys are so bold! They must have something
of everything!

My youngest sister-in-law, Berta, has become engaged. Her
bridegroom is prosperous and comes from a wealthy family, but
his father requests Berta should bring along at least 50,000 crowns.
Naturally, she does not have this kind of money, and since the
gentleman threatens to withhold his consent, Berta's brothers
must raise the money. For the father-in-law this money is a trifle:

he doesn't need it, it's just a whim on his part. Willi and the other brothers-in-law are, consequently, in a crunch because they don't have it. There are very disgusting people. You know, sometimes I myself feel a sort of an inclination toward antisemitism in me when such a fine specimen of a co-religionist comes my way. After all, Berta is ravishingly beautiful, and if my siblings had to make such a sacrifice I would have flouted the engagement in her place. But she doesn't care and there's no chance I'll put my foot in my mouth.

How are you with the dough? I'm materialistic today, am I not? But that's because after tomorrow comes the first, and I have had no money since yesterday. Brrr!

Will you see something of the coronation? I read the newspapers and simply wonder to myself: How can they? While in Spain . . . Come off it, after all I can change nothing!

Oscar, by the way, is no longer called that, but Abner Mareni. He actually became a Palestinian citizen and his name was unpronounceable. His divorced wife, Malkah, with whom I correspond, is in New York, where she has established connections with the press. That's an efficient fellow! Lacking the smallest spark of sentimentality, always set on a purpose, tremendously educated, reckless of herself and others. *That one* will have her way! Her and Oscar's child, little Leilah, is very sweet, to judge by the pictures. Gre Edelstein and her husband are going now to Paris for the World Exhibition. They are, praise God, doing very well down there. Dr. Spitzer[65] is in Stresa. Recently, I met him twice, but we both weren't too happy about it. It still makes me unhappy.

So now Willi has finished the serenade he sings every evening with the children. They sing eagerly and in tune. Hanuš is also beginning to plunk on the piano. He can already play "All my Ducklings" with one finger. He is capable of playing it 99 times in a row and Tommy sings along with ardent enthusiasm all 99 times. It is eerily beautiful! By the way, I do not think that he will be a second Mozart. Not even. . . But why anticipate events?

Yesterday I wrote an essay on the theme: "To overcome oneself is the most beautiful victory," for an academic high-school student. Today's girls lack inspiration; they cannot write essays. I find myself, on an average of once a month, obliged to give someone a hand. In one case last year I received a C-grade, but otherwise it's always an Excellent. Not long ago I delivered such a superb example that Judith had to read it aloud. The theme was: "The Street." I asked her if she wasn't terribly ashamed to have read it as her own work, but she wasn't. When I think about it, it always occurred to me weird that sister Stanislava, who didn't like me, ran down my essays and held up as an example my classmate's essay, which I wrote as well! I shall have, by the way, in May, a radio broadcast, with the assistance of the monastery-school headed by Sister Bernadette.

Now that's that. Greetings and kisses. Write to me soon!!!!!
Ilse

I believe today is September 24

My Dearest Lilian!
It has been a busy time, and as much as my thoughts lingered with you, I didn't get round to writing. I gave my maid notice. She had three suitors and had lost her head in such a way that it had become unbearable. And her replacement stood me up. Then I hired a second, who, one day before beginning to work, was killed in an accident. So I had to simply keep house with a two-hour temporary help, who on top of that was eight months pregnant, therefore demanded some consideration. And that was really strenuous! Wake up early, look after the children, in between read on the radio, mend, darn, it was a lot. We have cut our summer holiday short because it has rained incessantly.

I think about you so much! And I wish for you that the little one—how terribly unimportant whether girl or boy! —will make your life rich with joy. I've found out that as a mother one mustn't expect anything for oneself, but when one's lucky, a little happiness is nonetheless left over for us, and a lot should be left for you,

Lilian! I do have many worries with the boys because they are repeatedly sick. They are also so ill-mannered that I often don't know
what to do about them. Still now and then there are moments
when I am proud and happy to have them. Tommy is marked forever by his serious sickness. He must always be careful with his ears
(after all, he had an ear tube inserted on both sides and had blood
poisoning in his head). He lacks a piece of bone over the left ear on
a very dangerous spot; he can neither bump it nor get a blow, and
how difficult it is for such a wild boy to prevent this, you know
that yourself. But he makes a powerful, healthy impression, is way
rougher than Hannerle, and his feet are only one shoe size smaller.
Hannerle is so very fine-boned, the little girls his age have four
sizes bigger feet. Tommy is more popular than the older. Tommy
is so sincere and bold, speaks openly about everything, and yet everybody is fond of him. There was an old man in our summer resort who looked like our departed president. He used to always sit
alone at the table and was always treated with deference. Tommy
fell in love with him and one day he ran to him and hugged him
enthusiastically saying, "Že, ty jse můj Mikuláš?" (Say you, are
you Saint Nicholas?) It was very odd, but the old gentleman became his best friend.

Yes, our president died. He was a person whom we shall all
miss, especially we Jews. He was just, wise and great. We really
loved him like a father. The grief in our land is inconceivable to
an outsider. People cried on the streets. Businesses forgot their
financial interests and all the shop windows were cleared out and
displayed flowers and portraits of "dad." I had to help Hannerle
set up a "Masaryk Table." It is still standing in the living room.
Hannerle contributed the fine saying, "At least there will be no
war anymore! Our president is now in heaven, he will put things
in order!" Perhaps you have heard about the pogroms in Poland?
It started in Bielitz, a Polish town not far from here. A Jewish
restaurant owner (allegedly, converted for thirty years) acted in
self-defense and shot a drunken farmhand. This has such terrible

consequences for all the Jews in Poland: demonstrations, lootings, (not *one* Jewish apartment was spared in Bielitz), and bloody attacks. Isn't this a crying injustice? Masaryk cherished the Jews and always emphasized that one must be just. How much longer shall his moral influence last? When will his protection stop? It is an uncertain life now.

Hannerle takes next week the first class with Ernst Immerglück. I find that rather too early, but Ernst thinks one cannot start early enough. I would have loved it if the boy were talented. As a baby he was really a wunderkind, but that has been lost. At school, he's in the second grade now; he is doing well. He is best at reading (his writing is dreadful) and he loves it. Could you sometime get me a picture book with very simple verses? What would you like to have for the baby? I find it more helpful if you tell me openly. Maybe you need something in particular? I still own my boys' beautiful baby carriage set (cushions and quilt cover) which you could have if the measurements are right. Does Mutti send you the accessories for the pram? Is your husband happy? Has your marriage turned out the way you wanted? Liliput, I have to tell you something quickly. On your last visit here you left a styled dress of light blue taffeta with beige tiers. Now, I've made out of the taffeta the most wonderful temple flags you can imagine, for my children and two other little girls. We have now the Joy of Torah celebration. On the last day[66] the children hold little flags and march, singing, around the Torah. Usually one buys ready-made little flags from paper, but I find that uninspiring and always make especially beautiful flags. (Appreciated as the most beautiful here.) This time they're tailored out of your dress: two light blue stripes connected by a white one surrounded by gold braid trimming, and on the outer edges, gold fringes with little bells (they tinkle so playfully when the children are walking around with them) bearing a golden Star of David. Hannerle even has an inscription: "Praised be the Eternal, our God!" In this way you are somehow with me!

Presently we're having the marvelous autumn days, full of sun and beauty. Tomorrow a singer is singing on the radio songs that I have translated. I am already full of anticipation. On September 3, the program having been changed due to Masaryk's illness, I read "The Legend of Peace." You don't know this piece so I enclose it, but would like to have it back.

"Wu'd aunt Lilian be very scared, when she wu'd have a quintu-plet?" Hanuš wants to know. Please do not forget to answer that. He thanks you for the pictures, with which he runs a flourishing trade.

Willi wishes you all the best for your "difficult hour," and the beginning of a new happy time. I kiss you with all my heart.

Your Ilse

Witkowitz, December 8, 1937

Dearest Lilian!

Tonight I dreamt of you, and so vividly, that I'm sitting now at the desk, in the midst of all my numerous chores, writing to you. You were as charming today as in your salad days. Your hair grew back again and had its golden shimmer. We went together through Ostrava, and its Ostrawitzakai looked suspiciously similar to the Jungfernstieg,[67] and you always wanted to turn into that part of the city where the Dr. lived.

I stopped you with strange pretexts, always pretending to be anxious for you and your reputation; but in reality, it is clear to me now, in my waking state, it was out of jealousy. I have dreamt of him before: such a beautiful dream that what I like most would be to fall asleep again right away. I was very ill and he came to visit me. He sat at my bed and held my hand. That was all, but this "holding my hand" was so indescribably beautiful that I cannot describe it to you. Is it very bad to have such dreams?

Yesterday evening, by the way, I attended with Lizzie a lecture by Ludwig Hardt.[68] It was very nice; he read fine things: Claudius, Kleist, Altenberg etc.; but I find Yehuda Ehrenkranz nonetheless much better. I have heard only few elocutionists and therefore cannot presume to pass judgment, but Ehrenkranz speaks a marvelous, pure German and has a wonderful, pure and expressive face. I love him anyway very much, also as an other-worldly, childish and benevolent person. You would like him very much as well. Lizzie went out yesterday for the first time since she had her baby. They are in very tight financial circumstances, secondary school professors do not earn much here, and in the last months she has neglected her appearance. But now she is giving herself a fresh start, spent a long time at the hairdresser's, wore a nice dress, and in one stroke was yesterday not the old Lizzie, but still a new and delightful one. Afterward, we went to the café with our husbands and Mizzi Huppert and husband and my sister-in-law Erna. It was lovely to be among friends again and babble out freely. I'll have to do that more often; I am definitely starved for this.

On November 29 we celebrated Chanukah. You do know what "Chanukah" is? Our Makkabäerfest, at which we light up candles for eight days. I invited ten children, who came accompanied by 29 adults. Our Ernst came disguised as "Eliahu the Prophet" and brought presents, and it was very pleasant. The children were quite convinced of the heavenly descent of the prophet, very attentive and cute. Hannerle played with both hands Chanukah songs, and wasn't in the least unhappy when Eliahu told him the little angels in heaven always sang along when he practiced. He wished for "three soldiers on horsebacks with rifles," but Eliahu brought him a game of chess and said that the good Lord doesn't like war games. On St. Nicholas Day his friend Jenek (he lives in the same building as we do and his grandfather is Hannerle's principal and teacher) got soldiers, and now Hannerle asked me a tricky question: "Why can't Eliahu bring any soldiers and the Nikolo can?" "Is there a Jewish God and a Christian one?" or "Why do Christians like war and the Jews don't?" I very often don't know the right answers. Yet he doesn't wonder at all that "Christian Nikolo" had thought about him too and left gifts for him at the monastery kindergarten (where Tommy is going) as well as at Jenek's. (Even nicer than Eli-

ahu's, who always has money problems.) The other day Ernst Immerglück, effused with enthusiasm, smothered him with kisses. He
thinks he is very talented, but I remain skeptical until he has perse-
vered for five years. He has studied now for two months, plays flu-
idly all scales (also in contrapuntal motion), is learning the notes in
the bass clef, plays circles of fifths and fourths and knows them by
heart. Whether Ernst's method is good remains to be seen. At this
point Hannerle's lessons are seldom longer than ten minutes.

I myself have felt lately like working again, but the prose
refuses to allow me to get to the poetry. I am wondering if my
Christmas radio broadcast, *The Bohemian Christ Child*, will take
place and if it'll be successful. Until now I haven't been to a single
rehearsal. (. . .) This month I had some concern that the stork may
be coming again. Once I asked Tommy, who is literally wild about
little children, if he wished for one himself: "Would you rather
have a girl or a boy?" He reflected thoroughly, and then said, "I'd
rather have building blocks!"

But now I have to conclude. Please do not make me pay for
my long delay, you do know how seldom I get to writing!

Write to me before year-end, and a lot.

1000 greetings and one warm kiss!

Ilse

Witkowitz, February 13, 1938

Dearest Lilian,

How else could I enjoy this Sunday rest, which has materialized because Willi and the other two boys drove to Ostrava, but
by answering to you! I was already industrious, helped tidy up,
heat up two stoves, and put on the food, so I can reward myself
and chat with you. First of all, many thanks for the pictures of
Gillian. They are funny, like all little children's pictures. I observed
in today's newspaper that even the crown princesses of Holland
make no exception. Being twice a mother I know what to look for
in those pictures, and find that in the first picture the laughter is

sweet, in the second the little nose is cute, in the third the tubby little arms are to bite into, so you can be completely pleased with the impression your daughter left on me.

What an enviable modern mother you are! I look back on those nearly six years in which I haven't gotten a full night's sleep. Now, however, six children couldn't disturb me anymore, one can adjust to almost anything. How lucky you are that you can breastfeed. I always think that both my boys are prone to illnesses because they were raised on substitutes. I absolutely want to send them away this summer. It is right of you to want your child to learn to occupy itself. Hannerle could too; he stood for hours alone in his baby walker, sometimes having an excited conversation with my cooking spoon or a little piece of string. Another play-mate was his shadow, of which he never got weary. When did my boys start to stay dry? I don't remember and would have to check their daybook. But certainly not before they were one year old. I go more often to Lizzie now. Her little Danni is a charming, cheer-ful child who moves with dizzying speed around the floor and is oddly attached to Willi. Funny that all the babies are so fond of him. I believe it's because he grabs them firmly, throws them in the air, and has a lively way of having fun with them until they scream with excitement. Danni spots Willi in the biggest group of people. He crawls on the floor from one to the other, sniffs at the pant leg like a little dog, Lizzie must not read that! and lifts himself up on Willi, howling triumphantly. That, despite the fact he sees Willi rarely. Elli is visiting her now, but it really hurt me to see her. You know, the sword of Damocles of her family's insanity is hanging over them. Lizzi's grandmother, mother and brother are very ill, and now one fears her uncle Moser may be mentally ill as well (you know him, he's the handsome man who owns the pharmacy). And when I saw Elli again, after four years! I noticed the erratic, profoundly sorrowful expression in her eyes.

Her husband is good to her, anyway a fine guy, her daugh-ter Mirjam is in the fifth grade (ten years old), and Mischa, the younger one, is Hannerl's age. But she is ill nevertheless. Lizzie

is a constant worry for all those who love her. She doesn't live
in particularly good circumstances. When she married Otto she
counted on her parents' pecuniary support, but that has become
impossible due to the expensive stay of her mother and brother in
mental homes. Financial worries are nasty, as I know from experience. I get by very badly. I haven't got what it takes to be a good
housewife, even though I never spend anything for my own needs.
I am trying now again, energetically, to earn some money. On
December 24, 17.50 o'clock will be a broadcast of my radio play,
from Prague, *The Musician with the Flute*. Maybe you will be able
to tune in?

In addition to that I have received assurance that I will have
a reading of "my own works" from Ostrava in the coming month
and, further, a staging of a children's play for Mother's Day (May).
But for the time being, I have no children to perform with since
the nice teacher with whom I have worked for years has lately become infected with the antisemitism bug and makes excuses. Too
bad! Further, I sent a fairytale, "There Once Was a Rags Collector,"
to the radio journal in Brünn, with whom I haven't yet worked,
and, in a fit of megalomania, a movie script, rather a movie idea,
composed for the Vienna Boys' Choir competition. It is impossible
for me, as a Jew and Czechoslovakian, to be successful, but at least
I have enjoyed the process. I even had a really neat idea. Lastly, I
have two really good things on the way: a fantastic school radio
play, *Sanus Defeats Morbus* (in which the children's diseases are
the bad and the vitamins are the good spirits, with the cod-liver-
oil as Punch), and a dramatization of Andersen's "The Story of a
Mother," into which I put my heart. Ernst Immerglück selected
the background music. Now I am waiting skeptically to see the
children of my muse again since I believe in success only when I
hold the money order in my hand.

In any case, I put my heart into it this time. In the morning,
when I hear a heavy letter clamping through the mail slot in the
hall, I prefer not to go out at all. By the way, could you do me
a huge favor? The following has happened to me: I have made a

radio play out of Wilde's "The Happy Prince"* (Three years ago). It was very well received, was accepted, a very talented band-master wrote the music for it and then nothing came out of it. Suddenly last autumn, the work of another authoress, who hadn't made much of an effort, was put on. (This tale lends itself to dramatization because Wilde wrote it mostly as dialogue.) *My* piece is certainly different, has a background story, and is, without self-praise! more original than that of the competitor's. Now they want to make me believe that my piece wasn't taken because I didn't have the publisher's approval. If this is needed with Wilde, I don't know, maybe it is, but I would like to ask you, since you after all do live in England, to try and apply in order to get me the approval to dramatize Wilde's tale. Perhaps I will venture to dramatize a second tale. Will you do me this favor?

And yet one more thing: Would you know a good family that could host my eighteen-year-old nephew Felix for the summer? He should learn English. And how much would that cost? (Anything expensive is out of the question.)

That is enough for now. I, as well, would gladly learn English. Yes, Hannerle has gotten his report card and brought home a lot of A's. Who does *this* child take after! Certainly not me.

We're all sending our regards to you and likewise to your husband and your child!

I don't send her a kiss, because I'm sniveling.

　　Ilse

*We called that piece "The Unhappy Prince."

March 14, 1938

Dearest Lilian,

I'm just answering briefly. Because the overall decision only has to be made during the next days. But both your letters deserve an immediate response. You are a fine dear fellow, Liliput, I always knew that, and this recent test of our friendship wasn't even necessary. But the confirmation of your decency has made me really happy. You're "my" only person that I can rely on. Thousand thanks! Many thanks to James too: it's especially nice of him to have agreed to raise my boys, because this really isn't a minor responsibility. The thing is that I would send Hanuš away for a longer period of time only when life at home would become unbearable, which isn't the case so far (and with God's help never will). When Felix travels to England he will take the boy with him, and I will be very thankful if you want to keep him for the holidays. (. . .)

I am already observing my Hanuš with your eyes. I do not believe he will cause any difficulties except for his food habits. He eats very slowly and dawdles. To make it somehow work, it's best to let him eat everything with a spoon, which naturally annoys me and which, hopefully, you will be able to wean him from. He is, as regards independence not further along than Tommy, who is of a totally different nature. But otherwise he is well-behaved, compliant, and is good-natured. With love, he can be convinced of everything. He needs the so-called "twilight tenderness": i.e. when in the evenings you take him on your lap, give him a kiss and tell him a story, he has a warm spot for that. Tommy makes nothing of it; he is one hundred percent a man and, if he demands tenderness, it is only because, on principle, he wants to have everything that the older one gets. Hanuš is a bookworm, reading for him is above everything else; but next, out of emulation instinct, he loves uniforms, soldiers and puppet theater. I would readily leave him with you for at least one year but his principal, who likes him very much, advised me against it. Hanuš is not yet advanced enough in Czech and may forget it because of the new language. Czech, as you know, is very difficult, and being with you he would have no opportunity of speaking it, so he will forget it.

He is feeling, as far as this is possible for a child, as a Czechoslovakian, and his fatherland is for him presently the most supreme thing in the world. He has not yet been directly affected by antisemitism. Perhaps there will be a miracle and we Jews will continue to be equal here. Anyway, I consider your will as the deed and look forward to spending a beautiful summer somewhere in the Beskids with you and yours.

Should our plans materialize, then you must write to me what clothes Hanuš needs, provided the climate there is different from here. He has been, thank God, through all childhood diseases, so that we don't need to worry about that. He only gets a light cold and red throat, but usually it's quickly over.

I have to cook now. Once again, thousands thanks to you and your husband for your goodness, and for you a kiss

from your
Ilse

March 28, 1938

Dearest Lilian,

I really must ask you for forgiveness, for having aligned you, even for one moment, with people who until recently were my friends—or pretended to be— and now show an entirely different face. But when everything around is suddenly transformed, when all at once everything is filled with hostility and cruelty, one loses faith in everything. Your letter describing the demonstration on behalf of Czechoslovakia is good and comforting, but I fear the sympathy of the masses doesn't help as long as those who matter are content merely to protest "energetically," "resolutely" and "more resolutely." Lilian, for three weeks I have been ill, mentally and physically, in a way I have never experienced. I cannot read, write, work; nothing can keep me home; I'm drifting around the streets aimlessly and restlessly, which is for me very detrimental because I encounter people who feel exactly the same and who have no other theme than: What next?!?

Lilian, you must not forget that Germans live among us, Germans we have lived with in peace and friendship, but who, since the beginning of the Henlein Movement,[69] have all become Hitler supporters. I no longer know here any one of my, until recently, German friends, who doesn't ogle at Germany. I believe that our

Germans are the worst enemies of our fatherland. Since the coup in Austria,[70] they have exhibited their disposition quite openly, from the white half stockings of the young fellows (still forbidden last year), to the older generation's open demonstration of venom. And the worst is for us Jews. How Hitler must fear us that he persecutes us so! Up to this day I have believed in God; but if he doesn't give us a token of his existence soon, I can no longer. This persecution of Jews is inhuman. What should we do; *where* should we go? I love my homeland with an almost painful passion; I am Czechoslovakian through and through and no worse than those who make us out to be inferior, bad and depraved; no, on the contrary, I am *better*, I say that without false shame, I know what and who I am! Lilian, I do not think yet of a bad end for us; no, I hope and wish ardently that everything will soon take a turn for the better; but you and Gre, you are my hope for my children, who, if no one helps in time, shouldn't be trampled down and humiliated here. Then the both of you will help me, right? I think it doesn't come down so much anymore to Willi and me. We must do whatever we can to enable the children to go abroad. Therefore, I am taking your—perhaps offered without thinking—invitation to send Hanuš with Felix to you, seriously.

If something comes out of the thing with Felix, I will send the boy with him. You will love him and he will love you too. Felix is free as of June the first. He therefore can come in mid-June if the expenses do not exceed what his parents can spend on him. He should really learn English because he has a childless uncle in America who is interested in him. He is raised as Czech, however speaks German well. Some English, too. If—God Forbid! something happens: I mean war, then the difficulty of Felix's conscription in the army might arise. So please settle the matter soon. As for Felix, he is a handsome big boy whom I have liked very much as a child. Since then, his milieu has unfortunately turned him materialistic without any special intellectual interests; but maybe I'm wrong. He is, though, a dear young man.

We are all so desperate; each of us somehow connected to Vienna; each can tell something terrible. A cousin of mine, a lawyer,

president of a distinguished Jewish organization, "B'nai Brith," was
arrested and locked up. His wife hasn't heard of him since. We had
Yehuda Ehrenkranz over here. Willi convinced him not to go back
to Vienna but, if it's possible, to travel directly to Palestine and
wait there for his wife. He broke down completely; some of his
dearest friends were among those who had preferred to die by their
own hands. Now he faces the difficulty of procuring the money
for the ship tickets. His tour, which looked very promising, was
canceled because no one can be bothered with attending lectures.
Willi does for him more than he is actually allowed to. I arranged
a private lecture for him at my place that yielded something, even
though nothing worth mentioning.

Please write immediately this time! And write also if you really
want Hannerle. Regarding Felix, you must write exactly what are
the costs and *where* he will stay. What is the town near you?

Thanks for the picture of Gillian. I grant you all the happiness
with her! Attached is the photo of Sylvia, who is at the same age.
Apparently she cannot sit yet. But then she is not blessed with a
healthy mother who would breastfeed her. Send this picture back!
And I thank you a lot for the letter!

Your Ilse

Vitkovice, April 5, 1938

Dearest Lilian!

It's half past ten in the morning, the boys are at school and
the food is on the stove: the possibility to write to you presents
itself and should be used. I am happy when I can chat with you. I
have no one else anyway. Not long ago, when all attics had to be
emptied due to an air-raid drill, Mama brought me a pack of letters from you, and I realized that the friendship with you actually
transcends the scope of common friendships between two girls.
Praise God! I reckon we have known each other for 21 years now,
right? Since Nyköping. You are my "longest-term" girlfriend. And
actually, you know me best because I am more open with you than

I am with everybody else.

I hold on inwardly to the plan with Hannerle, even if I do not speak about it. But if the thing with Felix materializes, then the boy will come to you. Hannerle poses the funniest questions about this. He absolutely cannot picture England; you could probably write him one of your nice letters. What interests him mostly is: does he have to travel through Germany (at the back of my mind: is that safe?), with what sort of ship, and for how long, if the ship doesn't sink? Then, because he doesn't like meat, if one must eat a lot of meat in England, and if a lot of fish (he has never eaten one). Will he have a "friend? Will he see soldiers? That would be a small anthology of his most burning interests. I often now observe him objectively, trying to see him with your eyes. In comparison to your brothers he resembles, I think, Oscar mostly. He is quiet, at least as long as he's alone, but actually not always "good." He annoys me with his lack of independence. He laces up his shoes by himself, indeed, but can tie no loop, which however doesn't disturb him. He simply walks home with untied shoes (slippers must be worn during classes in our schools). To see him coming back from school is really amusing. The coat is buttoned up askew, the cap sitting adventurously on the head, the scarf fantastically knotted, unless one of his classmates or his principal who likes him very much has pity on him and dresses him. When he sees something gripping, his five-minute way to school takes him an hour. He cannot remember on what side he has his hair parted! He's not very organized either. In exchange, he has a completely good character, doesn't bear a grudge, is very corrigible and is not defiant. I count the fact that he tussles willingly, among his "good" qualities. His piano playing continues to please me. He has brought home for Easter an exercise that at first I couldn't play: a piece with six flats. But he knew it by heart before long. Now he's playing out of Schumann's *Scenes from Childhood*, "First Loss."

Frau Ilka[71] from Budapest visited here recently and on this occasion I was invited to old Frau Spitzer's. At the time of the coup the old lady was in Linz with her daughter Resi, and has suffered greatly. Her son-in-law, Dr. Morgenstern, a famous Zionist leader, was imprisoned on the first day and hasn't yet been released, while no one knows why he was arrested. An awful lot of people have been arrested only because they were wealthy or in good positions. Yes, Frau Spitzer had a difficult time there. Her passport was taken from her although she is Czechoslovakian, and it took much effort to bring her back home.

Now it is almost eleven o'clock. Fare really well, regards to your husband and take a loving kiss from

Your

Ilse

April (?), 1938

Dearest Lilian,

It is really almost the same as before my first journey to you! You haven't forgotten even the express letter. But unfortunately, poor Hanuš will have to stay home. The explanation—which makes me really sad! —follows. First, as I wrote to you, Felix has to complete his matriculation, and this will be only in May, or even the beginning of June. Second, he has difficulties with his passport, and third, he already has to enlist for military service. Please share all this information with the family in Stevenage. It's the teaching couple, isn't it, and we would have liked that very much. However, if they don't mind, leave open the possibility that Felix, his surname is Auslaender, would after all come, and write to me about your expenses so we can put that in order. I am so unhappy. I wish I knew (something has broken in my typewriter) Hannerle is safe. After the speech Henlein allowed himself yesterday, we can expect anything. Willi behaves very peculiarly regarding the England affair. When I try to make it clear to him how fortunate the boy may be that, under the circumstances, he can come to you, he asks in return whether I don't think about the thousands of children who just don't have this luck. Is that the standpoint of a father? I do not want him to leave, but I would like to protect my child from humiliation and persecution. But what is clearer to me than Willi's explanations is the possibility that you will decide to go with the little one to Sweden. It will be hard enough for you with the baby without having to provide for another dependent child. However, I consider it risky to travel with Gillian. You want to wean her; she will therefore have to change the milk twice within a short period of time, which would easily cause intestinal catarrh, especially in the summer. You should breastfeed Gillian as long as you can, Lilian! Unfortunately, I wasn't so lucky to be able to feed my children by myself, but I would have done it for quite a long time!

Now you should learn what worries me. I would have happily sent Hannerle to you because I most likely have to go to a women's health resort. I had a miscarriage at Easter and the physician determined on this occasion that my womb is one single wound. I have had months-long pains and discharge, but unfortunately, I never dare complain about pains because I'm afraid to be suspected of indulging in self-pity. So now I am in danger if I don't do anything. But: *me* in a health resort, the children in a summer resort, the (household goes on), Willi, who lately has afflictions again, finally in Karlsbad, *that won't do!* However, if the older would have been with you, somebody from the family would have taken the little one, and I would have maybe cured myself at home or even in a bath resort! Anyway, one of the two of us would have been sent to a health resort: the doctor would have decided where. But if Felix doesn't go, Hannerl must stay here, and everything will be different. I must again go to some primitive summer resort where I'll have only work and no recovery, and my condition will not improve. I would like to once have a good time for at least 14 whole days!

My physical and mental state is wretched; I had a disgusting experience during my last radio lecture (it might have really been the last one) which proved that the Nazis are already at the helm. My literary career has likely ended.

I don't want to spoil your mood. I very much hope I will still be able to send you the boy. He himself is already very happy. If it doesn't work this year, then perhaps another year.

Give regards to your husband, and here's a kiss for you, and for the little girl too, who is hopefully already healthy!

From your Ilse

23. V. 38

Dear Aunt Lilian!

I thank you and uncle James for your lovely invitashion. But my daddy does not let me go, he shais that I am too little. I was already so happy! Maybe I will come, when I am older.

Fine, that at your home I have to eat no meat.

Many greetings to you, uncle and your little girl

Your Hanuš

Greetings from Tommiček

Dearest Lilian!

Thank you for your letter! Good for you, you're going to Sweden! Can you imagine, we nearly went to the Adriatic in Yugoslavia? By bus, very cheap, the stay there would have been inexpensive. But on Saturday came the mobilization [of the Czechoslovakian army], and now we naturally have entirely different worries than travelling. We are quite depressed, as you can understand, although mobilization supposedly doesn't mean war yet. We are so close to the border, around 50 km.

Those Sudeten Germans! I cannot describe how vile their behavior is. A few days ago, a five-year-old whippersnapper said to one of my acquaintances who wanted to joke with the fine fellow: "Are you a Bohemian or Bolshevik? Then I am not allowed to shake your hand!" "Wait only, until Hitler comes!" has become a frequent threat. Suddenly one half of town has become German: many, who aren't German at all, out of fear for their existence. As far as I can see, fear is the main inducement that has made the SdP so popular, for everyone who hasn't joined the party is threatened

with a note on the "black list." Up until Thursday all Germans
wore dirndl, that is, Tyrolean costumes: loden hats and white calf
tights. But on Thursday evening during an election rally of the SdP
in the German House, some youths flocked before the place and
began hunting down white calf tights.

I am sorry it has come to unrest, but on the other hand I can
understand the Czechs, for whom wearing Tyrolean costumes must
be a provocation. Since Friday they have disappeared completely
from the scene.

I personally feel bad about this because, well, as you know, I
liked to wear dirndl dresses. But that has come to an end, and the
boys too will have to cast off this lovely and practical attire. We Jews
are naturally hit the hardest again. Our children are all Czech, but
we adults have always spoken German between ourselves, which
is our mother tongue after all. Now the Czechs declare: "How can
you use this language when the Germans inflict on you so much
injustice?" But on the other hand, when we make the effort to speak
Czech, they scornfully say: "Look at the Jews! They know how to
readily adapt!" Apropos, at the demonstrations there are not only
"Germans out!" shouts. We are mentioned as well. In the autumn
I am going to the volunteering nurses. Lilian, do not forget that I
am bequeathing my sons to you if anything happens to us! Isn't this
terrible that one cannot plan anything a week ahead? Everything is
uncertain. If England, France, Russia promised to help us, Germany
wouldn't dare come near us. I would have travelled so gladly to Yugoslavia. It is wonderfully beautiful over there; the sea and the warm
sand would have done all of us so much good. My nephew Felix
wants to enlist voluntarily. There, you see again how pointless it is to
make plans.

How is Gillian? How do you actually call her? Does she have
no nickname? And Oskar is Papa! Little Ocki![72] "Kristen" is a very
nice name. How is Acki's little one called? And how is Aunt Gertrude as a grandmother?

I have to take Tommy for a walk now. He is so sweet nowadays
I could eat him up: so joyful and loveable. Poor children!

It's a good thing that I'm already finishing this letter. Let me hear from you soon, your letters are so beneficial for me these days. Farewell, Lilian!

    Ilse

June 14, 1938

Dearest Lilian!

My typewriter is broken and I have to write with a pen, which isn't at all easy for me. I wanted to send your mother a congratulatory telegram because your letter did arrive the day before her birthday, but it cost more than I had; she will surely accept my wishes in retrospect, right? I decided, after reading your letters, to pack both children and travel to you! Willi has done me the favor and inquired at the travel agency, and it wouldn't be that expensive at all. But these days, to travel with two Jewish-looking, Czech-speaking children for almost 1½ days through Germany?! Through Poland it takes too long and is too expensive. So although I had to abandon my bold plans for this year, it would interest me how expensive life is in Steninge[73] itself. Please write to me accurately how much a day of modest living would cost for a family of two adults and two children. Lilian, our mountains are certainly beautiful, but I would so much love to be again by the sea!

I want to tell you what has been my most ardent wish for years: to spend one summer in Fünen, in Denmark! Since I have read Pontoppidan,[74] since I began to love Anderson, it has been my dream to get to know this country. Do you believe it's so unattainable? You are now, after all, in the vicinity, I venture to note, relying on my frail geographical knowledge. Please try to get some information! And then: how would it be, if we resolved to meet there next year? Willi, and perhaps also your husband, would surely say: "crazy!"; but these two men do not know what you and I are capable of when we want to see each other, isn't it so? It can be a quite small place, the sea is after all infinite, and I am willing to do without meat and "comfort" if I can only be there! *How long*

will you be staying in Steninge? When does your husband arrive
there? Are there many foreigners over there? Many apartments?
Answer everything accurately and at the soonest! I am already in the
know regarding the climate etc. Is there a shallow beachside? How
is Gillian coming along? Does she still crawl in the sand? Does she
eat well? How is her relationship with her grandmother? (Does
James still have parents and siblings?)

I find the abbreviation "Lill" delightful, but if you do not
want it there is nothing to do about it. When Gillian will someday come to me she will be called "Zillinka," and if you go nuts,
ha-ha! Who did she get the beautiful dark eyes from? Lill, I am
not as amusing as it seems! I am sunk in an abyss of sadness and
despair I simply cannot come out of. That I am Jewish is beginning to appear like a curse to me. Being Jewish means being
without rights, defenseless, a scapegoat for everybody. What have
we here in the Republic, for which we are willing, with trembling
fear, to sacrifice our lives? The German plague infects everybody
and the Czechs have never loved us, just as other nations have
not. If you want to give me some help at one point you could,
and without even special effort. It would suffice, every now and
again, to write in a foreign language (which is highly regarded
here!) to one of the bigger newspapers and express discontent over
an allegedly barbarian incident. We're striving after all for tour-
ism, and that is why they listen to the voices of foreign countries.
There is, for example, the following case. Recently, an acquaintance of mine who was speaking, really discreetly, German on
the "Nádražní třída" (the train station street), was accosted most
viciously and insulted by a gentleman of higher standing. ("Are
you still speaking German, you stinking Jews? . . . etc.") The next
day, in Prostějor (a big Moravian city) my sister-in-law, who was
speaking Czech while crossing the street with my mother-in-law,
was accosted again for that reason ("Now you can suddenly speak
Czech, you stinking Jew!") These two scenes must be described
with the voiced disapproval of a foreigner who *otherwise strongly
sympathizes with the Czechs.* Would you be party to that? Believe

me, you would do a great service! Another matter is the boycott.
The members of the SdP were told in the rally to buy only from
Germans and Christians. Consequently, the Czechs boycotted the
Germans in return. The Jews are doing very badly; *they* cannot
and do not want to boycott, but this rabble-rousing is advanta-
geous to nobody! Lilian, there has never been such an atmosphere
of hatred, envy and contempt! "The Jews are to blame for everything": this is hammered into children with the most ridiculous
and bogus proofs. In addition, the different nationalities hate each
other after having lived side by side for 20 years in perfect peace.
Yes, there are state-of-emergency regions: in the German Ore
Mountains, the Weavers,[75] maybe also in others areas. But also
in the Carpathian Rus there is suffering and hunger; Jewish and
Carpatho-Ruthenian craftsmen are living there under the same
wretched circumstances. These are the results of the crisis, not
the vicious intention of the government. Yes, it is simpler to take
money from rich Jews and use it to start "public work." It is certainly easier to put Jewish employees, who have no one to turn to
for help, out of work and assign their posts to "Aryan" contenders;
but that is unjust, mean and illegal. To what end am I torturing
you with those reports, Lilian, you who despise any injustice, you
who are decent through and through?!

I cannot free myself of these things and I cannot forget that,
for instance, a Christian lady, whom we've asked to enquire after
a cousin in Vienna who has stopped writing lately, has told us she
was walking in the street with Olga (that's her name) and Olga was
spat on! Olga already lives under the poorest conditions and she
and her son have barely a piece of dry bread. *That* is Hitler's sow-
ing. How can God, if there is a God! just look on!

Ach, I stop already. I wish I were with you, but will I ever be
able to forget what we are going through now?

You see, now I can't after all congratulate Mutti. Please, tell
her I wanted to do this, that I wish her happiness with my whole
heart, which she anyway already has because she has a lovely peaceful homeland and doesn't have to fear for her children.

Kissing you,
Your Ilse

Lilian, are you expecting a baby?

Witkowitz, October 10, 1938

Dear Lilian,

Your letter arrived in only four days, which is clearly wonderful
when one thinks that it takes six days for the mail from Moravia.
I was really yearning for news from you! Ostrava stays Czech for
the time being. However, the Polish and German borders are only
minutes away; this hair-raising new demarcation disrespectfully
overrides all human rights. Ostrava is completely cut off from the
rest of the world. Since Schönbrunn (Svinov) was occupied by the
Germans yesterday, we are left without milk and electrical power.
The broadcasting station is in German hands as well. Lilian, what
we have been through during the last weeks here is an unparal-
leled mental martyrdom. We all love peace for we know what war
means, especially for us who live on the border. The conscription
of men was portentous, yet it was mostly observed willingly, and
those who stayed home volunteered for air raid duty, the women
for the Red Cross or, like me, at least donated blood. We hoped
for help from our allies; it was after all clear that our small country
could not stand up against a mighty Germany. Our nerves were
on the verge of breaking. Especially since the German radio propaganda has stirred up the agitation without limit. Nevertheless,
no German was jostled, even though the Sudeten-Germans spread
the nastiest atrocity propaganda—which, by the way, reality has
surpassed! —arousing hatred against the Jews. Then all the radios
were confiscated, which at least has provided respite from unnerv-
ing contradictory news. In front of our window they dug shelters
and the children played in them. All people with any means left.
We stayed, but in what state! Especially as we began to doubt our
"friends" would help us. Every evening there was a blackout. There

we sat from six o'clock, in the dark, without the consolation of the
radio, mostly with no candles or batteries which were sold out immediately, feverish and filled with terrible fear. The suitcases of the
children, who were supposed to be evacuated with their schools,
stood already packed. Each child had been given a medallion with
our picture put in it. The children were mischievous and carefree as
always, and we were very impatient with them.

And then, at the last minute, came the Four-Power-Confer-
ence. Lilian, we were still hoping for an amicable solution, but the
masses knew it at once: "Oní nás prodají!" They are going to sell
us! One could hear in the streets. But they didn't just sell us; they
bartered us away! Never have souls been sold off so basely! Hitler
wanted to have "his" Germans. Good, but why did England permit him to seize so many hundreds of thousands of Czechs and
Jews? Lilian, completely Czech regions, where maybe not even one
citizen speaks German, were taken by Germany. And we Jews?!
The Germans who are living in those undivided parts don't even
consider migrating to Germany. Why should they? They have their
nice properties, their well-paid positions, which they will not give
up. Yes, they were an excellent tool in Hitler's hands. They have
undermined the Republic by fomenting artificial hatred between
Germans and Czechs. But they are staying here because Germany's
freedom doesn't seem desirable to everyone. Yes, and after the prey
had fallen came the vultures and pounced on the corpses. Poland
has taken lots from us: the wonderful ironworks of Třynietz, the
many, many mines which were our source of life. And again the
same injustice to Czech towns and villages.

My maid comes home with red eyes from crying; she has just
read that as of tomorrow she is becoming Polish. The girl from
downstairs comforts her: "Ach, God, you are only Polish but I
belong to Germany, and in my whole village, Polanka, not one
person speaks German." Wilma has become Polish and so have my
relatives in Oderberg, but they are nowhere near as unhappy as
they would be had they become Germans.

Why has no one over there in Munich thought about us Jews?
Didn't Chamberlain know the danger in store for the Jews when
he bartered them to Germany? What will all those poor people do
who now increase the droves of "tiresome refugees?" We're reading
in the newspapers about all sorts of touching funding activities in
England. But it doesn't affect us; it is a screaming mockery when
measured against the disaster which England has brought upon
us, and not even for its own advantage!!! How can Chamberlain,
damned by the many hundreds of thousands whose homeland he
had taken, still live in peace?

Our homeland here is destroyed. Ostrava has no rail connection
with the surrounding world: its food supply is endangered. (Willi's
livlihood is destroyed as well, but he is only one out of countless
thousands!) It is overflowed with refugees, which number would
have been significantly higher had not the government, using great
caution, announced the occupation of the respective zones only two
days in advance. We are devastated over President Benesch's resignation[76] and we (this time I mean us Jews) fear the new government,
which, as it has declared, will "conform to Germany." The Slovakian
Government has officially declared itself against the "Marxist-Jew-
ish ideology." It so happens that I am reading now André Maurois'
book, "Benjamin Disraeli." Chamberlain, it appears, had a predeces-
sor. Antisemitism here rises alarmingly. The people are shouting: "It
is all the fault of the Jews. The Jews have sold us out!" Where is the
logic? But hate does not require logic!

Yugoslavia has invited many Czech children for one school
year. Lilian, what if you could prompt anyone to take on a similar
initiative? I still would happily send the boys to you, now even
more than before, but I cannot do that considering your present
circumstances. By the way, don't you have a "Lady's help?" I know
a young Jewish girl, can run an efficient household, especially fond
of children, who would love to go to England: Judith Birn; you
met her as a child. Please, dear Lilian, overcome your exhaustion:
try to help! We Czechoslovaks urgently need help, help of any sort,

if we want to successfully rebuild our fatherland.

I thank you many times for the lovely picture of you! Is that James? He looks very nice. And the little one is sweet! I have written to Eli, but I don't think she will reply.

Kissing you,
Ilse

I am sitting on your bed,[77]
watching you asleep,
your cheeks are red,
your sweet rest nothing stirs.

May you never learn
what your mother senses—
may you God's protection gain
for you are defenseless.

The loveliest hours a mother has,
are by the children's bed,
in bitter fruits of hate,
our people are immersed.

Dangers woven by envy
lie in wait for you.
May you find God's mercy,
unfortunate Jewish child.

Witkowitz, December 1, 1938

Dearest Lilian!

Your last letter was a sad surprise for me. It pains me that you had such a misfortune. I believe it's among the worst things to watch such a little being dying no sooner than you had held it in your arms. But how did it come to be a premature birth? That rarely happens without any reason? You will probably not be able to forget this little girl for the rest of your life. But perhaps one day you will be happy that it parted from you without having to know the cruelty of this ugly world and its despicable people.

You have no idea how unbearable life here in the Č.S.R has become. Ostrava is swamped with refugees from Poland, Germany and Slovakia. Saddest of all is the way Jews are being treated. In Slovakia, old people were hunted out in the middle of the night, brought to the border in their nightclothes and abandoned in the harshest cold. Even here, Jews with Polish citizenship are deported immediately, without giving them valid passports or allowing them to take their possessions which, as is often the case, they've acquired over thirty years or longer. Among others, Frau Birn was deported with her family, so my inquiry regarding Judith is now obsolete. We have just received an urgent letter from Wellner[78] imploring Willi to try and arrange a delay for his old parents' deportation until their Palestine certificate is obtained. In the so-called "no-man's-land," the small piece of land between the borders where the stateless refugees stay in roadside ditches, shocking scenes are taking place. A few days ago, a young woman, who gave birth for the first time, died in a tent with her newly born child because no one would help her. Is it so, that misfortune makes people inhuman? I have always thought that misfortune makes the suffering of the other understandable. Can you understand why I'm looking away when I see my former German acquaintances? They disgust me, and I'm ashamed for them. Almost all the people whom I had loved have disappointed me deeply; only a handful have shown themselves to be truly human and decent. One of these rare exceptions is my childhood friend Zdenka[79]. (You may remember the neighbor's girl, with whom I always brought the cows to pasture.) She came to see me and cried with furious indignation. Then offered me help in case I needed her. She herself has four children and her husband is a policeman. She brought three freshly laid eggs for my boys. Isn't that touching?

What shall become of us, we have no idea. Willi thinks we still don't have the right to go away when so many other Jews need asylum more urgently. Many of our friends emigrate and want us to join them, mostly for Willi's sake. I now realize how popular and appreciated he is. A prominent and wealthy family wants to take us at their own expense, all for Willi's sake. I would very much like to start a small account with you for Hannerle, if I knew how. If it's somehow possible, he should come to you, even if only for the summer months.

And now, a happier note: my English classes. I'm teaching a young woman (what a joke!). I cannot afford to buy the textbook, but she owns the Ullstein edition of *Tausend Worte Englisch*[80] The way I do it is that first I learn the material by myself, and when I master it, teach it to her. That way I memorize it more thoroughly. For several days now my sister Mutzi has been studying with me as well, so I'm repeating each lesson three times. You may recall I used this method to learn to play the lute. I'd be very thankful to you and James if you'd like to assist me. I would gladly get newspaper excerpts, feuilletons and, eventually, old magazines in English. (. . .) I'm hungry for learning just as in my best days as a young girl. Do you by any chance have also an old English-German dictionary for me? **I have never money to buy ist. Kiss your little Baby,** regards to James from me; his affection honors me! Take a loving kiss from me and lots of regards from Willi.

> **Always Your good friend**
> Ilse

Witkowitz, December 25, 1938

Dear James,

Many thanks for your lovely letter, which I understood well except for three words I had to look up. I also understood you mean us well, and I am even more thankful for that than for the **English lesson.** I'm glad Lilian has such a loving husband! The two books also arrived on time, but you shouldn't spend so much money on us! I will learn from the books twice as happily, first because they're from you, and second because they're good. My son thanks you as well for the rabbit story, but it will still take a while until he'll be able to read it. I don't teach him English yet; it would be a burden I do not wish to impose on him. But he can count to one hundred in English, add and subtract, and is terribly proud about that.

I would like to write you something happy, Christmassy, but my heart is so heavy that I cannot. The measures against us Jews here in the Č.S.R have nowadays taken such harsh forms that the thought of staying is no longer relevant. My husband is in Prague since yesterday—when one wants to travel from here to Prague, one must, thanks to Munich, travel through Germany—in order to seek advice about emigration possibilities. The options include China, Haiti and—unfortunately, only as faint hope—Palestine.

Elli Wendland has recently written very nicely and lovingly, offering her help. Now the question is how she can, and how far her willingness goes. Emigrating to Argentina is still very promising, but perhaps she doesn't mean *this* kind of help at all. Unfortunately, it takes so terribly long for her answer to arrive that until then, many bad things can happen. We no longer hope for good things. Life has become unbearable for us; we live here almost like among beasts—forgive my expression: I hope the real beasts will forgive it, too! —and not like human beings. The Germans, with whom we have always lived in harmony, are the worst. All the suffering that we endure still seems insufficient to them. They, who betrayed their fatherland, agitate and lash out at us who were loyal to it. Sadly, the Czechs must dance to the German tune. What do you think about such consulates, it involves two different ones, who, when asked by despairing, deported people, "What should we do?" come up with answers: "You can go hang yourself as far as I'm concerned!" and "You still have a gas valve at home!"

I know personally the people who have received these advices. I think England, which played such a fateful role for us, should now intervene. Huge donations streamed in from England, and it was explicitly announced they would be distributed "regardless of race and ethnicity." But it so happens here that the Jews have either to take care of their own refugees or pay for them when they are put in refugee asylums, which isn't the case with other refugees. One becomes hard and wicked now: my heart is filled with thoughts of revenge, hatred and ill wishes for those we have to thank for this nameless disaster. God works in mysterious ways—he lets monsters like Hitler and Goebbels live, yet a human being, as our great, generous writer Karel Čapek, who has written works like *Die Weisse Krankheit* and *Die Mutter*,[81] must die so young! A week ago friends of ours lost their only eight-year-old daughter, a child like a ray of sunshine, sweet and loveable. These are good and serious people who lived only for the sake of that child. Where is the justice in that? You are writing so full of trust, so beautifully, that you believe in a good future, really, also for us? You see, if we emigrate now to a climate that Willi, my husband, can't cope with—he already worked as a settler[82] in Palestine for eight years, and returned back to Europe seriously ill—how would we feel about such a "new" life?

I am still hoping to send you my boys, but now everything is doubly uncertain. But I would like to draw your attention to one thing: we know a boy who a few days ago was taken by an English Evangelical Mission (for the protection of children, I think) to London on an airship. It would feel good to have a way out in case of an emergency. Couldn't you find out the exact address of this Mission, and maybe get in touch with them? I am now clinging twice as much to my children, I don't wish to see any other people anymore: I either pity or despise them.

But now I should stop writing. Otherwise you will lose any desire for any further correspondence with me, if that hasn't already happened. I am working hard on my English tasks; just now I am learning the Lord's Prayer. **And forgive us our trespasses, As we forgive them, that trespass against us**—He who taught this prayer was also a Jew. He too was persecuted and tortured. I don't believe I would ever be able to forgive those who sin against us.

Live well and may you and Lilian be so happy, as one must be when one still has his fatherland and freedom. Believe me: this is infinitely a lot!

And once more thanks for everything!

Ilse

Dear Uncle, I thank you very much! Hanuš.

Witkowitz, January 5, 1939

Dearest Lilian,

I am rushing to answer for a childish reason: I want to give you the opportunity to respond sooner so that your letter, and a detailed one at that, will arrive in time for my birthday. This is my birthday wish: that you, James too, should write to me around this time. I want so much to get as many letters as possible now, perhaps out of feelings of anxiety, out of an awakened need, to feel that one is, after all, not entirely alone?

I have tuned the radio to London R. and hear English spoken, very excited; the wind, the radio wind that is, roars; now a woman is crying: more terrible wind; and half an hour ago I heard the German news. I do that every evening because I dread the German news. I thank you so much **for your kind letter, you are a fine fellow** meaning to say: a good sport. Lilian, I will never forget how thankful I am for your letters since May. Never!!! My belief in humanity clings to you, otherwise it would be reduced to nothing. Your plan to establish a home for ten children is beautiful. Do you have any particular children in mind?

Our situation here is unsettled. We are caught in a mouse-trap. There is no way out, and when there is, then we cannot take any money. And without money we cannot go anywhere. How does one judge a world that so calmly overlooks this violation and robbery of the Jews? Look, we ourselves can't do a thing, neither protect ourselves nor write against this. But there has to be an opposition abroad in articles that expose grievances, condemn short-comings and in this manner take our side. There is, for instance, the issue of expelled Polish Jews. On the day of the expulsion they had to leave their homes and businesses, but were not allowed to enter Poland. The majority registered for the emigration group to Haiti (Santo Domingo). This, of course, doesn't run so smoothly as they are wanting experts, organizers, foreign currency. But at least they are allowed to live somewhere until everything is sorted out and they have the prospect of ending this dreadful state. But there again among them are those who won't be permitted to go, some due to advanced age, some because of poor health, and some lacking the required money. They are not allowed to remain here any longer, cannot enter Poland. What then? The Birn family is among these unfortunates; not long ago I applied to you on behalf of Judith. I hear so much about the Baldwin Fund,[83] ach, if only it could help all those unfortunate people! What a mean thing that one isn't allowed to take along one's hard-earned money. To make people poor and stateless, this is the fruit German "culture" has yielded.

And on top of that, to squeeze out profit from the suffering of those miserable Jews. I want to tell you a contemporary joke: A Jew enters a travel agency. He can't answer the question where he wants to travel. The manager finally places a big globe in front of him. The Jew spins the globe in all directions, studies it attentively, and finally asks timidly, "Do you have nothing else in stock?" Or a riddle: Who is the greatest chemist in the world? Hitler. He has made gold out of Grünspan.[84]

Regarding my level of English, I have actually reached the next-to-last booklet in the *Tausend Worte*. Both my students are working on the third. Grete Rosenberg is a bit lazy and studies only whatever I drum into her; Mutzi, on the other hand, is very conscientious and doesn't proceed until one thing is well absorbed. That way I know the first three books almost by heart. I'm convinced that I am also learning things I will never need; or do you believe I will ever have the opportunity to say, **Could anyone be happier than I rushing on my motor-bike with my best girl behind me on the pillion-set?** But perhaps one day one of my children will say that to me. Just now there is a man singing the Hindu Song on the radio,[85] the one you loved so much during your last stay with us. If anything happens here then you or James should come and take the children, all right? That's, after all, the easiest, and I will save the money for this. I'm afraid I cannot send you anything, allegedly the letters are being X rayed. Is that true?

So now, servus[86] dearest girl. How's the child? What can it do now? I'm glad you liked the set. Yes, Mutzi has made it. By the way, Mutzi is looking, until she receives her permit for America, to find employment in England. She can do almost anything: run a big household; do splendid handwork; sick-nursing; social work; was administrator of a retirement home; is conscientious and extremely industrious. Wouldn't you be interested? She is, however, already 46 years old, but makes a younger impression. She would gladly settle for a lower salary in order to learn the language. Perhaps you can contact an employment agency. She can pay for the journey, but the work permit and the prospective position must be arranged. Please, be patient with this new appeal to your kindness too, and do whatever you can. She is eating up her hard-won savings and cannot and doesn't want to find a position here. Whoever employs Mutzi is scoring a hit. We have long forgotten the things she had done to Mama and me; anyway, only the initiated know about this, which doesn't make her less unfortunate and needy. She is a refugee who has fled from the occupied areas, should you need to provide information about her.

One more time goodbye, regards to James, and kiss the little one. It's so good that your husband likes me. Imagine, what if he didn't like me?!!!!

Heartfelt greetings,
Ilse

February 1 and 2, 1939

Dear Aunt Lilian,

I want to tell you something today: I can already count up to hundred. But also english. Tommy can also little english. He says always **ei em e's lai** and **haudujudu**.

How are your little girl and uncle James? We have in the house also a little Suse. Now I am sick for three days. That was fine, I read the whole day. I have a new game **Business** game. In next letter I will rite you bout my report.

1. II. 1939

Also I have three B-grades, for writing, drawing and needle-work. In all the other objects I have A-grades. For these Vati gave us a gramophone record: the dwarfs' song from *Snow White*.

     Do you like to go to the cinema, too?

2. II. 1939

Dear aunt Lilian do not count the mistakes, now I end because I am going to Suse. Your Hanuš.

Vítkovice, 18, Švecová, February 3, 1939

My dearest Lilian,

     (. . .) I tried a little poem again, but it will not be admitted (accepted?) in the literature. It does run so:

The best things of the world are these:
A little home full luck and peace,
Without the neighbors envious looks,
With silent hours in homely nooks.
A sound of music, a children's song
And far away are hate and wrong.
No one is there who grieves my heart,
But You shall come and never part.

Please, correct the faults. We want to go to Palestine. It's very difficult to get the certificate. One must have thousand pounds and then it's not sure. We have friends, which will send us the thousand pounds. Until the march 15th is nothing to do. Later will be distribute again some certificates, —shall we be so happy to get one? We should establish together with our friends a little fabrication or a shop. It's good to live in Palestine among mans with the same ideas, experiences and with the same ardent. And it's not so far like San Domingo. The world is such inhuman, such unnatural at present. —Elly hasn't answered. What can she help?

It's uncomfortable to write in the knowledge that one is constantly making mistakes. You have no idea how willingly I'm learning English. It's an outright pleasure for me. I know enough vocabulary, but not how to use it. I simply lack the conversation. Since last week I have a third student of English. Isn't that funny? But I can study with them based on the textbook and they don't ask for more. The third one has even asked me about the fee, which hasn't happened so far. Naturally, I don't ask for any payment for *I am* the one who is learning the most. The basics are already embedded in my mind. Recently I have started to learn Ivrit, Hebrew, by myself. This is certainly one of the most difficult languages. At least that's how it feels to me. The script alone, written from right to left, I am unable to figure out. But I read fairly well the printed letters from school and from learning with Hanuš; the written letters I picked up recently.

I'm glad you received my small packet. Can Gillian wear the shoes and is she happy with them? You know, let me give her presents as long as I can. Who knows how long before I will be dependent upon the presents of others? I sewed for her two panties again, this time with a better cut. As soon as I have time I'll add underwear. At least I'm learning. If we go to Palestine I want to have one more child. A free and lighthearted child not haunted by envy and hatred.

That would be nice. Won't I be too old for that though? Frau Sternlicht, the mother of little Hanna who has died recently, is at times of unsound mind with grief. We are encouraging her husband strongly to have a new child soon and he understands that this is the last hope for Hilde; but *these* are uncertain times, and one doesn't know where one will be next week. Still, I advise him to have the child: many children have been born on ships or even on trains, and precisely such a child could bring consolation and joy to his parents like no other. I have faith in the future, a future in another country. *Here* I could no longer live. All, *all* people have become too appalling. We Jews are once again facing new ordeals. However, our own suffering is but small in comparison to the inhuman wrongs inflicted upon republican Spain.

Now, returning to the currency exchange issue. Do you know that the official rate for the English pound is 124 crowns? Or is it only on paper? Just imagine how much money we'd need in order to go to Palestine when, to attain the certificate, one must have one thousand pounds. You can get those thousand pounds for 124,000 crowns at the National Bank. And the Sternlichts have money to pay for us only at this rate. Pity, pity, that you are not rich. If someone in Palestine could deposit for us one thousand pounds, we don't need to see them at all: we could immediately go there. But unfortunately, the best people have the least money. But it would be nice, right? It would be a matter of pure trust, because one must trust a person for whom one deposits thousands of pounds in the bank.

Now I must prepare the boy for his piano lesson. He is presently playing a rondo by Kuhlau. Very nice and expressive. If we end up going to Palestine you would be able to visit us, wouldn't you?

Lots of Love,
Your Ilse

Witkowitz, February 22, 1939

Dearest Lilian,

I simply cannot understand why you're not writing. Hopefully everything is O.K. with you? I could really think of no other reason. You do know *how* I'm waiting for mail from you. Especially now. Tommy has been at the hospital for a week now. The poor child had to endure a trepanation already for the second time. Three years ago his scarlet fever led to middle ear inflammation and thrombosis with sepsis; we were lucky he came through it. However, not only was there no improvement in that matter over the last three years, but it has become so bad lately that I grabbed the boy, so to speak, on the spur of a moment, and took him to another doctor and, following his advice, immediately went to the hospital, where he underwent surgery the next morning. Awful as the situation was, it became even more upsetting for Tommy because during the examination it turned out that his tonsils had not been properly removed, which made a second operation necessary right after the first bandage-changing. Strangely enough, after the tonsil operation he felt much worse than he had after the trepanation. He had a high fever and I was so anxious that I spent the nights at the hospital with him.

Feb. 23. Today we brought him home. Over approximately seven weeks he will have to go every second day to the hospital to change his bandages, and after that he will, hopefully, be healthy. My new typewriter doesn't have exclamation marks, otherwise I would have expressed my longing for Tommy's recovery with at least three exclamation marks. As the physician explained, it was bad. The bone was affected and there was a big suppuration. I do not need to describe to you how miserable this child is at the moment. At the same time, the little guy is such a touchingly good patient that one could cry over him. He has actually suffered now more than an adult could take, always remains sweet and good at that, and when afraid, he's hiding his fear in a nearly manly way. The physician is a notorious brute and I could murder him when he shouts at the child or even touches him rudely. The first time we went for the bandage exchange we had to go to the outpatient clinic. Now, imagine how a child feels when he finds himself placed in the midst of groaning, bleeding, agonized people, "treated" one way or the other by an intern or a nun, knowing that soon he himself will be agonized. All of a sudden he hid his little head in my coat, and by the twitch in his shoulders I noticed he was sobbing. To bawl aloud was beneath him. Why do some children have to suffer so much? Why does my little boy have to go through the same severe disease twice?

Your silence really troubles me. I'm racking my brain what

could be its cause? And right now we have so many worries and concerns, and it's such a relief to be able to talk about everything with someone close. Elli hasn't written yet. Pity: somehow I did hope for valuable advice. We would like mostly to go to Palestine because we no longer trust people. We're afraid of being persecuted everywhere by antisemitism. However, it is apparently impossible to immigrate to Palestine. Allegedly all the Czech certificates for 1939 have already been allocated. That is unfortunate. It's terribly humiliating for us to live here. At the same time, we are not allowed to leave. We cannot transfer money and without money one can't travel anywhere.

Now the following thing transpires here: As the Jewish misery began here, when so many people became stateless and were deported into a no man's land, the Santo Domingo-action emerged. That is, all those people who didn't have a homeland anymore, and all those who had one but couldn't bear to see the changes it has gone through, grouped together to form a collective in order to emigrate to Santo Domingo. It wasn't an easy decision for any of them to move so terribly far away from parents and everything dear and familiar. But they nevertheless made up their minds to go, for anyone with a strong personality can't live here any longer. Everything was well organized, they received the permits to take money, and they learned and worked feverishly. End of January, then middle; end of February; finally, by the beginning of March the journey should have taken place. The people sold everything they could not take with them, also in order to raise the necessary money. And now the government suddenly refuses to allow any transfer of funds. Yes, England has indeed put money for disposal, it claims, but for *refugees*, and the thousand Domingo expatriates cannot be regarded as refugees. Emigrants too would not be refugees. The people's despair is immense. Now the leaders of the collective are trying for the last time to find salvation in London. What will happen if this fails is unthinkable.

I wish you were here. If only Gillian weren't so little so you could leave her for a couple of days; I believe we could have even funded your trip. What would James say to that?

Couldn't you make an inquiry whether in some fairytale way one could get hold of a Palestine certificate from England????

This letter should be sent by the airmail—I simply *must* receive an answer from you. By the way Ernst's younger son has gone with the last children's transport to England. His mother travelled with him but, since we have no opportunity nor wish to contact her, we don't know where he is. She ostensibly had them both baptized before the trip. Will hardly be of any use to him.

Lilian, have my letters become too tiresome for you?? I very much hope you'll write soon.

Your Ilse

Witkowitz, UL.Pluck. Šveca
March 10, 1939

My dearest Lilian,

I would already send a telegram, because I understood not your long silence. Hanuš awaited (?) a letter from you. I am very sorry, that Willi allow not to send him. Here is so a bad situation. Sunday the Germans may hang out her flags. I fear the view of the "Hackenkreuze."[87] That's a great provocation to the jewish and tscheck people.

One speaks of a new "Anschluss"[88] and you can imagine our mood. Therefore I can't appreciate, that you are discordanced, only because your husband is not at home in time. We have so great sorrows, for little blunders ("Dummheiten")[89] there is no space. Lilian, if you have an influence to lose the humour, you must remember to me. Please, do it (. . .)

Yes, we have applied for purchasing a settlement estate in Palestine. It consists of a little house, a field, fruit and vegetable garden, a cowshed and a chicken farm. But now Lilian, see to it that the resolution of the Palestine question will be favorable for the Jews, otherwise we, and with us thousands of other Jews, will be miserable. I can hardly imagine myself switching to something else

now and becoming a farmer in a hot climate; on top of that without help. But the circumstances are such that this settlement has
become our ardently longed-for destination.

Incidentally, it is not Otto, but Erwin Sternlicht (his brother)
who wants to actually give us the funds for emigration.

Tell me girl, how on earth you imagine handling Hans without a maid or any other help? You simply *can't* do that. Such a boy
needs after all a lot of help, even if he's good, reliable and plays
no tricks. But he lacks independence, is untidy and a bad eater.
Nevertheless, it is my heart's desire to send him to you, but Willi
is most reluctant to do it. You know, I fleetingly really had the ex-
travagant hope you'd come here Lilian. (. . .)

Who knows what the future brings? Anyway do not forget me
if something happens. Cataclysmic events took place today again
in Slovakia. And Hitler is always to be blamed for everything. How
long will he continue to bring calamities? Is the number of people
he plunged into misery still not high enough?

And to you I say once more, with heartfelt love and sincere
sympathy: don't make your life and James' hard with unnecessary
acrimony. You know that he loves you. That must be more important to you than anything else. Don't be sulky with him, stay
friendly also when *he's* ill-humored, because men are mostly angry
for a reason and we women have to be patient and swallow the bitter pill of their displeasure. Life is so hard and bitter anyway. I've
become very modest in the last months, Lilian, and I know *that*
life for my husband, my sons, or anyone else close to me, shouldn't
be even one shade darker because of me. I hold almost no one as
dear as you, and nevertheless there has been ill blood between us
because you're so easily hurt and react harshly. I thought you overcame that. Does this still agonize you? That is a pity, for it surely
brings you many gloomy hours.

Now live well, my dearest girl, regards to James, and kiss the
little frog for me.

> Kissing you heartily,
> Your Ilse

Vítkovice, March 17, 1939

Dearest Lilian,

You always were a decent person, and that you involved yourself in my illness so devotedly proves your friendship as well as your decency. I don't know for how long my heart will hold out. Anyway, taking care of two boys is now a too big burden for me. Hanuš could come, and it could be with Mutzi, who would obtain a passport when she's able to produce evidence that she can take up a job in England. You have in the meantime, received her references, and in case you still have no position for her then please ask my friend, Frl.[90] Löwenadler, to accommodate her for the first period as help for her household. I know that Frl. Löwenadler doesn't like strangers around her, but when you tell her that I earnestly ask this of her because I feel very ill and don't want the boy, who is already sensible enough to suffer from my illness, to witness all that, then she would give Mutzi the position, especially since Mutzi could really be of help to her. Salary is out of the question as Mutzi must first learn the language. With her skills she will surely find a position. Moreover, she has an affidavit[91] for America, but it's not her turn yet. She will be looked after in America. Frl. Löwenadler must send with the employment certificate the permit as well.

It would be nice also for Tommy to finally meet his aunt, but first he needs a lot of care, medical help, and every second day new bandages. You simply can't handle that. And then: we do want a little sunshine for us too, especially since my illness casts so many shadows. Did you understand the reference to the Barbican Mission?[92] Recently this mission has taken several planeloads of evangelical children to England. However, the air traffic is disrupted now. In any case, inquire, and say that Hanuš has to be taken only up to London and that we'll try to cover his travel expenses.

Hanuš sends you his best regards. He's erasing your postcard so that you could use it again. These last days he's a bit dazed by all the changes here. Now that a separation from him moves into the not-so-distant future, I realize how much I love him. It is endlessly difficult to send away a child. He realizes how I feel and is doubly affectionate. Every evening he crawls into my bed, naturally immediately imitated by Tommy. And so I end up lying with my two rascals in bed and Willi's heart sinks even further. I am worried that you will have to invest too much effort into the boy and you'll eventually suffer. I can't even promise to send a little contribution since Willi has no income anymore.

I just hear him coming. Supper time. I haven't been able to eat for the last couple of days. The mere thought of a meal makes me sick. My nerves are awful. It is all connected to the illness. Hopefully everything will be good again soon.

I'm kissing you, you dear good person, and thank you both. Frl. Löwenadler should let us know immediately. I believe she can do this.
    Ilse.

Your telegram has arrived just this minute. Thank you. I will instruct my brother-in-law in Prague to make an inquiry with the same mail. If it's possible, we'll do it. What were you told? But please do not telegraph anymore: it costs an outrageous amount of money and I can't accept that. Ilse

Does Hanuš still need a permit? Please ask for more details.

III 39

Dearest Lilian,

Since your card from four days ago arrived only today, you won't get my letter from yesterday as fast as I wish. My illness makes terrible progress and it's definitely possible that we will have to send Tommy away as well, although my heart bleeds at the mere thought of being separated from him. Anyway, provided he can be accommodated in a home where he can receive medical treatment. Rumor has it that his previous physician shot himself, which is regrettable for many reasons. I have no idea what will become of me here. If only I could have a change of environment; the local air is detrimental for my health, and the exhausting worry for Willi and our existence adds to that.

I will never forget what you and James are doing for my children these days.

Ilse

March 24, 1939

My Dears,

Your express letter just arrived at ½ 8.[93] Although I have nothing special to tell you, I'm answering immediately. The Mission is closed; at least it was when I sent there my brother-in-law, who is an attorney in Prague. And I have no idea what papers the child requires. They say that up to eighteen years no papers are necessary except for the parents' permission. But this is all pointless as long as the office stays closed.

Please send an urgent notification to Elli via airmail, which is impossible from here, to send the invitation she offered for me and my family *regardless of the circumstances*, with all the paperwork, in order not to miss anything. It is not easy for me to accept her offer but today I cannot afford to be picky. What Elli has suggested, as it seems to me not *very* eagerly, is what is called here an affidavit. I will use it only in case of emergency. We have made an application to emigrate to Palestine, but that is currently impossible.

I still think Mutzi could leave. She falls under the category of Sudetenland refugees and would surely be allowed to leave upon producing the permit. I will visit her right now. Her affidavit is, I believe, not yet approved, since the administration does not operate properly anywhere. I haven't studied English for a long time now because of my illness. Willi's family has experienced a lot of disasters so one has enough to think and worry about.

The children are **all right**. Tommy has lost his physician but it appears as if his wound begins to slowly heal. I don't think he will be able to travel. It's indeed egoistic on our part, but you have to consider that his presence here can prevent even thoughts of suicide. He is so joyful and has such a sunny disposition. Hanuš is way more serious. Him I'm sending to

you, honestly believing that apart for his outward lack of independence you'll have no trouble with him, and that he can be a
little companion for you and James.

Although I keep on telling myself again and again that it's
absolutely necessary for us to emigrate, I cannot come to terms
with the idea. I simply *can't* grasp that I have to leave everything
I love. I have never done anything wrong therefore I don't need
to fear the Gestapo. On the contrary, behind all the swastikas
that lavishly adorn many windows now, there are likely very few
people who have worked as enthusiastically for German culture
as I have, a Jew, who loves and respects the Czechs. Whoever
wants to be a *mensch*, in the true sense of the word, doesn't separate his fellow human beings by language and race, but by *good*
and *bad*. People who let themselves be told whom to respect or
despise; whom to love and whom they should hate; when to be
thankful and when not; who forget and remember by command,
such people *I* cannot respect. I am aware that hard times are approaching us; isn't the parting from my child already endlessly
hard? And even now at this point, every day brings a new burden; but I am becoming calmer.

I have never been ashamed of the fact that I am a Jew. But
now, when we are being hunted down like animals, when we are
robbed of our homeland where we've lived decently and honorably for centuries, when the biggest and most powerful countries
indeed regret our fate with indignant words, but otherwise secure
their gates against "undesirable elements," today I'm carrying
my Jewishness as an honor. Today, I believe in God again and in
divine providence. Everything that is happening now surely has
a meaning we can't yet see, but is nevertheless in everything that
transpires. We Jews are the victims, but not the only ones who
are unfortunate. Are not my compatriots miserable too? But they
are at least allowed to stay in their homeland.

And here is my last English assignment. Is the word **man** to
be used in the same sense as the word 'Mensch' is in German?

Live human, Thou my God, that's what I might.
All human's[94] right shall also be my right.
I am a man like you, I suffer and love,
My heart is so like yours. I weep, I laugh.
O help us, God. Give justice us and peace
And let us live like other people, please.

Please, wouldn't James write a few lines to Willi? Men aren't as flexible as we are in getting to know each other, especially Willi, who is so terribly closed. But I believe that a few lines from James would do him good. Willi, by the way, doesn't disappoint me. He is truly *the* man whom I love and look up to.

If it's possible, I will enclose international stamps so that you can write more often. Please don't be offended, your letters are like medicine now. And the letter to Elli will cost too.

Goodbye and think of us.

Ilse

Write no sender!

Witkowitz, April 2, 1939

Dearest Lilian,

This is no longer an *exchange* of letters, but more just me keeping a diary sent to you for reading. Well, you won't have any time now, but I still need to chat with you.

As most important news, I must first tell you that Elli wrote this week and made us a positive offer. It concerns a settlement in *Parana*, Brazil, and Elli had, by coincidence, the opportunity to speak about us with an influential personality. The letter I've asked you to write to her and send by airmail has therefore become superfluous, but if you have already written it, no harm done. I would like to learn more about Parana. We only know what is written about it in the encyclopedia, and that is not much. I would be most happy if we could get away from here. It's just so bitter to leave to a foreign land without means because one isn't allowed to take anything.

You can hardly imagine our life now. Willi continues to go to
the office,[95] which he gradually liquidates. Hannerle goes to school,
but how long remains uncertain since the school buildings will
be taken over as quarters for the German army. For the children,
the German soldiers are extremely interesting. Every morning
they can, from our windows, watch them exercising. The boys can
already sing their songs. Tomorrow is Seder Evening, you know,
the most solemn evening in the whole year, when we celebrate
the exodus of the Jews from Egypt. The *Stürmer*,[96] which is carried
by all the bookstores, calls our Easter "The Jews' Murder Feast." I
would like to speak sometime with the author of this article and
similar other pieces and ask why he writes them. Aren't we Jews
sufficiently miserable? Of all the malicious stories spread about us,
this ritual myth is the most evil. I can only think that it must be
embarrassing for the local Germans who have, over decades, eaten
our offered matzos with big appetites, to read such stories and pre-
tend to believe them.

Tomorrow evening we are invited to my mother-in-law. It was
always wonderful when all nine children, with their wives, husbands and children, sat at the long table. Last year, Tommy, the
youngest, recited the Hebrew questions and I was so proud of him.
This year we'll have several empty seats around the table . . .

Lilian, you have known me since my school days and have always been well-informed about my friendships, right? There were
many German girls among them and we have been until recently
on good terms. These days, when I run into them on the street,
which is after all unavoidable in such a small town, they quickly
look away. Only one was able to smirk at my face without a greeting and, interestingly, it is the *one* for whom years ago I had done
such a service that, on the verge of tears, she assured me to *never*
forget it. But there are some who laugh spontaneously and call,
"Servus Ilse," and one who quite demonstratively comes toward
me and walks beside me, though I feel uncomfortable with such
heroism. How do I feel? It is appallingly painful, Lilian, so painful
that I can't think of anything else for a whole day, but at the same
time I'm also thinking: how does *she* feel when she doesn't greet

me? I think every decent person must be inwardly ashamed. Do
you believe that, too?

There is still no answer from the Barbican mission. I even
wrote them in English. Perhaps they didn't understand me for that
reason? However, if they haven't yet reopened I can get no answer.
Lilian, wouldn't it be a good idea to write to the English consulate and plead with anyone who is leaving for England to take my
Hanuš with him? However it's *you* who must do that. I wanted
also to ask you to write to me if he should take anything in particular; perhaps his bedclothes and cover? He was given two nice suits
yesterday so that now he's well-equipped for a good two years. And
you should have no unnecessary expenses incurred by him. I'm already enormously indebted to you. Even if the child will not travel
to you—one never knows—I will take your word for the deed.
What you and Elli have been doing for us these bitter days we will
never be able nor willing to forget. Without you two we would
have lost faith in humanity. I'm sending Hannerle to you calmly
and without worries. I'm firmly convinced that he will receive the
love and attention you would give your own child. He should also
go to school right away, all right? He'd learn the language best over
there since you will speak German with him from time to time so
that he doesn't feel too deserted. When we emigrate I would like to
still leave him with you for a while. But these are questions that we
will still have to discuss in detail once he will be with you. He himself is looking forward to meeting you though he also fears parting
from us.

I haven't learned a lot in the last weeks; to be honest, I almost
don't learn at all. I can't concentrate.

One more thing: a friend of Lizzie has been in London with
her husband for a few days. He's a physician and she has two little girls; one of them, five years old, is very well looked after in
a home. But she and her husband, with the second child, who is
very little, live in a wretched apartment. The little one is apparently sick and they are in a bad situation. Will you allow us to
send her your address? I've just remembered you know the husband. He is Dr. Leo Hornung. Perhaps you can assist her with

some of Gillian's clothes? She couldn't take anything with her. You may face, in the next days, an invasion by members of Willi's family. Don't be alarmed then dear, and think that the people see in you a little of me.

So now I'm completing this letter which was my Sunday afternoon activity. Regards to James, kiss your little girl: how is she making progress? Heartfelt hugs and kisses from your

Ilse

Mama sends you her warm regards. I'm looking forward to seeing you! Hanuš

Witkowitz, April 14, 1939

Dearest Lil,

I want to try to see if I find someone who would mail this letter from Poland. I'm very worried about your long silence. Over here a storm is gathering. We listen to your news because ours is dictated and false. It very much looks like there is going to be war and as if our children won't be able to reach a safe haven. Everything has terribly changed here. Nothing but swastikas wherever you look, even on chests beneath which no German heart beats. Nothing but open gloating on part of the Germans, wailing and silent dignity from the Czechs. The Czechs are waiting however . . . I wish I still had this faith. But there is no hope left for us anymore.

Willi's family is in great misery. My oldest brother-in-law, the attorney, lost his office and is wanted by the Gestapo. He is safe but his poor wife and the little girl are not. By the way, this child should also go to England if, as previously discussed, the opportunity arises. Two other brothers-in-law, from Ostrava and Prague, were arrested and locked up but have already been released, and one of them crossed the border. The third, rather the fourth, whom I had not mentioned here yet and who flew here from the Sudetenland, must report daily to the Gestapo. I'm afraid of what might happen to Willi although our conscience is clean and we have never belonged to any party. Willi's livelihood is, of course, bust. There is hatred stirred up against the Jews, but the Czechs, except for the Gajda Party[97] and the Fascists, treat us more like fellow sufferers. It's so dreadful that one wishes to be capable of hope it will change soon. The German soldiers behave decently without exception. These are very young fellows who feel uncomfortable under the hate-filled glances of the Czechs. All of us worry now about Hitler's birthday, for already with the "moving in of the protector" the town was a sea of swastika flags and illuminated swastikas. The girls in the Czech schools had to sew the flags. They did it with tears. Many just stopped going to school.

We're enclosing in the letter a five-dollar note. Please confirm its reception with the following words: image of Uncle Lincoln bears great similarity.

If the opinion where you live is that war is coming then write: It begins to be very hot. Anyway, write about everything. Strain your imagination, I will understand.

Farewell: hopefully this attempt will be successful.

Your *Kränzchen*-sister

I.V.39

Dearest Lilian,

That was quite a Sunday breakfast today, with the arrival of your letter. (Exclamation mark.) Otherwise we get no mail on Sundays. They made an exception today only because tomorrow is May 1. Fine that Uncle Lincoln arrived at your place. He should visit you often and think of me as well, for it is required that friends or relatives abroad will pay the initial sum for our new life abroad or for the deposit. This, for instance, was one of the conditions in the letters from Chile, where we needed 150 Lp[98] for settling. *Please* tell me *right away* whenever Lincoln or another valuable guest visits you. I'm terribly interested. A postcard will do.

Elli wrote yesterday, briefly, but per airmail and warmly. Heavens, heavens, where would I be today hadn't I known the

Kränzchen? And to think Hertha had to force me to write my first
Kränzchen-letters. You can't imagine what you mean to me, you in
particular, for Elli has only lately emerged as an important factor.
At the same time, I find the thought of going away ever so dreadfully difficult. All the "familiar" trees are blooming now, the mountains look down at me as if they wanted to call me and I love them
so much. Yes, Willi is serious about Sweden. It could also work financially, but it won't be possible, I feel that. But please, you must
give me your mother's address or any other Swedish address so that
we can re-establish contact should anything happen that would
render direct correspondence between us impossible. I consider
this very important.

Your remark that James was an aviator left an overwhelming
impression on Hannerle. Aviator is *the* most awesome thing for
him. Now James has won him over completely. Today I went with
the children to Zdenka, my youth friend from the "Erbrichterei."
She married a policeman and owns a small farm. We were formally
invited and were served with coffee and cakes. Ach, you, it does
one good to be among people who don't treat you with contempt
but with compassion and sympathy.

Who knows whether Walter can come to you, for he has
no money. I don't like him much, neither do I like his wife, my
youngest sister-in-law. But now he's in a bad state. They have a really sweet little girl, Evička. How long did Uncle Lincoln's journey
take? Can you determine that?

**I am very lazy and I learn not English. I had to learn a poem:
Solitude. But I have no patience. My brother, who is now called
ABNER, is an English soldier in Palästine.**

So, and now I simply must go to sleep. I'm so tired.

Lots of kisses, or **Good night everybody.**

Ilse

Some Mr. Winton[99] in London is leading the Ostrava Children
Action. But we haven't heard anything more about it.

To Zofiah Mareni [100]

Witkowitz, May 6, 1939

Dear Schusch,

I now, so to speak, have met you personally because Gre described you so thoroughly that it's as if I saw you before me with my own eyes. Now I will find it easier to write to you, and hopefully you're also inclined toward it—to be your friend. Since I'm reluctant to kiss women I warmly give you my hand, in my mind, and thereby seal our friendship, agree?

You will probably be happy to know how do we live here now? Well, at least we're not pestered by boredom. It's like dancing on a powder keg. The air is impregnated with insane rumors, which we no longer believe. Anyway, we allow for all possibilities since the wildest rumors have turned out to be true. Oscar surely told you that we have always lived in peace and warm friendship with all the people, regardless of nationality. I was deeply rooted here, so much that Gre was surprised about it. I loved my hometown and found inspiration where no one else saw it. Witkowitz is, for all that know it, an interesting but sooty and sober town. Nevertheless, I discovered beauty in its chimneys and wrote poems about the fiery glow that painted the evening sky red. I would weep full with emotion over each insignificant little willow tree that sprouted from the heaps of rubble. The dirty water of the Ostravica seemed more beautiful to me than the Adriatic. And what the Beskids have meant for me I can express only in verses, and even then, in my opinion, very inadequately. I've never wanted to go away. As regards the people, I loved them just as well and had an excuse for their conspicuous unpleasant features.

And now? I want to tell you what I experienced for instance today, a weekly market day, on my way to the market. I live next to the market so that my walk there isn't long. First I encounter Frau Rohrer (Oscar can provide you with the necessary commentary).

She was an intimate friend of my sister and we liked each other very much. At first she greets: "Good morning!" Immediately after she sneers at me and says: "Heil Hitler!" A few steps further I meet Frau Hocke. Oscar doesn't know her. This is a working-class woman who came to me when she was in dire need. I employed her and since she was pregnant, I helped her whenever I could. She told me three times a day how kind Jews have been to her. Now she's pushing the baby stroller with her one-year-old boy, who looks very nice in his light blue suit and matching cap. Both belonged to Tommy. Suddenly, she stares in the air. Next I encounter Frau Rozehnal. Oscar can tell you a great deal about *that one*. If I hadn't taken care of her little boy he would have perhaps run wild. She herself presented him to me last year with the following words: "Look, little Otto, this is Aunt Ilse who raised you." In addition, Mama taught her to cook and to keep house, for she was terribly inexperienced and helpless. Now, meeting me and Mama, who's with me, she's looking at us with no expression on her face and no trace of recognition. Other German friends stare at the floor. Only very few greet warmly, but, to be perfectly honest, there are still some who do. I don't care much anymore. Sometimes it still hurts a little, but then comes a beneficent wave of contempt that quickly washes all the pain away. And when I have some peace and time to reflect I try to put myself in the position of those *friends*, convincing myself that they must be ashamed inwardly. Because even if I can imagine that I could be filled with enthusiasm for an idea, for a person who has the halo of glory, surrounded by greatness and God knows what heavenly miracles, even so, I would *never, never* be carried away emotionally so as to betray my friends or condemn an entire nation and find people despicable just because my idol demands that from me.

During the nasty September days when all the people who had the means fled the town in wild panic, only we and a German tenant stayed behind in our three-storied house. We bonded with such harmony that can only develop in times of commonly felt danger. When she moved out she thanked me sincerely and emphasized that she would never forget how I treated her. At the time, the Germans were in *the exact* situation we Jews are in now. Still, I would prefer not to meet her now.

You will be surprised that I unburden myself to you like this. But apparently, everything I laugh about contemptuously on the surface, I nevertheless subconsciously take seriously. And I must somehow provide myself some relief.

Talking about the weekly market. On most Fridays we have lungs hash, which goes by the name of *Beuschel* here. Oscar says you would like to know how we prepare that. So: the lungs, together with the spleen and heart, we're talking, naturally, about calf lungs, are cooked like soup meat: around half an hour together with parsley, a small potato, celery, onion, some peppercorn and a bay leaf. Then the meat is laid on a board. I'm making it so that I put the lungs and spleen through the meat grinder, but I chop the heart coarsely. Then I prepare a roux, pass some of the meat stock into it and spice it with lemon peel and juice, a little sugar, some mustard and, optionally, also anchovy paste. Finally, the chopped mincemeat is added and is brought to a boil. Once you have the sweet sour taste, you'd have it right. *Beuschel* is served with bread dumplings, not potatoes. But I myself don't make it first class because my husband shouldn't eat any bread dumplings. He's not allowed to eat Beuschel either, but for the things he relishes he makes an exception. Such are men. Is Oscar annoying you with the food? But that is how most men are. Mine, too. Sometimes I think the whole love affair is a question of the stomach. One of my friends' husband is happy when he receives coffee, bread and butter. The man is my ideal.

You know perhaps that my older boy should go to England for a longer period of time? It won't be easy for us to separate from him, but we'd nevertheless be happy when he will get away from the bad atmosphere here. He's a little Czech patriot and already understands too much about politics. That alone is a reason to send him away, for politics as it is now is a bucket of dirty water.

So, but now the children want to eat. Give my regards to Oscar and write sometime soon, all right? You don't know how we're starving here now for letters from a better world. And write whatever comes to your mind.

Meanwhile have warm regards from your sister-in-law

Ilse

May 31, 1939

Můj zlatý Hanušku! (My Golden Boy!)

Good day in England! You see, I'm travelling with you and am right here by your arrival to welcome you in your new home. Can you feel the kiss you're receiving from me?

We were awfully sad when you left. I have to tell you that I also cried. Wasn't it silly of me? You're going to Aunt Lilian and you'll have a great time there. I can't wait to see if you write to tell me how was your journey, if you ate properly, if you drank your tea, and if you washed during your journey? You were already terribly dirty at the train station! Hanušku my darling, I must tell you how happy I am that you've adopted our president's wonderful motto. Don't ever forget: the truth prevails, but the lie dies![101]

You know, unfortunately I can't write correctly in Czech; but you know that and wouldn't laugh at Mutti, right?

It's so empty here without you. But on the other hand I'm happy you're going to Aunt Lilian and will see so much of the world! You have to describe to us exactly everything you saw and did. Everybody here is waiting for your letter!

Stay always good my dear boy, obey your aunt and uncle. See that you will become a proper big brother to the little one and

love her. Don't be disorganized! Keep your things in order so that
the Aunt won't have any unnecessary work on your account! Get
dressed on your own and help whenever you can. Ask for nothing:
you have enough toys and the Aunt must save money in order to
keep you in England.

Nazdar[102] Hanuš, I'm sending you 155 kisses and 398 greetings. (How much do they add up to?) And I'm pressing your little hands so tight that you scream

"Au!"

Your Maminka

At' tě husa kopne![103] (The goose should kick you!)

We don't want to be sad because we know you will come
back to us, and we also know that you will live by the motto:
"The truth prevails!" Stay healthy. I'm greeting and kissing you,
Aunt Lilian, Uncle James and Gillian.

Your Tatínek (Vati)
Willi

Last photo with Tomáš, Hanuš and Willi

Going-away party for Hanuš, May 27, 1939

June 1, 1939

Milý Hanušku! (Dear Hannerle!)

It is so sad here at home without you, and yet I'm happy
that you're with Aunt Lilian and that you get to know another
part of the world. You must write to me about everything: what
you experienced and saw during your journey, what did you talk
about in the train, whether you were together with Bobby, how
long was your journey, how long you stayed in Holland etc. All
our friends are waiting for your letters. Bobby Fuchs was very
happy with the picture postcard that can be rotated. But Jenek
was sad he didn't get it. Did Uncle Walter[104] wait for you? Did
you sleep at his place? Do you already know a few English words?
Babička[105] sends you a thousand regards.

Tomík is running around the whole house like a lost little
sheep and doesn't know what to do without you. From Prague
I brought Marta a beautiful apron on your behalf, so you know
about it when she writes to you. Tomík is very proud of his

necktie, Hanušku. I went yesterday to the Vyšehrad.[106] It is the most beautiful place in Prague. I visited the graves of our Greatest and laid lily of the valley bunches on three of them and said: Hanušek sends them for you. I picked up from each of these graves a little leaf that I'll send you as a little greeting from Karel Čapek, Božena Němcová[107] and Bedřich Smetana. You should receive them quite soon. Tomíček sends you many regards; he hopes you're well, that you don't forget him, and that you also buy him candies.

We're going now to grandmother. Be good, my golden boy, behave properly, be obedient and don't forget to brush your teeth! A kiss for you, a kiss for Aunt Lilian, and a kiss for the little one. Do you like her? I can see, Hanušku, how you're laughing at me when you see how many mistakes I made?

Your Mamička

5th June 1939

Dear James!

I thank you very much for your good and kind letter. I was so glad when it came. This day began so sad and terrible. When I awaked, I saw burn the jewish church. I don't weep so soon, but at this sacrilege I could not but weep. Then came your and Hanuš's letter and my first thought was: "God be praised, that the child must not see this horror!"

Don't be impatient, when I shall write too often. Hanuš was my little friend and it will give me new strength, when I know that he is happy. You want to know his habits and tastes. As to that he must accomodate to you. He has to eat, what you eat too. He doesn't like meat, but it is necessary, that he eats meat also, and Willi was very rigorous in this respect. Hanuš is not fond of dainties, but he likes a piece of sugar, green peas or a little kohlrabi and bred with butter and radish. His greatest luck is a slice of pine-apple. Every evening he drank milk.

Take care, please, that Hanuš doesn't read too much and in bad light. He is such a bookworm.

Have you received Hanuš's chest? I hope it has well arrived.
Preserve it well, please, as long as Lilian is not in Hitchin, it is
very precious. I shall now give to each of my letters a number
and beg you to relate to it in your answer to have a control that
you get all my letters. I fear, many ones are lost.

I look forward to your next letter. I myself am unable to
write more today. I am so in dispair and it is almost impossible
for me to write in English.

Many regards to Lilian. For you a handshake!

Your friend

Ilse

June 6th 1939

Hanušku!

Bobby has told his mother much more about the journey. I
would also like to know how it was, if you all were in a good mood
along the way, if you sang, if you had enough to eat and why you
drank the tea only after you'd arrived in London? Was it still good?
Who was waiting for you? Both uncles? If I only knew where you
are now, if still in London, or in Hitchin, or in Sweden? Bobby is
already going to school but on Fridays he's always allowed to go
to his grandma. You did not eat up on the way the confection for
Aunt Lilian, did you? If you did, no harm done: maybe I can send
more. Tommy is now very lonely. He collects stamps for you, but
then it occurs to him that you're gone and he throws them away. In
the evening when he's in bed he says, " . . . and protect all Czechs
and Hanušek, good night!"

You remember that you promised me to write a lot?

And don't forget Aunt and Uncle Immerglück, and for heaven's
sake not the two grandmothers! You can send another postcard
to the boys at school and an extra one to Jenek, all right? They
will also write to you once they have your exact address. Anyway,
I wrote also to your Swedish address but maybe you have not arrived there yet? I would happily write to you in Czech, but then

I'm making so many mistakes and my Herr son laughs at Mutti, don't you? I'd only try it occasionally so that you don't forget how we used to talk to each other. You, however, can write to me as you wish.

Hannerle, please be good and decent. Eat everything like you had to at home. You know a soldier has to be able to swallow everything, and you're an army general after all. Brush your teeth properly and wash your ears properly. Speak loud and greet people so that they can hear and understand you.

The photographs from your farewell party have turned out lovely. I'm sending them to you little by little. Today I'm enclosing in my letter the badge from Bobby and one more beautiful thing, a forget-me-not from Božena Němcová's grave. Ask your uncle to stick it in the *Babička* book and take good care of it. It's like a greeting from her. Next time, you're getting a bay leaf from Bedřich Smetana's grave. I've picked it up myself along with a flower from Karel Čapek's grave, but this one I wish to keep for myself. Then you're getting an answering stamp. You do know that you take it to the post-office and can exchange it for an English or Swedish stamp? I wanted to send you more of these so that you could also write to your grandmothers, but we received only one and we're allowed to send only one.

If Gillian's grandmother pays you a visit after you arrive in Sweden, please give her my best regards. I liked her very much and she surely remembers me. You must tell me a great deal about the sea. I love it so much, especially when it makes those big waves. Is the sand nice? Do you play nicely with the little one? Don't ever leave your scout knife lying around open when she's nearby, and don't bang with your pistol when there are adults around: they don't like that. What did Uncle say about the belt and weapon? Didn't he feel like playing with them? Well, you'd surely let him play with them if he behaves well. How do you actually speak with him? That must be funny! Aunt Poldi showed me how you two talk with each other: for example, *he* wants to ask you if you can swim. He taps on your shoulder, swings his arms around and nods his head. But you think he's asking if you washed yourself and you nod. Then he throws you in the water so that you'd show him how you swim and you start shouting dreadfully. Is that so?

You also must tell me what you're doing the whole day and what you did with Uncle Walter. Write to me how you find your uncle and aunt. Do you like them? You don't know how good they are. You're very lucky to be allowed to stay with them. Everybody sends you regards: the boys, the aunts, the uncle, the principal, Frau Juřicová, Marta, big Pavel, and the little one from Ostrava, Aunt Poldi and Aunt Weiss. And Tomíček asks about you a thousand times a day and forgets to annoy us. And Vati and I? You do know we long for you so much, but when you're fine we're happy too. I'm hugging you, my dear boy. I love you and remain for ever

Your Matička,
who loves you "from heaven to earth and Marienberg," as our Tomíček says. And don't forget your motto, "The truth prevails!"

Give Aunt Lilian a firm kiss from me! You can sometime kočkenen[108] with her. Just try! Mutti.

Witkowitz, June 15, 1939

My Dearest Big Boy!

Tommy and Aunt Hilde wrote you such beautiful letters, now it's my turn. Today I cannot write you anything amusing: I'm a bit sad. It's no longer pleasant here and I'm really completely happy that you're away. Besides, it has been raining for two days and so one's in a bad mood anyway. I very much hope that this letter doesn't have to wait too long for you in Sweden. I wish you a really nice time by the sea. Be brave, go into the water and see to it that you learn to swim. A boy must know how to swim so that he doesn't go under.

When I'm in a happier mood again I want to create stories for you, you know, like back in the days before going to bed. Can you still remember Tommy's favorite story about the Ball-Ball? And I will also send you songs; you will have to sing them by yourself though. Do you sing at all sometimes "Kde domov můj"[109] and the other beautiful, lovely songs we have always sung together? And the song "Doctor, what should I do, my head aches so?" You should once sing that one to Aunt Lilian: she'd like that; but *all* verses!

Bobby is drawing beautiful pictures for you and will send them to you. Sunday is school festival of the Czech schools but this year we're not allowed to have a parade. Tommy will go there if the weather improves.

How were the rest of your days in Hitchin? Did you behave? You know, Hannerle, I don't want to always tell you: be good, be good! Because I don't want you at all to be so terribly polite and good and utter no word except "yes please" and "no please." When I'm telling you to be good I mean you shouldn't do anything nasty, yes, not even *think*: not gossip and not lie. But you don't lie anyway. Think of us and don't forget us. But at the same time love steadfastly your aunt and uncle and be to them like their own child.

I think a lot about you and Vati does too, and we speak about you every evening and are a bit sad that you're so far away; rather, that you had to go so far away. Write diligently in your diary, but not just what you're doing and eating, but also what you think. This is very important. You will see, such a diary is almost like a friend. You can tell it everything; it doesn't let out anything. It just can't answer.

I'm now taking you very tightly in my arms and giving you a heartfelt kiss. And here's another one you should give Aunt Lilian and say, "Mutti thanks you!" Understood, Hannerle? But say it so that she hears, not through your teeth.

Goodbye my little boy, and write diligently to us. Stay healthy, and be strong and happy so that everybody will enjoy being with you.

    Your Mutti

Dear Hanuš! Apart from us your letters are read by Omama[110] in Ostrava, Aunt Erna, Paula, Else, Uncle Karl, Pauli and many others, and everybody shares our happiness and yours. Ať tě husa kopne! Soon, a detailed letter. For now warm regards to you all and kisses, Willi

Prague, April 6, 1940

My Dear Hanušku!

It is Sunday afternoon around five thirty. The sun is shining but it's pretty cold outside. I've just returned home from the cemetery where I visited grandmother. Hanuš, it's a beautiful cemetery with mostly very well-kept graves and lots of birds sing there. A blackbird sat on a gravestone singing so wonderfully that I stood still and had to listen. I went quite close to it but the bird didn't notice and continued to sing. The name Isaac Fuchs, died 1905, was on the stone, which was almost ruined, but the bird was singing so lovely as if it wanted to say, "Even if everyone has forgotten you, I will sing for you."

When I arrived home Tomík and grandmother sat in the kitchen eating. They had big pieces of Buchteln[111] in their hands, and as I saw them I became hungry and took a few bites. Now Tommy is outside on the street again, playing with marbles. Do you still remember how it goes? All the children here play marbles in the spring; you should see that. One can meet them at every corner, big and little, as they're trying to land the little balls within the holes in the ground. And naturally, Tommy plays with them. I bought him a whole full bag, a hundred marbles, and every noon when he has eaten up properly, he gets ten. So after each lunch he dresses quickly and says, "*Ahoi*, Mutti, now I will earn a couple of marbles for myself." And gone he is. Two hours later, or even later, he comes back and doesn't have even a single marble anymore. The reason is that he prefers to play with the bigger boys who play much better than he does. It's so beautiful now on our street and I often miss you. And then I think again that so much of what we're experiencing here would have made you sad, and that you wouldn't even be able to enjoy all that beauty. And then I imagine how much you've already been able to see during the year since you've gone away from us: foreign countries, the sea . . . And how much you've learned: Swedish, English and German. Do you know this is very, very important for your future? "As many languages you know, as many times you're a mensch!"[112] Do you still know who said that? But, my little boy, don't forget your Czech mother tongue! When you go back to Uncle James you may meet Aunt Selma and Uncle Walter more often. And with them you can talk in Czech, right?

Some time ago I met Kurt Lichtenstern. He lives here as well, with his mother. His father had the same fate as Bobik's and Erik's father, and like Uncle Otto. Aunt Lilian will explain it to you. I received two letters from you yesterday. Did you receive the writing books I sent you? There were six altogether. How old is Bertil whom you write about? Are you going to the Aronssons for the Seder evening? Can you still recite the "Manistana?"[113] The Aunt will practice it with you if you ask her to. Why do you like Alistair more than Gillian? Is it because you know him from the cradle? You will always protect him, and Gillian as well. Your last letter was nice. I really liked it, but see to it that you always answer my questions.

I'd like to advise you that every evening when Aunt Lilian bids you "good night," that you talk with her about everything that interests you and whatever lies heavy on your heart. Maybe you've never had yet a heavy heart my young boy, but if you feel that way, open your heart to her, my boy. Remember that Aunt Lilian is there for you like Mutti, and you'd surely tell me everything, wouldn't you?

You must write to me a lot this month because when you will be going away who knows what will happen!

Do you sometimes think about how it'd be when we see each other again? Whether you'd recognize me? Little Tommy's growing fast; he's now as big as you were a year ago when you went away. Unfortunately, your shoes don't fit him any longer. What shoes are you wearing now? Still the same you brought from home? Are you still reading my letters aloud to the Aunt? Give her a kiss and my regards, give Gillian a tight hug, but not so that she screams, and caress Alistair's little head!

I'm sending you a thousand kisses
Mamička

Prague, seventh of April, 1940

Dear Aunt Gertrude,

I thank you *very* much for your kind letter from the 28th of last month which I received today. I think you'll still have your hands full with me when Lilian is away, but I'm convinced you'll do it willingly because you had your boys abroad too and were happy to hear from them. And to *me*, "mail from Sweden" means everything: happiness, distraction, consolation; for me, these letters have to replace cinema, radio and theater. You may perhaps recall my passion for music. Music is equally essential to my life as eating and drinking. (By the way, do you still have your mandolin?) And now I can go to no concert, can't listen to the radio; my sole friend is my guitar, but now it does not feel right since I'm rarely in the mood to sing. After eight o'clock I'm not allowed in the streets; now in summer it's bitter. Willi is at work the whole day after all; our only chance to take a short walk and be able to chat with each other without being disturbed was after dinner. These walks are now cancelled. There's little left for us that can bring us joy. I would have perished from despair, humiliation and hopelessness had I not left my old hometown. Over *here* it's even nicer though. The city is wonderfully beautiful, especially the city part where we're living, the Vineyards.[114] Narrow alleys and lanes, with beautiful villas and marvelous gardens, and the streets that go up and down are constructed in terraces. Everything is quiet and peaceful and so remarkably familiar, even when you see it for the first time!

Homeland. I feel again and again how deeply rooted I am here against all the assertions that we don't belong here. Mama is even longing for the "Erbrichterei" although she went through so much misery and hardship there. Just now she has cried with homesickness.

Yesterday, Sunday, I went to our cemetery to visit the grave of my mother-in-law, who'd died here in January. I liked her very much; she was a wonderful woman. She could write and read only Yiddish and had no formal education at all, but for that, her nobleness of heart surpassed that of a queen. She had nine children; five of them had to flee and she couldn't survive the separation from them. She has a very nice place at the Olšany Cemetery. And I love cemeteries above everything. I pass strangers' graves and dream about the fate of those who lie in them. Yesterday a blackbird on a weathered gravestone was singing as beautifully as I've ever heard. I came quite close to it, but it didn't notice me at all and continued to sing further, undisturbed. The man lying in the grave has been dead for 35 years and had a grotesque Jewish name. It was comforting that the blackbird sang its song over his grave. Only the new section is awful where, on freshly thrown-up mounds, two, three, and often also *four* names stand with the same date of death. One needs no imagination to sense their terrible fate.

Is Carl-Axel's wife nice? She's Hungarian, isn't she, and *they* do especially suffer from homesickness. It will be difficult for her when Acki is away from her for so long. But her boy looks as if he doesn't leave her much time for herself. He's very handsome! Does he look like Acki or like his wife? And how are Ocki's children? I find those questions odd myself because last time I saw the "boys" they were nine and thirteen years old, and I still imagine them that way.

What does Acki do for a living? Is he doing well? You must be very happy and thankful for your children. Imagine how terrible it is for Jewish mothers whose husbands and children are far away from them, mostly without the faintest hope of seeing them again. Take for instance my mother: Ernst is somewhere in Russian captivity, Oscar in Palestine, *we're* supposed to go to San Domingo. And Mutzi, who temporarily still runs the old people's home in Ostrava, has an Affidavit for America. And what will become of Mama? that's still a complete mystery. And her fate is the common fate of Jewish mothers.

You're writing you've often wanted a set of baby clothes. Shame that all the cute things that I'd sent for Alistair's birth came back. They were quite lovely clothes which my sister-in-law had knitted. Now they're lying in my wardrobe and Alistair grows out of them.

Hanuš wrote me on Saturday. I, irrespective of all the yearning for him, am so happy that he has had this marvelous year in Sweden which improved his health and maybe also his character significantly. He loves his "siblings" very much, but especially the little boy. You must, dear Aunt Gertrude, tell me more about him if you see him one more time on his departure. It only grieves me that Lilian, who anyway has barely enough money, has increased expenses because of him. I don't know how we're ever going to be able to repay her.

My little rascal has just come home for lunch. Since he's lacking an Aryan certificate and therefore can't go to kindergarten, and I have little time for him, he's looking for distractions on the street. Luckily, we live in a good area and he plays with nice children. He is very independent and mature though, completely different from "Hannerle." He is completely different anyway. But cute.

Now I have spent a wonderful hour chatting with you and plan to send the letter in the afternoon by airmail. Write to me soon how long it was on the way, all right?

Warm regards to you and to your boys!

Your Ilse

Prague, May 26, 1940

Můj milovaný chlapečku! (My dear little boy!)

We were so happy with your notebook and what you wrote. You are so knowledgeable and capable of so many things when you come back home again everything will be different: then *you'll* have something to teach me.

I'm not making any progress with my English: I've studied hard but then my head was so full of worries that I didn't make any progress. **But I understand all you have written, my boy. I was so glad that you are able to count. I never could count, when I was** a school-girl and my friends made my lessons. And "Geographie" I liked, but I never knew how long a river or how high a mountain is. But I always had good reports in Geographic and in count also.

So, and now back to Czech. I find that about your teacher amusing. Do you like her because she's nice or because she's giving you chocolate? We haven't had chocolate for a long time but we can do without it. And now I want to tell you something. I received a new beautiful mandolin. It's not completely new, it is from Italy and is 33 years old, but Vati bought it for me and I'm very happy with it because it has such a beautiful sound. In the evening Uncle Karl comes to us and we sit, always in the kitchen; he plays the mandolin and I the guitar. We Jews are not allowed to come out of the house after eight o'clock and so we open the window to the courtyard, play and sing. And Tomíček sings with all of us the songs that you liked: "Ach, synku, synku"[115] (Ach, my son, my son), "Water, water, we don't drink," "Dance girl," and many others. And all of a sudden children are coming from all over: Miluška, Jiřinka, Marcella, Peter, Blanka, Evička, Zdenka, Mirek; all gather in front of our window and sing with us. And then one window after another opens in our building, the people look out and suddenly the whole joint sings. (Here they call each building a "joint.") You can surely imagine how lovely and funny it is. You see, my Hanušku, that music is our friend and comforter. How sad would it otherwise be for us as we're no longer allowed to go to the park or the cinema, can't visit the concert halls nor the theaters; and we must remain sitting at home in the evenings even now that it's summer, when everything outside smells so wonderfully and blooms beautifully. So we are happy when we can play and sing a bit and for that reason I've wished so much that you, my children, would also learn to play some instrument. You probably have already forgotten what you learned, haven't you? I'd like to see Tommy learn an instrument soon. You can't imagine how big and strong he's become! He plays the whole day outside in the street either with a ball and a bat, or with a hoop or his scooter.

You want to know if you're allowed to write on Saturdays. Of course you can; as long as we live among Christians we must live like them. In Palestine one celebrates "Shabbes"—that's a lovely day over there, no cars are allowed to drive in the streets, men are not allowed to smoke; it is really a rest day there.

Today is Sunday. Tommy and Vati are taking their Sunday stroll right now and Babička is tidying up. Yesterday, father, Tommy and Uncle Jacob (it's Herr Meller, but Tommy still calls him that) went to the children's fun fair at the King George market place and Aunt Meller[116] and I followed them secretly. That was funny. They rode the carousel, sat on the swing, shot the air guns and had no idea they were watched. Vati has a good aim, do you still remember? Everybody admires him. Both children won prizes. I think you would have liked little Fella very much. She's the same age as you, clever and sweet. She always reads your letters and each time asks me to send you her regards. Now I have to prepare lunch. I so much want to cuddle with you, my little boy. Do you think about it sometimes? Everybody is kissing you and sending regards, but mostly your loving

Mami

August 13, 1940

Můj drahý Hanušku! (My Dear Hannerle!)

Your notebook finally arrived today. I couldn't wait for it any longer! You should know that I'm sick and that I even have to lie down for a while. I have arthritis and can't walk. Little Tommy is now with Aunt Erna. He didn't want to move to her and asked the whole time: "And who shall go shopping for you?" However, Aunt Erna was lonely and wanted his company, so he finally had to go there. (. . .)

Tommy starts school next month. If he gets permission he'll go to a very nice school on Kladska Street. If not he'll have to go to the Jewish school; but it's really far so that he'll have to take the streetcar. You should have started school as well by now. Be happy, Hanušku, that no one's mocking you, that the children like you, and that you

have a good home with the Aunt. Which of your old friends
can swim? One or two at best. Who has seen as much of the
world as you have? Not one! Not even Bobby Kohn who lives
in London. You must learn to *see*! Now you're surely laughing
my little boy, thinking: Well, my Maminka is funny! But you
know, Hanušku, seeing and seeing are not the same. When two
people look at the sea, each one of them sees something else.
While one sees only endless water the other sees different kinds
of waves, how the foam is glistening and glittering; he sees a
white sail in the distance and much more. It's a real shame that
my Czech isn't better. I'd so much like to give you other examples. You know, for one person the forest is nothing more than
a row of trees, for another it's a whole world. Do you understand what I mean? I hope that you learn to see the right way.

　　Don't forget, my little one, how I always told you tales,
how we sang together and hiked in the mountains. Can you
recall how we, you, Tommy, Eva and I, always "conjured" in
Čeladna?[117] How we found the "conjured-up" money first on
the street and then later at home in the pajamas? Now children
are often gathering under our window pleading, "Please gra-
cious madam, play us something!" Then I take my mandolin
and play and the children sing and dance. Or they want to play
hide and seek. Then I get a whistle; one of the children runs
away and hides, while I must watch out that no one peeps, and
whistle when a minute has passed. Tommy too loves tales, but
only if they aren't sad. When tales turn evil he begins to cry and
says reproachfully, "But I told you, you shouldn't read any sad
tales!" (. . .) Hanušku, do you still remember the song, "My little boy, my little boy, the moon is shining in your little room?"
Now I must conclude: the physician has just paid a visit and
told me I still have fever. Give Aunt Lilian a kiss from me, and
to Gillian and the little one too, but you're getting a hundred
thousand kisses (can you bear that at all?)

　　　　from your Maminka

August 24, 1940

Nazdar, Hanušku!

Your second, incomplete notebook arrived yesterday and I want to answer you today, immediately. I'm still sick, but your letters are a better medicine than those the physician prescribed, my little one! If only you didn't scrawl that much! (. . .) On page one you ask if we can guess what you want to tell us. That was really a difficult question: Vati: "Maybe he had to follow the captain onto his ship?" Grandmother: "Or he learned to dress up Gillian since Aunt Lilian is so occupied now?" I: "Perhaps he saved someone's life, since he can swim so well?" And finally Tommy: "Vati, what do you think, maybe he learned to dig up potatoes by himself?" (He would like to be able to do that by himself.) There you see, we didn't come up with the correct answer. We were curious to know the solution to the riddle and then we read: "I've learned to cut bread by myself." But you wrote that so messy that we had to guess our way to the answer. (. . .)

The tent you wrote about must be very big! A heap of bricks was lying around in our courtyard and Tommy's friends, with his assistance, used them to build a hut with it! Actually, it was almost a castle. They made it as nice as real bricklayers. It also had high castle walls and inside, an oven, table and chairs. Whenever there was a thunderstorm they all crawled inside. But the joy lasted only a short while. The foreman told them they should tear up everything immediately so that no accident happens. It was very nice of the Gullander family to invite you to their house. But I think you shouldn't have taken any presents from little Bertil. He likes you and that's why he's giving you his things, but maybe his parents frown when he's giving his things away. *Never accept gifts from younger children, Hanušku!!!* You know, not long ago your cousin Pavel visited a lady with a little son who gave Pavel a pair of very expensive stamps. Three days later the boy's father came by, very furious, and demanded the stamps back immediately. The whole affair was really embarrassing. So think about what I told you! Sometimes, it may be difficult to say no: perhaps the present is really nice, perhaps it hurts to give it back, or maybe one doesn't want to snub the giver. But as a proper boy one *shouldn't* accept any presents from children! Do you understand, Hanušku?

Are you meeting little Karin from Bårarp sometime? (If I wrote the name inaccurately it's because your writing is so fuzzy.) How old is she? Do you think I would like her? For when you take a bride you must always ask yourself: What would my Mutti think about her? Your future wife would be my daughter! You take that into consideration, don't you, my boy? Tommy has a "bride." Her name is Eva and she is four years old. She is quite beautiful, with big blue eyes, but sometimes she is a bit cheeky and I don't like that. Maybe he will reconsider it still. I'm concluding this letter now. I think it contains at least as much as your notebook, but I hope that you can read it more easily.

I'm sending you thousands of regards and only one, but sweet, kiss!

Your Mamička

Dear Hanuš!

I haven't written to you for a long time because now, during the harvest, I'm coming home late in the evening, and Mutti takes the letters she writes to the post right away so that you'll get them soon. Mutti writes to you about everything in great detail so that I don't have to write to you separately. I also always tell Mutti what she should ask you and what to tell about us. Today I went with Tommy again to Strášnice, to Aunt Erna and Pauli. They had a visitor, Herr Director Kohn. Everyone is sending you regards. Then we went to Omama at the cemetery. On the way Tommy picked up flowers from the fields and put them on Omama's grave and said with each flower: this one is for Tatíček, this one for Maminka, this one for Hanušek, and this one for everybody. You too would have gotten a kick out of our walk. But when will that happen? One day for sure. Stay healthy and many kisses from Tatíček *Willi.*

Tomíček sends you best regards and "the goose should kick you." Give regards to the *Aunt* and *all children.*

October 9, 1940

Můj Hanušku! (My Hannerle!)

You see how fast I'm answering you: I've just received your notebook and I'm already sitting down and writing to you. I think I have never received such a long letter; I read it like a book! In return you're getting a nice kiss, my little boy! And now I'm going to answer all your questions one by one. First: I don't know anything about this Swedish cowboy story. I've never been to Sweden after all, and I can't speak Swedish either. Vati is taking now a master-builder course. He leaves the house at half past six, goes first to the synagogue and prays for grandmother. It's called Kaddish, and each child is obligated to pray it on the anniversary of his parent's death. Then he goes to work not far from Prague. 25 Öre[118] isn't so little for a boy your age. When I was eleven I got one Czech crown a month, and even this was withheld by my mother when she noticed that I didn't write down neatly all my expenses. Try to save, Hanušku; that is something I never could do, but I regret that! I always had the money fly away from me like a flock of sparrows. Don't buy yourself a scooter! Uncle James still has your scooter and maybe you'll get it sometime. (. . .)

Here is the German text to "My Little Boy."[119] It's your own song, which I myself composed for you when you were still little, even younger than Alistair:

> My little boy, my little boy
> the moon looks at your toys,
> my little boy, my little boy,
> the moon looks in!
> And when my little boy's asleep,
> the moon is happy then and pleased,
> and looks so joyfully in.
>
> My little imp, my little imp,
> the moon an angel brings

my little imp, my little imp,
and he is white.
He opens his wings
and guards you from fear,
so sleep my little child,
so sleep my little child!

You sang that too, but with the words "the moonlooksin." What a
good laugh we always had! Sing it every evening and think about
us just as we always think and speak about you. Tommy is forgetting slowly how you looked. He's very big: the biggest in his
class. What does "farbror"[120] mean? I always called grandma in
Stockholm "tant."[121] I sent Herr Aronson good wishes for the New
Year. This week we're celebrating the highest of all holidays, Yom
Kippur. On this day one asks God for forgiveness for all sins and
fasts strictly. You too fasted once and ate nothing for twelve hours.
Then comes "Sukkes." One lives in a decorated hut, and the whole
thing ends with a celebration in which the children walk around
with flags. Do you remember you and Tommy always had the
most beautifully adorned flags? I always sewed them for you with
beautiful blue and white silk. Well, times have changed and now
we no longer have time for celebrating. We are all sad and miserable. Only you are still doing well, and it pleases us all. You must be
thankful, Hanuš!

Naturally, we thank all who sent us their regards and we send
our warmest regards back!

Yes, it's true that we use two, sometimes even more, lemons
every day. First we prepare a salad and some vegetables for Vati,
who suffers from kidney disease, with lemon juice; and then Vati
drinks his tea also with quite a lot of juice. But you mustn't write
to us anymore in the toilet. I do not like that at all! One doesn't sit
there after all, in order to read or write, but to carry out as fast as
possible a nasty but important business. Or do you have there such
a lovely loo with marvelous view and musical accompaniment that
you cannot part with it?!?! The fruits of wild roses are called rose

hips. One can make from them good marmalade. Some pages in
your notebook are written very nicely; wouldn't it be possible that
you write everything so nicely? You'd bring us a great joy with it! It
made us very happy that you did so well in dictation. Learn well,
my Bubele: knowledge is more valuable than riches and power.
Hanušku, did you receive the packet of clothes from Stockholm?
I'd advise you to write the boy there a few lines in Czech, his
name's Hans Fischer, and thank him. Maybe you'd meet each other
one of these days and then you can speak sometime in Czech with
him. It's nice for you they celebrated your name day, but we Jews
don't celebrate that. Didn't Herr Aronson tell you that?

We're sorry the Aunt broke her finger; that must have been a
very severe pain!

I still haven't recovered fully either and the joints still hurt very
much.

I think this letter has become quite long hasn't it, Hanuš? I
hope you don't get sore throat so often, and no sniffles.

I'm kissing you a thousand times in my mind and wish you to
stay healthy and happy!

Your Mamička

Tommy and táta Willi are also sending many kisses.

Regards to Aunt Lilian, Willi

19.10.1940

Hanušku,

Today only a few lines so that you can't say I don't love you.
Tommy sends you warmest regards. He's outside in the courtyard
playing with the children. He carved a bow and arrow and they are
now playing Indians. Tommy is incredibly skillful: he can do everything by himself; the bow too works excellently. You will receive the
Mladý hlasatel[122] for half a year; maybe I'll continue to pay for it after.
Herr Limek was very happy with your letter. Do you know Tommy's
feet are already bigger than yours? He's the biggest in his class. Only he
doesn't feel much like going to school. Each morning something hurts

him; sometimes it's the stomach, sometimes the head or a knee. The pupils are getting no homework; sometimes he'll draw whatever he feels like. I wonder if he'll learn reading and writing at all. Sometimes I feel that he may even forget the little he has learned.

What are you actually studying at school? Give your teacher warm regards from me, all right? And Hanušku, you're getting now a nice kiss from me; stay healthy, kind and cheerful, help Aunt Lilian and love the children. Take care especially of the little girl; she needs a papa she can play with. Try to replace him for her a little, and learn with her. Maybe you'd tell her a tale sometime or teach her a song? Imagine, Hanušku, that she is exactly the same age as little Zuzinka Rosenberg with whom you so loved to play. Don't think she's "just" a girl. There must be girls; I too was a little girl, and my brother, Uncle Arnošt, never wanted to play with other children unless I was there. You're surely a gentleman, aren't you? Boys who despise girls are idiots. Take Tommy for example, he's a one hundred percent boy. But he has a little girl friend, Eva, he plays with, and he doesn't care if anyone laughs at him. Some girls have more brains in their little finger than some boys in their head. I hope that in the future you'll take a bit of care of Gillian. I'm really asking you to do this! You will do that, right?

Give the Aunt a nice kiss from me, and one to Gillian as well. And then write to me how she responded. Shalom, synáčku (my little son)!

Mamička

The goose should kick you! Many kisses, Willi

2.11.1940

Milý Hanuši! Dear Hanuš!

Now you're in a new environment once again! You can hardly imagine how restless Vati and I have been since the Aunt wrote to us that she's going away and would leave you behind. Poor children! I can imagine how much Gillian cried as her mother went away. Alistair doesn't understand that yet but you surely understood this, my little one, don't you? You're a brave boy and you understand that

Aunt Lilian was longing for Uncle James and wants to be with him again. You already understand all sorts of things, Hanušku, since already at your young age you've experienced a lot. I'd like to write you something funny, something you could laugh a lot about, but it's important to remind you of something serious. You're after all my friend, aren't you? I want to talk to you as to an adult and hope you want that too and that you'll understand me. According to what the Aunt wrote to me, you're with strangers. I don't know them but it's very kind of them to take care of you: not many would have done that. For that, Hanuš, you must be thankful to them; be as thankful as a ten year-old boy can only be. Be obedient, polite and help whenever you can!

And one more thing: you can surely imagine how worried we are for you. That is why we're asking you to write to us, sensibly and clearly, where you are now actually, about the people who have taken you in, if they have children, if you're going to school, if that village is far from Steninge, and if you are treated nicely. Hanuš do not forget to answer all my questions!

Today is Saturday. Tommy has no school; he sits at his little desk singing: "The fox sits under the oak, he has a whistle and a drum. The fox blows his whistle and plays on his drum." Sometimes he blunders and sings "plays the whistle and blows the drum." He can write now ones and fours. Vati is coming home shortly and then we will have lunch.

Hanušku, I hope that you write to me soon and that it will be a long letter! I hug you and kiss you on the small scar on your forehead and wish that you always be very happy and stay healthy!

Your Maminka

November 8, 1940

Dear Aunt Gertrude!

A letter from Lilian arrived today and I can't tell from it where Hanuš actually is, whether in Bårarp[123] or with you. My husband

and I are extremely worried that our poor boy has apparently
turned into a cuckoo's egg, everywhere in the way, and we're the
more miserable as, after all, it isn't within our power to change
this state of affairs. We've already undertaken everything possible
so that the Jewish congregation would do something for H. but
please, *if at all possible*, let the boy stay with you so that he doesn't
have to go to strangers. I'm begging you fervently—you can imagine how I feel. Please, let me know as soon as possible what actually happens with the child. I would be very grateful if you could
give me that information.

    In a hurry,
    Ilse

The Jews[124]

No homeland do we have,
nowhere finding peace,
further we must wander
always search and seek.

Despised and eschewed,
defenseless, with sorrow mute,
for us no peaceful harbor beckons—
Why is that O God?

Even the hunted animal
has God's protecting roof . . .
Harassed by envy and rancor,
where do we find refuge?

O Heaven your hand
hold out kindly to us,
and give the tired wanderer
a homeland at last!

Ilse and Willi Weber, Prague 1940

Prague, November the 8th, 1940

Honorable Madam!

I've received a letter today from my friend Frau Treen,[125] from which I gather that my son Hanuš has temporarily found a home with you (or had, which unfortunately I don't know for sure), for which I thank you from the bottom of my heart. You can surely imagine how worried I am about the fate of my child since I learned about the imminent departure of Frau Treen. First, Frau Treen wrote that Hanuš would stay with a certain Frau Gvarn-ström. I wrote this lady immediately and also sent Hanuš a letter to that address. I guess those letters wander around ownerless in the world now.

Since my poor boy is now, unfortunately, dependent on the charity of strangers, I would have been happy if he could have stayed with you. Your name and brief reports about your children appeared repeatedly in Hanni's letters. Gathering from his letters that he loved you all and that you've been good to him, I had the feeling that he wasn't with complete strangers. Forgive me therefore, when I regret so openly that he could not stay with you.

Frau Treen wrote that she did not know yet (on 28. X.)[126] where the child would go. Can you understand what worries this remark has triggered in me? He is after all a little boy who already has a hard time not being able to go to his mother when his heart aches. Perhaps at one point you wondered if it was really so necessary for me to have separated myself from my boy. But I can assure you *that* even if the poor child has no home now and is sent around like a postal package, even when he himself would perceive his sad situation and shed tears over it, it is nevertheless much better than if he would have stayed here. One and a half years ago, as we sent him away after difficult mental strife, we certainly had no idea that we'd be separated from him for so long. We thought we would emigrate and build a new existence for us in a foreign land. Then our child could get back to us. We're suffering mostly from the fact that our plans did not come true. However, being in Sweden, Hanuš was spared many difficulties. He could live in peace and freedom among loving people; he was allowed to remain a cheerful and unsuspecting child, which wouldn't have been the case here.

If I've been so detailed with you then please attribute it to the wish to be understood by you. I thank you profoundly for all the kindness you have shown my child, and wish God to repay you through your children.

Your grateful Ilse Weber

Prague, November 20, 1940

Dear Aunt Gertrude!

Since you will have received my card in the meantime, I no longer have to tell you in great length how happy I am that my Hannerl can stay with you! It was a bad time for us when we had to imagine that Lilian would leave and he would have to stay alone with some strangers. Today I was freed from a cruel nightmare because I know you'll love him and be good to him, and that is most important for him, much more important than having his own room. (Which we also won't be having anymore soon.)(. . .)

I would be also happy if Hanuš would soon go back to school. Otherwise he reads too much. You'll have to curb him a bit in this respect; he needs not bury himself so much in books and ruin his eyes even more. Well, you will be soon perfect in haircutting if you have him around you from now on. Say, does he have anything in common with your boys? How is his appetite? And his manners? Oh, I'm already looking forward to your letters! It would be very nice if he can have music lessons again. You can't imagine how delightfully he already played! He knew Schumann's *Scenes from Childhood* by heart and he gave us so much joy. Now he has probably forgotten everything. But as compensation, the time in Steninge was so good for him physically and mentally that one happily does without his music.

Obviously, one can't have *everything*. Tommy has a long way to school, but is so independent that he travels by himself back and forth between school and home. Only in the morning I bring him to the streetcar. It's always so dark at that time, which makes me feel so sorry for the little boy. And when he leaves, waving to me and blowing kisses, I can't help but remember how Hanni left, his face besmeared with overflowing tears.

As reluctantly as I think about Lilian's journey so I feel sorry for her for not being yet able to leave, being forced to lead a gypsy life in Stockholm. Poor Lilian! She's heading toward no beautiful destination! Sometimes I'm trying to imagine that there is peace again and we are all united with our loved ones. But that is so incredibly beautiful that I cannot picture it to myself. Often my longing for the child is limitless! (. . .)

Do not be angry with me for the confused letter! It is what the inside of my head looks like!

I thank you a thousand times with heartfelt greetings!

Your Ilse

Prague, December 3, 1940

Dearest Aunt Gertrude,

Now I already have to answer *two* cards from you. I am very happy that you plan to write to me every week, and if it suits you I will write to you whenever I find time, but then in a more detailed manner. Please excuse my choice of paper. I am using it because it's thin and that way I can write you more. And one more thing: I do not wish that the expression of my deep gratitude would become an empty phrase for you. I will not always write to you how *very* happy I am that my son can be with you and how much I feel I'm in your debt. This feeling is indelibly embedded in my heart and I swear to you that I will never cease to aspire to repay you for your great goodness!

I'm very worried about Lil. According to my calculations though, *I* can receive mail from her from Moscow no earlier than the 20th of this month, in case she wrote to me from there! Why didn't she write to me before?!? After all, she promised that. Lil has been my dearest friend since my salad days, you know that. We

met under somewhat unusual circumstances but we understood
and loved each other. Years ago I had the opportunity to do her
a service (about which she doesn't even know) and it was self-evident for her to help me with Hannerle in this difficult situation;
which is naturally much, much more than I will ever be able to do
for her, and a thousand times more than anyone has ever done for
me. And for that reason you can believe me that I now love her
more than ever before, and that no person is as close to me as she
is (except for Mama and Willi). Hopefully she'll get through this
trip well, and be able to look back upon it in a happier future as an
interesting yet not a nasty experience (. . .)

I am occupied all the time. We have no maid, Mama is tidying
up the rooms (she is very diligent), and the kitchen is mine to take
care of. I wash socks and children's laundry once a week, also our
underwear; iron, patch, sew. Mama mends and knits. After lunch I
play patience, that is my relaxation, sometimes also in the evenings
when I'm not reading or singing to some old ladies who live in the
same building. I've learned to play the guitar quite well. I also have
a friend from back "home" nearby who sometimes comes, but generally we younger women have little time. Everybody is learning:
sewing, languages, millinery, baking; the men too are being "re-edu-
cated." They're taking the most unusual jobs: on the country road, in
construction, mechanics, repairing fountain pens, optometry, cooking, farming. And everything without complaint and unnecessary
reminiscences. We've really learned to accept the unavoidable with
dignity and just hope that we'll be able to put these newly-acquired
skills to good use soon. This aimless and vague living for the day is
nerve-racking and unbearable! Unfortunately I'm not as healthy as
I'd like to be. My joint rheumatism has indeed improved but the
right hip is still very bad. I'm also emaciated and not very productive. Other women can and must achieve more than I do. Mama is
sending you warm regards. She has finally, after one and a half years,
received news from my older brother. He is healthy and working,
and that is already a lot! Oscar, the youngest, is in Palestine. We hear
nothing from him now. He has a little boy. My sister Mutzi is in

Ostrava administrating an old people's home that she directs excellently. It is a really model home. Every now and again I'm invited on Sundays to a private chamber music performance, a beautiful experience from which I draw strength for the whole following week. I'm very much starving for art and music, but maybe it's good that way, so we learn to appreciate again these things. We have been taking them too much for granted!

Goodbye for now, Aunt Gertrude! Give Hanuš a kiss from me and many heartfelt regards

From your grateful
Ilse

How are you doing, Hanušku? Write soon! We're looking forward to your notebook!
Maminka

Ilse Weber, Praha 1, Norimberská 10
(at Dr. Weidmann)
[no date] End of Dec. 1940

Dear Good Aunt Gertrude!

Just now I received your lovely letter from the 15th of this month, the first letter that arrived to my new home, and it is also to you that I'm writing the first letter over here.

For three days we've been living here at Dr. Weidmann's, a pediatrician, though now without a practice. We're "subletting" as the ugly expression for it goes. We moved from our three-room apartment into a room, can you imagine that? I'm writing without bitterness, but have bad weeks behind me and was mentally and physically really sick, but it's foolish to mourn an apartment when there are other things that mean more to us.

Yes, and now you'd definitely enjoy it if you could look inside my place! We have this room, which is 23 square meters big, divided into two by my crosswise-placed three-piece wardrobe. The wardrobe's doors face the entrance of the room. This half of the room is Tommy's bedroom, but my kitchen table and two kitchen stools stand in it too. A tiled stove stands by the right wall, and next to it there's a washbasin with cold and warm running water (an enormous advantage, which I surely appreciate!), right next to it a small gas stove. Next to it, the smaller half of my kitchen cupboard with the most necessary kitchen utensils. The kitchen cupboard already borders our living room. My secretary and Willi's wardrobe next to it, these two furniture pieces already situated in the superior, cozier half of the room. The aforementioned "cross-wise-placed wardrobe" is covered from the back with a lovely carpet, so one of our two sofas leans on it. The second stands at an angle to it since there's no room there for a proper table; in front of it stands the machine, also covered with carpet. The "living corner," which contains the laundry bench as seating accommodation, is quite comfortable.

(An hour later.) I just had my first guests: my sister-in-law with Tommy, who this year spends a very long Christmas holiday with her. Conclusion: A visit is a catastrophe in *this* apartment! Unless it's very tidy and guests who don't leave things lying around. The day before yesterday, an acquaintance who had helped us left by mistake a small packet at our place, and today we had to literally turn the place upside down in order to find it. Yes, we don't just have the one room, but also two walls of a small foyer against which we placed the bigger half of the kitchen cupboard and a foyer wardrobe.

The kitchen cupboard must replace the completely absent pantry (which works during the winter, but what will happen in the summer?), and half of the chest in the foyer is Tommy's property, since the poor guy lost his lovely little room. We had to give away almost all his toys because we literally had no room. He was looking for them today quite distraught. Our subletting owner has a ten-year-old boy who, for his part, was expelled from his room. His name is Peter and he's a handsome and intelligent boy. I often compare him with Hanuš in my mind and the comparison is unfavorable toward Hanuš because Peter is really very clever. He installed a chemical laboratory in a room corner and tinkers and cooks the whole day. So he makes everything, himself included, dirty in the process. A third room is occupied by a young bachelor, a fourth by an old gentleman, and the fifth by a married couple. Nevertheless it is bearable. We have the former physician's office therefore occupy the most remote space.

I actually have *two* letters from you to answer, but, you see, don't you, that I couldn't answer the second-last; it simply was not possible. But the letter made me very happy. Now I know Hanuš' entire day plan. I would be happy if he finally learned to eat properly! That he's good at school pleases me greatly! Only, that he fills his notebook so slowly annoys both me and my husband. Please don't let him write in such thick notebooks in the future! We were very moved to know he received clothes from the Red Cross. We're no longer used to kindness by anyone. You know, all it takes is for someone to say to me a sympathetic word and I already cry. My nerves are so kaput.

The Lucia festival must be very lovely. I know this tradition partly from Carl Larsson[127] and partly from last year, when Rosa was Lucia in Steninge. What a beautiful time Hanuš had with you! I'm always happy when I think about it. Especially when, like recently, I have to live through hard days once more. I hope I'll yet receive from you a fine description of how you spent your Christmas? Tomorrow is New Year's Eve. Ach, may this last day of the year take with it all the evil that has come upon us. If we could only live again like other people, work and be happy like others!

Is your daughter with her husband already? Has she flown the whole way? What an adventurous life she has! I wonder if I'll also get mail from her at some point?! Does Hanuš still play so happily with soldiers? He could actually stop it. Don't you think he's becoming too old for that?

Tomorrow evening we'll be indeed sitting around gloomily, Willi and I. And on January 1 I'll try to be with you—if I only could do that in reality for this *one* day! How happy I was on the day Hannerle came into the world! In my view he was the most

beautiful and lovely child. I was more critical toward Tommy.
Please do tell Hanuš that Pauli broke his leg skiing. Now he's lying
down and suffers from strong pains. I myself won't be writing to
Hanuš so soon. I'm angry with him because he has been writing in
his notebook for a quarter of a year.

I wish you today, with my whole heart, that the new year may
bring you only goodness and beauty, that God will reward you
amply for what you're doing with my child, and that you will have
a lot of pleasure with your own children and grandchildren, dearest
Aunt Gertrude. And continue to write to me in great detail; you
have no idea what your letters mean to me!

Your grateful Ilse

At Dr. Weidmann, Norimberská 10, Prague 1
Prague, January 3, 1941

Dearest Aunt Gertrude!

Thank God you don't write a "notebook" like my son. That
would be unbearable. Imagine, I haven't received a line of his
writing for a quarter of a year! That must already have become
a thick book! Well, hopefully, it will arrive real soon and then at
least one every few months. It doesn't need to be so thick! Your
postcard from December 21, which just arrived, delighted us. I'm
proud Hanuš recited well. In his debut at the school in Witkowitz
he was so bashful when he had to recite a poem that he constantly
looked aside instead of at the audience, and caused general amuse-
ment. He will surely always remember the Christmas holidays in
Sweden and all the love he was given. But you know, the book
from us was not meant to be a Christmas present but one for his
birthday on January 1. Because we don't celebrate Christmas, only
Chanukah, which this year, coincidentally, started on December
24 as well. This one too is a beautiful holiday with candles and
presents and chanting. I anyway must ask you to make sure he
visits the Jewish religious classes. When one has paid dearly for

something then one appreciates it; and we have paid for our belief very very dearly. That is why it is our wish that our boy stays Jewish. We haven't denied our Judaism even for one instant, and he shouldn't do it either. He is still allowed to take the Protestant classes; each religion is beautiful and ethical; people just make a distorted picture of it. But please write to me openly if it's okay with you because I don't wish to do anything against your will! In the meantime I've gotten used to my new "apartment"; everybody thinks we have resolved the furnishing problem well. Through the crosswise placing of the wide wardrobe we have literally created a kitchen and living room. It remains unclear what will happen after Tommy's return (tomorrow). For the time being he's still letting off steam in Straschnitz. You know, what is really most interesting about Prague is that it consists of nothing but hills; each district has a few streets that make up a wonderful toboggan run, and my sister-in-law has outside her house a steep meadow, an ideal place for a boy of his nature. Tommy is exactly the opposite of Hanuš. He's outside in any weather no matter if it rains, snows or storms. We live now in the city center. We are no longer surrounded by dreamy villas and old gardens as in the Vineyards where we lived before; but there are beautiful old houses, baroque palaces, and right next to us, the old town square with the town hall and the famous apostle clock (have Hannerle tell you about it!), and the Moldau. Hanuš is a stay-at-home like his mother. There's nothing better for me than a warm corner and a book. But I'm not at all convinced this is the right thing for a future general. (He still wrote from Steninge: I'll be either general or sailor or policeman). Tell him please, that the three holy kings (My tří králové) were here. They send their best regards!

    Warmest regards to you in my husband's name as well,
    Your grateful Ilse

Nazdar, Hanuši! A happy New Year! And write more often!
    Mami

February 1941

Hanušku!

I would like to ask you, first, to read this letter only in the evening before you fall asleep, and, when you read it, imagine that you are lying beside me, hearing what I'm telling you. Hanušku, my dearest child, you're already ten years old. When I was your age my father died and many new worries weighed on my shoulders. I had to help with the inn and sometimes it was difficult and ugly to be among all the drunkards.

We sent you into the world in order to spare you worries and sadness. You're living now with Frau Löwenadler who loves you like her own child. You're still too young to be able to understand what this means for you. But you can no longer be so thoughtless.

Imagine, Hanušku, that I'm holding your little head in my hands now, looking into your eyes, saying: my dearest child, it is almost time you came back home to us. But you'd not be coming back to the home that you knew, where we were well and had a sufficiency of everything. We are poor now, quite poor; we're living in one single little room. Tomík receives free books from school, grandmother lives on the support from the Jewish community. Vati labors at work from early in the morning until late in the evening and still doesn't earn enough for our needs. All that is no disaster: the dear God will give us health and fortune, and we'll have a better life again. But you, my boy, have to adapt yourself. You have to be *hard working, modest* and *thankful*. Learn to wake up early each morning and be cheerful; you'll need that! Don't wait for Ruth to come and wake you up. Get up by yourself, get dressed quickly and you'll see how beautiful and long the day will be. Be at school just as good as you were in Vítkovice, and always imagine that your good principal Talpa is looking at you. Help Ruth in the kitchen with the dirty dishes; Tomík already does this by himself and so does Peter, who is your age and has rich parents. *Behave always very politely toward the servants.* Imagine that these are your Mutti or Vati who must work for strangers. No one should think he's better than the other. Arrogance is a big sin. The poor boy on the street in his ragged clothes can achieve in the future more than the one in the beautiful suit. No one can pick his parents! No one is allowed to place himself above others.

I'm writing you all this out of great love because I wish that your life would go well. I'm asking you, my dear child to keep this letter and read it every evening before going to sleep. Do you promise me that?

And try that with getting up, all right? I would like you to answer me to every line of this letter, Hanušku, so that I see that you understood me.

Dobrou noc, můj nejmilejší!
(Good night, my dearest of all!)
Mami

March 2, 1941

I've already written to you, Hanušku, that your notebook had arrived safely. It took only six days, and that is, after all, relatively fast. I'm starting this letter before Aunt Erna, Pavel and Fella Meller are coming. As you know, it's Tommy's birthday today and they let us know they'd come to celebrate together with us. Tommy is getting from us just a music stand. But I have also baked a small pie and a cake, and Uncle Karl, who's always very kind, bought him two books: the first part of *Ferda Mravenec* (Ferda, the Ant), and *V tajemné říši lesa* (In the Secret Realm of the Forest), as well as some candies. He got a beautiful pen from Peter Weidmann, but unfortunately he tinkered around with it so long that it broke. Yesterday evening, as we lighted seven candles, Doctor Weidmann, his wife, and the other neighbors came to congratulate him, and then they stayed almost until ten o'clock. Tommy has never before been allowed to stay up that late.

Your lovely letter arrived in time. Tommy will answer it by himself. The pictures you sent in the July notebook were very beautiful! There were six picture postcards and three greeting cards. I would visit you right away if I only could. Would you like that?

Hanušku, you wrote the following:

> In the cinema today I was
> this year for the third time
> it was terrible, it was fine,
> I had to be home at three o'clock.

This is a little poem, as you see. Did you want it to rhyme or was that just a coincidence? However, I was overjoyed. I wrote my first song when I was your age. At that time we had to write an article about "Münchenhausen" for homework. The girls in the class couldn't do it so I wrote ten different articles one after the other. But when I had to write my own article there was silence in my head. And then I had the idea to write some poem about it. It was successful, the poem; I still know it by heart; it was really good but the teacher didn't believe I wrote it by myself.

Today, like every Saturday, we had a small celebration in the Jewish children's day care. The children put on a play and Tommy was the old grandfather in "Budulinku."[128] Then we sang to the gramophone. We sing mainly in Hebrew; these are truly beautiful songs!

Vati and Tommy have just come home. They went to get a gramophone. An acquaintance lent us his beautiful records for one day. Therefore I have to finish now. Goodbye my boy!

I'm kissing you heartily!

Your Maminka

Prague, March 3, 1941

Dear Aunt Gertrude!

Your letter from the 19th of this month arrived this morning. Thank you very much for reporting so extensively! It's strange that it took my letter from January 11 more than a month to arrive, but the main thing is that it arrived after all! Yes, I did haul Hanuš over the coals; I almost felt sorry for him, but really, at the age of

ten one must already be able to write a letter, especially after practicing it for two years. You write again and again that he's gentle
and small. He wasn't smaller here than the children his age, though
not the biggest either. But the Nordic people are indeed generally
big, and it is certainly true that he's of a different nature. Hopefully, he's just good and honest. Life will cure him of being unre-
alistic and dreamy. He was always closer to me than little Tommy.
And you can't imagine how much I love his last picture! Tommy is
a lovely, hearty guy, once fresh, then affectionate again, very independent, a mixture of wanting-to-be-big and childishness, a bab-
bler who can be hardly silenced. But Hannerl was my little friend
who listened seriously when I spoke to him and who sometimes
expressed very deep insights. I know his many flaws; he is indeed
hereditarily burdened by both parents. But none of us is flawless.
God grant only that we be able again to live like people with a
purpose, with the vexations, but also the pleasures of everyday life,
in a home that unites us all. No one can compensate us for these
years in which we have lived separated and unnerved, tormented
and uprooted; they have made us so much older, and it will surely
have undesirable effects in the years to come. Look, Willi is now
seriously sick and unable to work. It isn't so easy, after all, to all of
a sudden take on quite hard labor when one has been working for
years in an office. And since we have consumed our savings this
unemployment is a catastrophe for us. But we trust in God! We
still have much hardship ahead of us. Even if there will be peace
soon, we will have to start all over again.

But now I want to put aside my worries. In the meantime I
took a break from writing, took care of lunch, washed the dishes,
and cleaned the bright furniture with petroleum. We have really an
incredible amount of soot here! I've polished the window, which is,
luckily, big and wide, and one casement is open, partly to let out
the smell of petroleum and let in the sweet March air. Our room
is becoming brighter already; we don't have to leave the light on
for the entire day. The ash and coal carrying will gradually stop
and my dear Prague will put on its most beautiful garment. I love

the spring above everything. But I hate taking walks in company. Can you understand me? Mama is sitting by the window mending socks; she always sends you her regards, but I think I don't always pass them on. Willi too, is rarely there when I'm writing, which is why I also forget to pass that on.

Please do tell Hanuš that the tough soldier, Tommy, really and truly shot himself in the hand the day before yesterday. He had actually received a shotgun and since shooting with a bottle cork wasn't fun enough, he charged it with a toothpick. The malheur occurred the evening before yesterday. He pulled the trigger with the left hand while the right one held the barrel. That was horrifying! The point of the toothpick penetrated the palm and broke off there, and Tommy screamed blue murder, although he's otherwise not oversensitive to pain. Luckily we live with a physician, but he couldn't take out the splinter because it sits straight down in the hand. So Tommy is walking around with a painful clenched-up hand and has an excuse to wash even more rarely.

Now it's almost three o'clock: shopping time! I'm therefore concluding and remain, with a thousand thanks for your love and kindness

Your Ilse

Prague, the 16th of March, 1941

My Dear Hanušku!

Today I want to tell you about what I'm doing at the children's day care and how it looks in there. The day care is about five minutes away from our house, and when I'm going there I have to go past the old city hall and the Tomb of the Unknown Soldier. Then it's right there on the second floor of an old house. When the children arrive they have to first sign in and put on slippers. After that they can either go to a room where they can play table tennis, or to another where a teacher helps them with their homework, or to the biggest room of all where there are various playthings, a library, building blocks and jigsaw. A young engineer works with the children who want to learn how to make things with a jigsaw. A physician·does gymnastics with those who like to exercise. I teach the children songs, mainly in Hebrew. They already know fifteen. At four o'clock the children get a snack: lemonade sweetened with saccharin, and bread with marmalade. You should see how quickly they devour the bread! These are poor children and they are always hungry!

But they don't look bad, they're really healthy and funny and make such a noise that one can get a headache. Worst is little Rudla who is the same age as Tommy, a clever and hilarious boy, small like a fist and a real clown. The best-behaved is a nine year-old-boy who helps us diligently and is always polite and cheerful. Among the girls there are also the well-behaved and less so. When I arrive with my guitar they all call, "Look, Fräulein Weber! Come and play for us, Fräulein!" And then they place a little table in the middle of the room, I write the text for the new song on the board, and we all sit down and start to sing.

On Saturday we always have a little party. We prepare a program, either a lecture or dances and songs, and the children receive a somewhat better snack.

Not long ago we celebrated Purim. Do you still know what it is? Maybe you can recall the biblical story of King Ahasuerus and Queen Esther, the minister Haman who hated the Jews, and upright Mordechai. The children themselves played that story and Tomík played an apprentice magician. He said: "I am the great magician Bubu and I know all the arts of magic. When I do magic I feel the best. I possess wagons full of gold. I will now present to you my world-famous magic free of charge, and should anything accidentally go wrong, that is only because my hand must have slipped a little." Then he "performed magic." I can't describe to you everything, but he did it well. He was indeed the best! As for his violin playing, he's doing excellently too. I would even say that he plays better and more on-key than Pavel.

Besides he is sweet. He's always cheerful and sings from morning till evening. Right now he's down at the Moldau with Judit

Birn. Do you still remember her? They live near us.

He has just finished this letter for you. It wasn't easy since he doesn't like to write. Now our Peter came over and he wants to write too. Every day he invents something new. Just now he invented a robot. Do you at all know what it is? Peter wants you to know that it's an artificial man. He needs the robot to prepare his homework for him. Do you know that Peter gets up only at ten? He is a lazybones, isn't he? But he promised to get up earlier from now on because he wants to earn money. I'm wondering at that.

Now he's standing next to me correcting my mistakes. Peter is a clever and well-behaved boy but sometimes he's rude to his parents. (He's standing next to me, reading everything I'm writing about him).

Farewell, my Hanuš; I'm looking forward to your next letter and am sending you a thousand kisses.

Maminka

25.3.1941

Dear Aunt Gertrude!

Sunday is almost over; I think we will have mail from you tomorrow. It often arrives at the beginning of the week now. Since it's uncertain when I'll have time to write I would like to chat with you a bit now. It's past five o'clock; I have already turned on the lights, Mama has just left for home, and Tommy's playing "pharmacy" with Peter, i.e. Peter, who really has a burning interest in chemistry, is selling drugs and Tommy's buying them. Every now and again I go there too and ask for rat poison or corn plaster, and since I'm paying with candies I'm a most popular customer. Such an hour of solitude as I have now has become rare, and I therefore appreciate it twice as much. In the next days a family of three will move into our apartment. Then four families will occupy four rooms, in addition to the "Fräulein" in the maid's room. As pleasant as one may be it's impossible to avoid a certain tension, and the nerves are overburdened. Well, but our case is fortunately not tragic because, touch

wood, we're a happy combination; we have the greatest consideration for each other, understand each other quite well, and help one
another where we can. Dr. Weidmann and wife are very kind and
really good people! It is almost funny when one goes through our
building and looks at the apartment doors. There are four, five and
even six calling cards sticking one below the other, and each notes a
particular ringing signal.

And we take all that with humor. Our guests are always amused
when I escort them from the "kitchen" which in the afternoon becomes the "children's room" to the "Persian Room." That's the name
of our living area. The space behind the window is called "fridge";
but unfortunately (from another perspective it is nice) the sun has
been recently shining into the fridge. However, since my supply
of fat is running out anyway, it may shine without causing dam-
age! When I need a glass of marmalade I must fetch the big ladder
from the janitress, which is allowed only between eight and nine
on weekdays, except Saturday. I am currently trying to find some
work at home, something that can be sewn on the machine and
requires no great skill. My involvement at the day care may consequently suffer but I cannot change that. If only there could be an
end in sight and some certainty one could lead an existence worthy
of human beings! Uncertainty is the worst and, for men who were
used to work, doing nothing is bad. Willi's sciatica still hasn't improved. I am very anxious to know, if you write to me tomorrow,
that you received news from your daughter! We're all very worried!

O dear! My beautiful peace is gone. The boys are fed up with
their game and have appeared in the room here, Tommy and Peter.
Now they want to make music, Tommy playing the violin and Peter
the mandolin. I find that Tommy is good with the violin. I've occasionally heard beginners play the violin, but Tommy doesn't screech
at all with his violin, and when he's giving Peter lessons it's *too*
nice! Peter always holds his tongue in the corner of his mouth and
Tommy opens his mouth at the difficult passages. Yesterday I had to
organize the "program" for the Saturday entertainment at the children's day care. I found a "circle" of around twenty children, boys

and girls, who were happy to demonstrate their skills. Do you know
what a "circle" is? Countless numbers of our children really can't go
to school (here in Prague we have only two, and no middle school),
so there are always small groups getting together with someone's father who's capable of giving lessons. (As a rule, they learn there more
than at school). And "my" circle consists of especially nice children.
I've received much credit thanks to them, admittedly undeserved,
because I knew only three of them and I saw their performance for
the first time; but I was delighted with most of them and their talents. It's so comforting to see that we do have at least *something* that
can't be taken away from us after all!

    Tomorrow I will write further! Good evening, Aunt Gertrude!

    Wednesday, March the 26th. By way of exception, your lovely
card arrived just today. Above all, we're very happy that James is
reunited with his wife. When you write to them please send our regards!!!! We're very much looking forward to Hanuš' picture. Many
many thanks for fulfilling my wish so lovingly! Willi and I very
much welcome his joining the Boy Scouts. This is just what he
needs. He is really too gentle and soft for a boy despite playing the
soldier, which he will hopefully give up now. Vati's birthday is on
May 21. The birthday letter with the picture came two months too
early. It seems he no longer knows the months' names in Czech.
"Květen" is May. Nevertheless we were very happy, and Willi will
write too. Hanuš had measles as well as rubella, chickenpox, scarlet fever, lung inflammation, and inflammation of the middle ear.
His tonsils were removed twice. Feel confident leaving him among
children anywhere. Yes, he already had whooping cough as well. In
this respect I have had nothing to complain about. Since yesterday
I'm working at home and I guess that is the reason that I am very
tired today. I'm making bags for soap and sponge out of Billroth
Batiste[129] for a business. It's a lot of work for miserable pay. Thirty
Hellers[130] per piece. Yesterday and today I made a hundred pieces
in ten hours; Mama, Willi and even Tommy gave me a hand. We
can't live even one day with this income. But maybe I'll get used to
the work and make more, although a hundred pieces in two days is

a good outcome. However, this is not for me. It is not good neither
for my eyes nor for my back, to sit bent over and work in the poor
light of our room. I'm definitely not cut out for manual work.
That is I'd rather do men's work, mechanics, or anything else; the
"feminine" handiwork is not in my nature. I also ironed a big stack
of laundry so that I'm ready for bed. Over here spring is hesitant
in its arrival this year; it snowed today and it's still really cold. But
like you *I* say: spring *must* come or, as the song of your beloved
mother puts it, "But God with his great goodness sends us again
the sunshine!" And as I can't think of a nicer ending for my letter, I
let these words conclude.

> All the love to you and my boy,
> Ilse

Dear Aunt Gertrude: Many thanks for the lovely greetings that,
hopefully, will all come true until my birthday.

> Very warm regards, Willi.

Hanušku, you are a real trulala: Vati's birthday is on May 21! But
because you have shown your good intentions I'll tell you something that will surely please you: I paid the magazine *Mladý hlasatel* for half a year in advance, so you should receive it for the rest of
the school year.

> Thousand kisses
> Mami

April 21, 1941

My Dear Aunt Gertrude!
    Today's evening belongs to you and Hanuš! I was today fabu-
lously diligent and, believe it or not, sewed thirty-five bags. And
beautifully sewn! True, self-praise stinks, but since the business
owner herself said I am her best worker I'm allowed to praise
myself this one time. You know, it's quite an unusual material,
so-called imitation leather, black. Each pocket panel gets a thick

layer of cotton lining, and when one just quilts a pattern on it,
it emerges beautifully and produces a lovely effect. It looks very
good. I created the pattern yesterday with an acquaintance who
used to be a physician, radiologist, an outstanding hematologist,
and promising scientist. Now he has switched to graphics and his
achievements in this field are equally impressive. I'm always very
pleased when I hear about someone who had to give up his profession and proves that he can achieve something in another field.
This young physician also designed a lovely frame for me that will
be used for the wall-newspaper in the children's day care.

But first I must thank you for the address in Hanuš' notebook,
which arrived on the 17th of this month, four days earlier than
the previously sent postcard, which I received only today, Monday. It seems to me that Hanuš is in the censor's good books since
his little notebook came through so quickly. The little notebook
provides me with a really good picture of his life and bustle; I am
pleased that he joined the Scouts. It will be a good counterbalance
to his stay-at-home tendency!

I have so much work that I often literally don't know whether
I'm coming or going. If I were able to get up in the morning one
hour earlier I would save a lot of time; but you see, *that* is precisely
what I am not capable of! In the evenings, if need be, I can work
until eleven, twelve o'clock, but I find it so difficult to be up early!
It has always been like that and at home was Mama's greatest woe.
The morning passes with cooking and tidying up. After lunch it
takes up to two o'clock before I'm done with the dish washing and
clearing up. Now comes the sewing, which is interrupted by shopping time; and only by multiplying my workload by three can I go
on Friday and Saturday to the children's day care. I'm quite indis-
pensable there; they would like to have me permanently but since
the Jewish Community can't expand the number of its employees,
and, on the other hand, I need an income, I must work five days a
week so that I'm able to follow my inclination: which happens to
be for the children's day care! for two days. It is, after all, amazing,
how much my bit of music-making helps.

At the day care the children are rather unorganized, each
doing something on his own: reading, carving, playing, gymnastics. When *I* come and sit down with my guitar my table is immediately surrounded and there's singing. (. . .) There are so many
nice and "picture pretty" children. They had been very neglected
before they came to the day care but now they're clean, bathe
once a week, are medically examined and treated, must wash
themselves, receive clothes, hair and tooth brushes, and the snack,
which is very poor though. Hanuš should see how they all pounce
on the marmalade bread and the tea, which is nothing but lemon
water with sugar substitute. But my Tommy drinks it just as eagerly and eats the doubtful marmalade and almost prefers it to the
one at home, which, after all, I made myself. The children were
touching. There are dozens of them who, during the holidays,
rejected the snack steadfastly, although their eyes clearly showed
their craving for it. I'm very happy Hanuš is not here, but from an
educational point of view I sometime wish to have him here. (. . .)

I was very pleased with Carl-Axel's greetings. I thank him
warmly and think he'll understand how happy I was to hear from
him that you all love to have my boy with you. I don't think we'll see
each other again so soon, that we'll see each other again at all, because even when once the war is over God knows where our fate will
take us, and we will have to banish the thought of seeing our friends
again from our heads. Ach you see, Aunt Gertrude, that is the blessing of work: it keeps you from thinking! Because if one would think,
one would become mad! We were torn off the tracks of everyday
life in a most terrible way. One reproaches us Jews for hubris. But
we must, after all, have something to give us the strength to endure
so much humiliation and persecution! In the last two years I aged a
hundred years, and almost everyone else with me.

You, dear Aunt Gertrude, I'd like to thank again from the bottom of my heart. Stay really healthy and happy and write often;
your mail is a celebration for the whole family. Hanuš still must
wait for a separate letter. I don't know when I'll have time and
feel like it. In the meantime I'm sending him a kiss with you. He

should answer Peter and tell him about the Scouts!

Wholeheartedly your Ilse!

Prague, the 1st of May 1941

My Hanušku!

Today is the 1st of May, a day we've always celebrated so beautifully with Vati. Do you still remember you always took the 1st of
May train to the city? And when you were little Vati carried you on
his shoulders.

Today isn't beautiful at all: it rains and rains; it's pouring with
rain. Our room looks gloomy but I have the day off and would like
to write to you. Grandmother sits by the window, darning socks.
Vati's lying on the sofa, snoozing. Tomíček went before lunch with
Pavel to Strášnice to repair Aunt Erna's sewing machine. Do you
know, when I'm sewing these carrier bags I told you about, I must
sew in such paper padding that it breaks the machine. I had to
call in already twice a craftsman to repair it; now I can fix it myself and do it daily. Tommy always helps me with my work and so
he learned it too. When Pavel was here today and told us "Mama
can't sew today, because her sewing machine is broken," Tommy
stood up and said, "I'll go with you and repair the machine." Pavel
laughed at him, but his laughter will fade away once Tommy will
have actually repaired it. I've already told you that Tommy has very
skillful hands. He loves to screw and repair, but books he doesn't
like in particular. He reads well but doesn't always feel like it. I'd
be happy if you too would be a little interested in manual work,
Janku, since we must now be skilled in everything because we don't
know where life will place us one day. I would have never dreamt
that I'd be able one day to feed all of us with sewing. Last month I
even earned our entire livelihood. And Herr Principal Brün, who
gave you the fine fountain pen as farewell present, this year works
as an ordinary worker at the railroad. Fella's father, who was an attorney at a big bank, is working this year as a carpenter. Everybody
is forced to re-educate himself and learn a new profession, and is

doing that willingly. The main thing is that one is allowed to work! We're very pleased that you've become a Scout! That's the only thing in the world I like for boys and girls. They at least learn how one should behave. Hopefully you stop now the stupid soldier game. You'll see, when the war is over no one in the entire world will want to hear the word "soldier" again. Better stay with the Scouts, learn to love nature, and act right. Isn't your motto "Be Prepared!"? It's a beautiful motto: Be prepared to help, be prepared to do good! It's almost as beautiful as your motto: "The truth prevails." But do you always tell the truth? I hope you do that. You write that you read a lot. But I'd like to hear from you what you are actually reading and *what you've learned from the book*. One can learn something from every book after all and, if not, then it's a waste of time! Hanušku, unfortunately we can't send you anything more, but if you save some money be a darling and buy and send Aunt Lilian's children some trifles. You'd give me a great pleasure! Write to me and report if you did what I asked you to. Those poor children are so lonely and abandoned and you, who actually don't belong to the family, are doing so well. But you're not allowed to read that to the Grandma, do you understand? You go often to the cinema! We're forbidden to go to the cinema and I haven't been there for a long time! It's nice of Hans that he's taking you to the museum so often; this is good for your education! Yesterday I went together with Tommy to the Church of St. Jacob and after that we went to the Týn Church. St Jacob's Church is really wonderful! Tommy goes to the Old Jewish Cemetery almost every day. He knows nearly everything there. We live almost directly opposite the old synagogue, which we also visited together with you. Maybe you remember the old flag the Jews received during the Thirty Years War when they fought against the Swedes. Now you yourself live in Sweden, Hanušku! We wrote Nana[131] but she didn't reply. Marta[132] didn't either. I must tell Tommy often about various discoveries and inventions, and that is sometimes exhausting for me, because I don't know enough about it. But now I figured out that I can read to him from a lexicon and he likes that very much.

Tommy also likes to fight with Vati. When I need a ruler or a carpet beater I can't find them because they are Tommy's "weapons," which he is hiding.

He doesn't meet with Peter at the present. Tommy's school is closed because of scarlet fever and Peter's father is afraid he could bring the germs with him. I'm happy about that because Peter can sometimes be a real devil. Once they both disappeared in Peter's apartment and, when they came out, they were dressed as robbers and attacked several neighbors.

We were very happy with the pictures. I made several copies from one; one I gave to Bobby, one to Aunt Haberfeld[133] and one to Uncle Immerglück. He sends you his regards and would like to know if you can still play something (on the piano)???

What rank do you have at the Scouts? Do you belong to the Cubs? Are you still so good at calculating? Tommy too has learned now to calculate. Sometimes we play this game: I let him calculate something, or we write letters to each other. What is your favorite subject at school? Are you still meeting the Norwegian Fräulein from time to time? How do you like the new tenant?

Hanušku, 29 kilos is very little for you. Erich Fuchs weighs already 35 kilos. That's certainly because you're so picky! I hope that you put on weight quite quickly! Please give Frau Lion regards from us. What kind of dog does she have? Do you always bring with you something for him? You should think of that!

We hung a green box on the window and today sowed something in it. But we don't know whether flowers will grow there since we have nearly no sun here. Tommy stands the whole time by the window to see if "it already germinates." He believes that it happens so fast! I'd like to know what you're doing in your club. Tell me about it! How many are you? And what are you occupying yourself with? Which of your friends do you like the most and what does he look like? Do you like Hans? I think it's nice to have an older, clever comrade like him. He can help you at any time!

Well, that was a long letter, wasn't it, my boy? But now I conclude and hope that you are healthy and good. Many kisses. I'd be pleased if you write again soon.

Your Matička

Prague, May the 5th 1941

My Dearest Aunt Gertrude!

Today I had a lot of mail, and later on even work. I sewed today almost ninety swimming caps and it stultified me. My head is aching the whole day it is such a disgusting work; a lot of work and poorly paid. But I must accept every order from this company. Next time I will get again something that is better paid. I receive sixty Hellers per cap;[134] the work process is the following: 1. sew together head-parts, 2. sew a small fabric-triangle to the frontal suture, 3. trim the upper edge, 4. trim an elastic band into the lower edge, 5. trim the lower edge and at the same time sew to it the band, 6. cut the band slantwise (I forgot to report that I first must stitch the band into a tuft, and then pull through the snap fastener.) Sixty Hellers is very little. Mama and Willi took turns in helping me. For tomorrow I have two more good hours of work. (Yesterday, Sunday, I sewed fifty pieces!) Yes, nevertheless I absolutely want to write to you today. While I sat at the machine I constantly thought about the contents of your dear letter. First of all, what you write about Acki's wife. I'm dreadfully sorry that you're not on better terms with her. Is there really no way for you to bring your relationship back on the right track? You see, I know this disharmony between mother and daughter-in-law unfortu- nately from my own experience and, therefore, wish you wouldn't have to go through all these unedifying things! I, as I have written to you earlier, very much loved my mother-in-law and she was my best friend. But unfortunately, Mama and Willi are not on good terms with each other. Both are to blame for that though it is mostly Mama's fault. She holds too high of an opinion of me. The man who, according to her, would have been good enough for me has likely not been born yet. I am really not subjective when I repeatedly say how good and honest Willi is; but Mama always

clings to petty things he's not a perfect example of and generally
fails to appreciate him. That he helps me with everything in the
household, that he doesn't smoke, doesn't play, that he allows himself nothing, all this is "self-evident"; whereas she, for instance, seriously urged me to keep the money I earn now for myself, which
is ridiculous. When my husband is sick *I am* working, I naturally
work in his stead, and I should not be so obstinate to obsess about
"my" and "his" money. Mama herself worked at Papa's side for
many years, and she never had her own money. I cherish Mama
very much and was always a good daughter but now I often lose
my patience with her and treat her harshly, especially when she
carps about Willi. Afterward I am remorseful. However, it happens
again and again. Yet between you and your daughter-in-law there's
an unfounded estrangement, twice as painful because you nevertheless love your boys so much. Isn't it at all possible to put this
right? If I knew her I'd advise her to bring about an open discus-
sion with you so that you can tell each other what actually stands
between you. It can't be her different nature only. I loved and
admired you so much I can't at all imagine that anyone wouldn't!
I know that you're very proud and very sensitive and *she* should
make the first step. But perhaps she's too young and stupid for
that? Perhaps when you meet her halfway and let her understand
that you wish to have harmonious relations with her, even if she
doesn't recognize your superiority and will not follow you, she will
perhaps be happy about it?! She is, after all, also in a foreign country and may need you! I would love to be with you and have your
love and friendship! That Lilian deposed her wish, with a lawyer,
that her children be raised in a home is surely because she had a
dangerous journey ahead of her and she thought of all the possibilities and wanted to protect you from all the worries and difficulties
that come with raising such little children. She certainly didn't
want to *hurt* you! Aunt Gertrude, we people are now all in such a
pitiful situation. The present times rob us all. First us, the younger
ones, of a bearable everyday life, of every joy, of the joy of working,
and the ability to strive for a purpose; but much more you, our

mothers. The older generation had to part with their children; our
Jewish mothers have no home, no family; they are starving, mentally and physically. And the children that still stayed with them
are no source of joy; they too are worn down by their own sorrows,
too unnerved by the events of their lives to still find patience and
love for their parents. I don't even have enough time and patience
for the one child who stayed with me! When he's joyful he gets on
my nerves; when I'm supposed to help him with his tasks I lose
my patience and become rude. At the same time I love him, and
sometimes I long for the older so much that I can't describe it. You
put it so well, Aunt Gertrude: "He sometimes annoys us but brings
us a good deal of joy as well." I wish he will give you plenty, plenty
of joy for your great selfless goodness! You don't even know *how*
well off he is!!! That he can live in a beautiful, quiet home, that he
can go to school, that he's treated as an equal, that he can go to
parks and cinemas, and is able to visit museums, ach, my sacrifice
was not in vain *after all!* You write that he's a child, a playful child:
that is exactly what I have to thank you for! Our children here
have unfortunately become too aware. Tommy, only seven years,
already knows exactly that the cemetery is the only garden where
he's allowed to go; he knows that during the afternoon shopping
time I must think about everything because otherwise later I'm
not allowed to get it. He pays attention to the time so that I don't
come home evenings after eight o'clock, and he quits playing with
his toys (only a few are left anyway because there's no place for
them in our small room) when he sees that I'm working in order
to come to my help. And Tommy is a joyful child whereas Hanuš
has a tendency to brood. Is that habit gone now? Write to me once
what he annoys you with and how he makes you happy, all right?
Please!

I'm only afraid that he's *too* happy with you and that he will
find it very difficult to settle back in when he returns to us.

It has turned ten o'clock now and I'll go to sleep. Tommy was
still awake half an hour ago. The poor boy doesn't get what he
needs.

I'm kissing your hands gratefully and keep on wishing fervently
for your mental and physical well being.

> Your grateful
> Ilse

May 16, 1941

My Dear Aunt Gertrude!

Friday evening: An hour ago I finished sewing my hundredth
bag (since yesterday) thereby breaking all records and securing
for myself a free, *sewing free*, day. Tomorrow I'm not touching the
sewing machine. I think this is work's greatest blessing: that one
learns to appreciate every free hour so much! I was so industrious
this week I never thought I would be capable of that. I literally sat
from morning till evening at the sewing machine and sewed; the
day before yesterday I did eleven hours (until after midnight). You
see practice is everything; I found the beginning so hard! The peculiar thing about my current work is that the harder it is the smaller
the income. At the beginning of the week I made swimming caps,
a kind of work I have never done: two elastic bands, one over the
forehead and one at the nape; the machine didn't want to stitch the
elastic ribbons and on average tore the thread twice with each elastic ribbon. You can calculate how often that happened! I was shak-
ing with nervousness and it wasn't safe to come near me. But now
I already sewed over three hundred swimming caps, the last ones
sixty-four crowns per piece. I left my old company because they had
held against me some rather inexactly cut small threads. The new
company asked me to sew swimming caps. They were more than
content with my work; they even showed it to the other workers
(although I don't sew nearly as fast as the others!) But I had hardly
worked one day for them when the old company sent for me, and
when Willi went there in my stead he received an order for one
hundred bags. That is a much more agreeable work and on top of
that, better paid. I worked for two days and can rest tomorrow. And

when Willi delivered the first fifty he was told that tomorrow I'd get
another hundred. This is fine! I also brought in Frau Fischer, Hans'
mother, as well. I really like her; she is such a lovely, brave woman
and they were so miserable. She had to assemble the bags; she does
it really well and liked it. But with those we're making now it has
to be done by an upholsterer, and so she switched to swimming
caps as well, which yield a smaller income; and so Herr Dr. Fischer
went around lugubriously. (Him I like, if it's possible, even better.
He is a highly intelligent, very educated person, and I know no one
with whom I'd prefer to talk.) When I recently visited the second
company I overheard by chance that they raised the question if
they shouldn't manufacture other relevant articles, and so I noted,
in passing, that I happen to be acquainted with the most efficient
worker of such and such company. The following conversation was
of no relevance; Hans' mother is already finishing her first week as
"first pattern producer" in the second company and I'm waiting
anxiously for her first weekly paycheck tomorrow. You see, these are
our worries. I hardly notice the spring at all. Our street has just one
single blooming tree and it stands in front of the ancient Old-New
Synagogue; the oldest synagogue, actually; the oldest place of wor-
ship in Europe in general. And when I long for more blossoms I go
to the old cemetery. I sowed seeds into a little flower box and placed
it in the window but the sun comes to us only for a brief moment
and whoosh, it's gone, and our place becomes very solemn; then we
open the window and turn the bulb's "eternal light"[135] off. Tommy
is sick; he has a sore throat since the day before yesterday. But today
he was already free of fever and helped me diligently. I placed the
machine next to his bed and he eagerly cut threads. After supper
he gave me his pocket money, two crowns, "because you were so
industrious." Isn't that sweet of him? For Mother's Day last Sunday
I got a heart he himself cut out and designed. I wonder if Hanuš
was clever enough to bring you a couple of flowers? *You* are now his
Mutti! He is likely too ignorant for that! Are the men in Sweden
wearing leather boutonnieres? Here they are trendy and I would like

to try and send you one. Please let me know what color you could use. Friends of ours are crafting beautiful ones. Make sure you tell me. I would really love to send you some if we are allowed to!!!

I'm pleased to know that the two little ones have recovered! How scared their mother must be! Have you received any more mail from her?

Dear Hanušku, today you're getting only greetings. Don't be mad when I don't write so much but you write very little too, and besides, I have an awfully lot of work. I hardly find any time to sleep!

Pac a pusu, můj hošíčku, od Tvé Matičky! (Be hugged and kissed, my little boy, by your Mama.) These couple of lines are for my boy. It really isn't enough for an extra letter. I'm dead-tired and am going to sleep soon.

Kissing your hands gratefully,
Your Ilse

July 6, 1941

Dear Aunt Gertrude!

I received back the enclosed letter from the censor because I had enclosed printed material for Hanuš which is not allowed. I didn't know that and much regret that our correspondence suffered a disruption. For the first time since Hannerle has been with you I have not received mail from you for a whole week. It seems to me strange but I think that it's for no special reason and that you are healthy and well. To Hanuš I wrote not long ago. The letter should have gone by airmail yet this wasn't possible as no such letters are going out right now.

I hope you're healthy again and can soon travel to your little grandchildren. I'm looking forward to your report: how they look and how are they doing.

I'm so happy that the flowers arrived. You'll get the others some time. I'd like to ask you if Hanuš can give one flower to the old lady who had invited him to her place for his birthday? And if yes, which flower should it be?

Today is Sunday. I am, like all the lazy people, industrious on Sunday of all days, and ironed, patched and sewed. After that, Willi and Tommy went to a playground and myself to the Moldau. That is my favorite walk! It's barely five minutes away from my house and when you go down to the quay you forget that you're in the middle of the city: before me the wide river with its beautiful arched bridges and small boats, in the background wooded hills. It is beautiful, even when you can only look at it, not being allowed to go there. Sometimes it really surprises me that we're not forced to wear black glasses. So we caress the green splendor with our eyes and remember past days when the trees still turned green indiscriminately for all people. Just now Tommy is calling me to his bed. He pulled out another tooth. He's going to look even funnier now! By the way, he brought home a nice report card, nothing but A's except for one B. We prepared a kind of lesson plan for him: in the morning he is supposed to write and practice the violin, in the afternoon he's allowed to go to the day care. He helps me a lot: tidying up, making the beds (no trivial work for us), and is very good-natured.

Willi is working again. I'm very happy because first, my work stopped and second, I've been so reluctant to work lately. I also have severe joint pains. Besides, I'm running around so much during our shopping hours in order to get hold of our food that I don't feel like doing anything after that. How is the weather where you are? I take very little notice of the summer, just as little as I did of the spring. On my way back today I visited the old cemetery. You would have liked it. It's the oldest cemetery in Europe. It has 20,000 gravestones that stand together asymmetrically. The graves of the pogroms' victims are embedded in the wall itself. Wild elder and jasmine grow between the stones, the black birds sing in the ancient trees, everything is so tremendously interesting: the old gravestones from the 16th century with their strange inscriptions; the grave of the great Rabbi Löw, creator of the Golem and adviser to the Emperor Rudolf. In between the gravestones old people put down their portable little chairs and enjoy a quiet hour. Tomorrow a new week starts

again. I will look forward once more to seeing the postman and will
be disappointed if he brings nothing. Do you have mail from your
daughter? I think it should have arrived by now!

Adieu now, good night! Warmest regards to you and Hannerle
and I wish you all lots of love and all the best!

Your Ilse

To Hanuš Weber at Frau v. Löwenadler
Stockholm, Oestermalmgatan 67/III

Sender Ilse Weber, Prague 1.
Nürnbergerstr. 60

Prague, August 9th, 1941

My Hanušku!

I received your letter but can't claim that it had a cheerful effect on me. You're writing worse than a six-year-old. I could somehow forgive you your mistakes but I find it difficult to understand
how you can't tell anything. On the first page you promise that
you will write more the next day when you're sitting in the train,
but in the end you don't do that. Then you want to report how it
was in Bårarp and in Steninge, but you don't do that either! Regarding Gillian and Alistair you can only state: "They are already
bigger!" I'm gradually starting to believe that you have somehow
become stupid, Hanušku! Your good school reports seem to be an
undeserved gift. I actually wanted to send you a nice book but I'm
not doing that. Yes, I'm ashamed to show your letters to anyone
here. "Does the little boy already go to school?" asked a woman
who accidentally saw your letter: and I pretended as if I didn't hear
that. Therefore: I will not send this book before I have received
from you a nice long letter with descriptions of the stay in Bårarp.
And one more thing: why did you leave there so early? Did you get
into mischief, Hanušku?

So that was my sermon: and now I don't want to be angry with you anymore but just write facts. A few days ago Tommy received twenty crowns and bought himself a ping-pong game. Now he's playing uninterruptedly and you can imagine how we feel in the one room we live in. One time the ball ends up in the soup, then in the cabbage, then on grandmother's head. It can drive you crazy. But where should the poor boy play? He's not allowed to play in the sports field neither is he allowed to be in the street; besides, that would be too dangerous; therefore, all that remains is our little room. The day after tomorrow Peter's father, our Herr Doktor, will celebrate his birthday. Peter and Tommy want to play for him on their violin "Gaudeamus"[136] for two voices. Whenever the doctor is out of the house the two practice like crazy. Sometimes it sounds so beautiful that our janitress says, "Since the two have begun to practice the violin all the rats have disappeared from the cellar."

Tommy always receives an "excellent" for his violin lessons.

Pavel prepares eagerly for his Barmizwah;[137] I hope you send him a nice greeting card. He received a bicycle and rides around like a lunatic! Hanušku, do you have no Hebrew lessons? What will happen when you soon begin with the preparations for your Barmizwah? I have to conclude now; stay healthy and improve your writing. I don't want to have a stupid son!

I'm kissing you,
Maminka
And tatínek Willi

19.8.1941

Dear Hanušku!

Actually I already wrote to you this week, nevertheless I want to immediately answer your Czech-Swedish letter which we received yesterday. Although actually: what should I answer to? You don't ask any questions! Even if you don't like what I am now writing I must tell you that your last letter was rather poor. You don't listen to my good advice, so write as you want. I have no choice but to come to terms with the fact that you're a little idiot. And besides, you have forgotten us a little, haven't you? (. . .)

You write: "When we were in Mostorp, she said that she liked me more than the others." That is very nice, but you don't write who told you that. Now, Hanušku, am I not right when I say you're silly?

There's a man who often visits us and of whom Tommy says: "This is the man who rides wild horses" (because Vati knows him from Palestine and said he can do that), and he has a little daughter, she's just turning ten, in Paris! You should see how charmingly and beautifully she writes! One can learn from these letters about everything she's been doing. But you wait, boy! I keep all your letters and make a book out of them, and when you grow up you'll be ashamed of yourself. Your first letters are really delightful though! Now I must conclude; Vati is coming for lunch soon. We are having vegetable soup, cauliflower and potatoes and apricot compote. This is a wonderful lunch but I would nevertheless have preferred a piece of meat.

Z bohem, milačku, darebáčku (Adieu, darling, my little robber), Handrla, Hannerle, Hanušku—what do you like most? When will we see each other again?!

A thousand kisses, although you're a little idiot,
Mami!

T.T.P! (The truth prevails!)
Aunt Poldi sends you her regards. Bobby works like a horse. Did you write to Jenda? If you haven't written to Pavel yet, then do that! And begin a new notebook again, and write in Czech! You *swore* once that you'd never forget your Czech, and what one swears, that is sacred! I'll wait patiently until your notebook is complete!
M.
A kiss from Babička and Tatíček

August 31, 1941

Dear Aunt Gertrude and Dear Hanuš!

Today I'm writing to the two of you together because I don't have much time. We received a letter from you both on Friday and on Saturday, for which I thank you warmly. Hanuš writes much more intelligent letters in Swedish and I'm hereby ceremoniously taking back my remark "little idiot" (claiming the opposite). Hanuš, here is a kiss, and we're friends again! (. . .)

Do you already dare to visit the city alone? Tommy is very independent. He travels on his own to his aunt in Strášnice, which is on the other end of town, goes to playgrounds and the day care by himself, and is otherwise also very brash. He always says, "I wish Hanuš would already be here, then I'd like to beat him up!" And Hanuš must eat very well so that he'll become strong, otherwise it will certainly come true since the "little brother" is already wearing shoes size 33 and is big and strong. He's also already muscular! Books don't interest him at all! Whereas the one reads too much, the other reads too little. Mama is just now also reading a book. She's sitting by the window and laughs out loud at certain passages. I am at a loss. I've lost my laughter! I'm always astonished how Mama can laugh so heartily after all the dreadful things she has experienced. I myself am a bundle of nerves, I'm no longer useful for anything, I perform my work mechanically but otherwise I am not good for anything anymore. I'm unable to write even one poem. Inside, I am like dead.

Yes, but the letter is intended also for Hanuš, so let us talk about something else. I'm already looking forward to hear about the new apartment. Is it somewhere by the beach or why is the street called so? Does it also have amenities, and what floor is it on? An intense thunderstorm just passed. I used to be afraid of thunderstorms but I've cured myself of it. When there's thunder and lightning Tommy likes best of all to sit by the open window and look out. Our dog Terry was badly bitten today by a Wolfhound during the walk, poor thing!

Last week I worked from home for another two days but it didn't go that well and I'll stop doing that. Willi is very industrious but much more nervous and tired than ever before.

So that would be everything for today. My heartfelt wishes to you my dearest, and write about good and beautiful things again real soon!

Your Ilse-Mutti

14. IX. 1941

Dear Aunt Gertrude, My Dear Hannerle!

In the last days I was too lazy to write; but one isn't always in a good mood, especially when one has sorrows. And in the circumstances we have to live in here something always happens that makes one sad. However, I am deeply grateful that you are punctual in your writing; you don't know what your letters mean to me! Once more I'm telling you from the bottom of my heart, my dearest Aunt Gertrude: thank God, that Hannerle is with you!!! He is still too stupid to understand what this means for him! For his little brother it surely will not be pleasant to go labeled to school, and he'll indeed sometimes come home scratched and thrashed because he's proud and defiant, but Tommy is a fighter and has character. Astonished, he told an old man who very much suffered from the new decrees: "Why shouldn't the people know that I'm Jewish? That is after all no disgrace?!" But Hanuš is soft; he wouldn't have gone about it without tears. My own attitude is very primitive: Why not? I'm not ashamed and need not be ashamed: I neither lied, nor stole nor murdered. (. . .) Since when does Hanuš have a name day?! We've never celebrated it with him; but in Sweden, where all the feasts are celebrated, he is obviously doing great. Hanušku, ty se ale máš dobře (you're doing well)! (. . .)

It's Sunday morning. We would have loved to sleep longer but we have a terribly vulgar janitor who starts to shout early in the morning. I've never known anything like that before! Willi and Tommy were good and dutifully helped me clean up so that I finished to prepare the cake earlier. Now Tommy has gone for "a walk" in the old Jewish cemetery as there is no other option.

Hannerle, how would you like to play in a cemetery? Supposedly it holds 20,000 tombstones, but the graves are stacked in three layers one on top of the other because there is too little space and reverence for the dead forbids digging out their remains. And so we're experiencing a strange drama: this place, so sacred and memorable as no other in Europe, where thousands of murder victims and the greatest men of our people are buried, resounds with children's laughter and singing, playing and joking. Our Peter botanizes enthusiastically there. At the beginning of June, the cemetery is covered with snow-white blossoms as wild elders grow there with luxurious richness. I'm now preparing myself for a long writing pause in Aunt Gertrude's writing since moving will demand a lot of effort. At the time, we "relocated" from our home in three hours and without any preparation. Whatever didn't fit in was given away. That way our maid came up with furniture for an entire room.

That's it! Writing is tiring for me because I'm no longer used to write by hand. But I'll get used to it again. Is my writing hard to read?

For both of you, most heartfelt hugs and kisses

from your Mutti-Ilse

September 20, 1941

My Dear Hanušku!

Today is our bathing day but since the water is not yet warm enough I have to wait a little longer and I will use the time to write to you a few lines.

Last week we received two letters from you and although you didn't write them yourself, we were happy over their contents. Do you know why? Because it was written there that you are now earning your own money. That is very nice Hanušku; feel free to try to earn a little because first, you'll understand how hard it is to earn money, and second, learn how good it can be to have your own money. Don't waste it on some stupid things though; use it only for things you need at school or to give presents to other people!

On the very day your letter arrived Tommy pleased me greatly as well. He received the mark "excellent with distinction" for his violin playing and was invited to play in a very good children's orchestra. Tomorrow is his first rehearsal and I already wonder how it'll go. Apart from that he annoys me a lot. He's a real daredevil and has ten answers for one question. Sometimes he makes our life very difficult.

Since yesterday he has been wearing a badge to school; it's a yellow star sewn on the coat or jacket. He's very proud of his star, pretty much as a general with his decoration. We too wear such a star and we all do it happily.

Now that you're earning your own money it will surely interest you to know what Vatti does. He makes insoles for shoes out of cardboard, that are then covered with fur. He gets a crown for each pair, and if you're very industrious you can complete 90-100 a day. You do know our Vati is most industrious. He works from six-thirty in the morning until seven-thirty in the evening. (. . .)

Next time I receive some money I'm buying you a beautiful book. It is a terrible shame that you increasingly forget your mother tongue. Should we ever see each other again you will no longer be able to speak with me. And all I can say in Swedish is "Jag elsker dig" (I love you). That will be something, boy!

But now I'm finally going to take a bath. So farewell my darling, sleep sweet!

I'm kissing you a thousand times!

Mamíčka

28. Sept.1941

My Dears!

Today came a nice letter from you dated the 21 to the 24th of this month. Thanks a lot! Don't be surprised if I won't be writing so often now.

That is to say: I can *write* just as often as before but we have been assigned now to a post office that first, is very far from my apartment and, second, it's always so overcrowded that I repeatedly went there with my last letter and had to return without achieving anything. It grieves me much, but there's nothing I can do about it. Now to your letter, my Hannerle! I'm so happy that I have such an industrious child who already earns his own pocket money. But I think you're going to the cinema too often. *Once* a month would be enough, don't you think too? You shouldn't just read but also understand what I'm writing, Hanušku! When I'm writing to you that I haven't been to the cinema for two years, neither to a concert, nor theater nor elsewhere, and that I also have no desire for it, out of heartache and worry, then you should be more than content that you live as a free human being with such good and noble people. You should thank the Lord for it every morning and evening and not be presumptuous. Look at everything you've already seen and experienced! You had beautiful journeys other children have at best read about, you spent a long time by the sea, you have friends with whom you can play without restrictions. You go so often to the beautiful zoo. And now compare *your* life with Tommy's: he's not allowed to play anywhere, at best in the little space which he has in our room. It measures hardly two square meters. Draw this space once and try to play Indians, soldiers or hide and seek within those two square meters. But he's not allowed to do even that because we don't live alone. Our children have such a terribly hard time with the adults. They have really great sorrows and difficult worries and grow sick of it; you know that the adults often say they are "nervous." Then they become impatient and unfriendly, don't they? But we are not just nervous, we are suffering from a nervous disease, and now the poor children should live with us! They aren't allowed to make noise, to sing, to romp about; we simply cannot bear that! How many slaps are given that are undeserved, how many blows in general! Take for instance Pauli. Aunt Erna had a nervous breakdown. She takes out her illness on Pauli. You can't imagine what the boy endures. Hannerle, I know that you are a nice, kind boy, but think once about everything you have,

that the children like you, that no one mocks you and that you
have a beautiful home, and how well you're doing, and you'll do
everything you can to please Mormor![138] That your "forest spirit"
was displayed in class is fine. *Who* drew it then? But tell the truth!
I didn't send you the book yet because Vati earned less last week.
Hopefully he's getting better work soon and then you'll get it!
Uncle Oscar's wife must have been very pleased with the furniture,
right? Did you help nicely with the moving?

Now a few lines for Mormor: the fact that Hannerle goes
to sleep with a stuffed dog proves that he's still his old self. He's
especially affectionate before going to sleep. When he could
hardly speak he had two rubber dolls, "Fitzebums" and "Dola,"
that he loved dearly. Sometimes he woke at night crying because
they weren't lying next to him. Tommy calls his small pillow
"Maminka" and also must have it by him. But he's considerably
rougher. Tommy is now the youngest orchestra member.

You see, we humans should make no plans. *My* goal in life was
to lead a simple beautiful life with a good, hard-working husband
and to raise my children according to my ideals.

Since they're both musical I thought it would be great to give
them musical education. And truly, we lived beautifully. Willi
worked hard the whole week; on Sundays we went to the mountains or went out with the children. And as Hanuš made such
good progress with his piano playing we had great joy.

And now? Everything is destroyed, everything is dubious. I
try hard to have Tommy learn whatever little is still possible even
if it takes sacrifice and strong nerves. But the other goal? To live
a peaceful and modest life? Will I ever see Hanuš again? Yes, you
should know that Lil is in touch with our relatives and that they
must take care of our child if we no longer can. Please keep that in
mind, just in case!

I might write to my brother-in-law today. If I'm already taking
the long way to the post office it should at least be worthwhile.

Hanušku, stay healthy and good! You don't need to be as
strong as Tarzan. It is unlikely you will have to kill lions with a

knife. But be strong in spirit and do not forget your promise: always tell the truth, my darling, můj miláčku, and be grateful! I think very very often about you: I love you so much and hope to be with you again!

God-willing we'll be together again and experience beautiful things and, if not, don't forget your parents and little brother: we love you all and hope that at least you will be happy.

I'm kissing you a thousand times, Maminka

And you, dearest Aunt Gertrude, I'm sending also a thousand regards, your very very grateful

Ilse

December 6, 1941

My Dear Aunt Gertrude!

Your letters take now significantly longer to arrive and that is a pity because we always wait with such longing for them. *You* write on Saturday, and today I will do the same because Mama will take it for me to the post office. I shouldn't write letters in the mood that I am in today but then you would never get mail from me and that would not work. My nerves are on the edge and a small trigger could make me weep. Perhaps that would be a relief. But I find it difficult to cry.

Our application for an entry visa to Sweden was rejected. We didn't seriously believe for a moment we would get it. Therefore the rejection meant no disappointment, at best I'm interested to find out why it was rejected. I will likely never find that out. So my boy will have to celebrate his eleventh birthday without his parents. I sent him a beautiful book, hopefully you didn't give it to him beforehand. Babi paid for half of it, he should therefore thank her separately. We found out today Hans' father's address: Litzmannstadt, Franzstrasse 21(Germany). Hans should write him real soon! I congratulated Lilian by mail and calculated carefully so she'll be getting my congratulations on time. However, the delivery time for letters to Panama varies. It's careless of her not to write a thing about herself and her husband. But apparently they're doing well and she takes it for granted and doesn't think it worth mentioning. How are the little ones? Do you have interesting news about them? Please allow Hanuš to light a memorial candle for Omama on the eve of January 11. It is her second death anniversary. What a lovely time December is for you! Soon it will be St. Lucia's Day then you have Christmas, and after that comes the New Year with Hannerl's birthday. On this day our thoughts will be especially with him. I still remember *my* eleventh birthday well. First, because it was my first birthday without my dear father who had died the previous December, and then because I received my first watch. And as long as I live I will never be able to be truly happy on my own birthday because, two years ago my mother-in-law, whom I loved very much, died exactly on this day. And her death is linked to many other sad memories . . .

And now, if you allow, a few lines for my boy:

My Dear Little Hanušku! There is still a bit of time till lunch so I can write to you. I'm happy you're doing so well and that you met so many interesting people. That man who showed you his dagger and all his rifles has certainly seen a lot of the world. Did he tell you about it? He knows fourteen languages! This is amazing. You see? And you forgot your mother tongue! Think about it, if your principal Talpa knew that! He would definitely be sad. Are you actually able to read the Czech books that you received? Don't forget to answer that question, Hanušku; and generally, I would like to ask you to write us something in Czech again. Can you read English? It's my birthday soon. May I wish for something? Then I wish for a *long* Czech letter from you, and tell me everything about school, which are your favorite subjects, how are your teachers, etc.

Tommy got into the habit of coming for "a visit in my bed": "Hanušek always did that, too." So he's allowed to do it once a week on Friday evening. He has a new violin teacher now but I'm afraid he doesn't like him quite as much as the former. Next week they will celebrate Chanukah in Tommy's school; he will act in a theatre play and also play the violin and the accordion. He's big and strong, has bigger feet than you do, and is sometimes really fresh. Can you imagine that I have no idea anymore what it's like in the *cinema*? Never forget that you have a little brother; you loved him very much when you were still at home, and he loved you too. Although you're not together you must always think about him! Some day he will be your best comrade and friend. Imagine how beautiful it would be if I had the two of you here again, if we could sing and read together in the evenings! Luckily, last week Uncle Sternlicht came home completely unexpectedly. He was away from home for two years and Aunt Hilde had to be without him and little Hanička. Hanička will never come back!

Aunt Erna was operated on, but she's getting better. Imagine, Pavel manages almost everything for her: he lights the fire in the stove, he tidies up, shops for her, and generally cares for everything so that he very seldom goes to school. Think about how fortunate *you* are!

Uncle Manek went away to work. Do you still remember Ossi Tauber? He lives in the Wild West and has already become a real cowboy! The Aunt wrote to me she was surprised that you didn't receive a better mark in "music." I couldn't understand that at all. Do you always sing from the songbook[139] you received from me?

Hanušku, I'm now concluding my letter. I'm sending you a thousand kisses but paper kisses aren't so nice. When you fell asleep and I kissed you, you always opened your little mouth in your sleep and returned my kiss. I would love so much to see this once more, my darling!

Cheerio, kiddo, farewell, my darling; stay good, cheerful and healthy and be kind to your

Mamička

17.XII.1941

Můj milý malý synu! (My dear little son!)

It is already the third time you're celebrating your birthday

in a foreign country. You have no idea how much I would love
to set your birthday table and with how much love I would have
prepared your presents and baked a real birthday cake. Think of
how beautiful your birthdays were and how we celebrated! Yet fate
wants something else. You have to stay in a foreign country and we
have to stay here. But we shouldn't be sad! You have everything I
can wish for you. You have love, a home, freedom and peace. You
see, here with us you would have had only love! and especially my
love for you; it's a lot, but I wanted you to have all the rest that we
here at home no longer have.

Therefore today I can only send you my warm kisses; I'm kissing your dear eyes and your forehead. I wish your future life will
always be as happy as today and that you'll never have to know a
life as ours!

Always keep us in your heart, my Hanušku; perhaps that
happy day will come, despite everything, when we will all live
together again and be able to celebrate our family celebrations exactly as before.

On January the first our thoughts will be with you; remember
us too and write to us how you spent the day. I hope you will like
Mormor's book (the Babička book); read it slowly so that you'll
enjoy it for a longer time. And don't forget to thank Mormor on
this day all the more for her love and care. Z bohem: God be with
you, my Hanušku.

Kissing you,
Your Mamička

January 9, 1942

My beloved boy!

We had no mail from you for many, many days. I was very
worried, although perhaps it was stupid of me, but the times
are such that one immediately fears the worst. On top of that
I received a letter from the consulate early in the morning be-

fore yesterday, and when I *got* it and recognized the stamp (it is actually written on the back "Consulate of Sweden") my knees began to tremble so that I had to sit down and at first didn't dare to open the letter. That was stupid because had I opened it at once I would have seen that it only stated that I should come and collect the money I had paid there for a telegram. Finally, I did read it and was much relieved. The next morning, yesterday, I received *two* letters and a card (from Christmas Eve) at once and I was overjoyed!! Quickly, a big kiss for the good report card my Hannerle! It makes me happy most of all that you study so well in a foreign country and in a foreign language. By being good at school you're proving your gratitude to Sweden for all the goodness it shows you! There is no other way for children to be grateful so continue to be good and industrious: at the end of the day it is you who profits most; no one can take away from you what you have learned! If you know many languages and know them *well*, many jobs will be open for you. Then I hope you will change your plans and won't become a soldier after all. Look Hanuš, to be a soldier doesn't just mean wearing a nice uniform and marching in step to music, oh no, little boy; imagine you had to be today *in the freezing cold* somewhere in the open for hours, maybe hungry, and there would be no Mormor who brings you tea and no warm bed that you can crawl into "with a cold." Look, you're not at all such a friend of freezing and hiking, I know that very well. Therefore think over very carefully about becoming a soldier! One can help his fatherland much more in other ways. If you learn well you may one day perhaps think of a marvelous idea: perhaps how to build beautiful cities, or how to cure a nasty disease; there are enough things that are needed! Each little wheel in a watch is important, the smallest just as the biggest, the smallest screw just as the hand. Besides, you want to become a millionaire in order to be able to do *a lot* of good. This is beautiful and good but one doesn't become a millionaire easily, least of all when one has so little talent for saving as you (and

Tommy and Vati and I). Earning money isn't that nice either, you know: I mean earning a lot of money! One should earn so much as to live decently, that suffices; but if one wants to have a lot of money one must be careful to stay decent and honest because money tempts one to do evil. One always wants to have more and, one day, one doesn't make it his business anymore to see that the money is honest and clean. One can do good without millions! Look at Vati! Do you remember how he threw a football over the fence once, to the children from the asylum? He saw how the poor children played with a stuffed sock and quickly bought a nice football, and the next time he walked by the playground and the children were playing again, he quickly threw the ball over the fence and ran away so no one could see and thank him. If I didn't happen to go with you toward him at the time and see that, *he* would have never told this. And Vati never had a lot of money. But he did not spend his money on cigarettes and he never went to cafés. Instead, he preferred to make others happy. When you grow up I want to tell you about the many people Vati helped and the many he still helps. People love and respect him for that and we are all very proud of him. Do you remember, Hannerle, how you always shared your presents on your birthday and carried the most beautiful ones to the children in the asylum?

I'd be happy to know you continue to be like that. The children in Steninge were surely also poor, right? You're receiving so many beautiful things! Here you wouldn't even be allowed to have them. And Mormor surely wants you to share what you have. I sent you a very nice calendar and hope you'll be happy with it. How do you like the book *Sailors and Discoverers*? I think it's a fine book! What other books did you receive? Which book is actually your favorite? Jenek congratulates you for the new year and sends you best regards. Out of 150 children only 40 were accepted to high school, and he's among them. He completed the first half year with honor. Now he's in the mountains for the Christmas holiday, which this year lasts a month. Sunday is

my birthday; I was never so sad! I don't want to have anything.
It is no longer nice at home, boy! The guitar is gone, the violin
too; I can no longer sit by Tommy's bed in the evening and sing.
Another child lent Tommy a little violin and he's now practicing
Schumann's "Dreaming" for my birthday. Yes, Babi's birthday
is on September 15 and Tommy's on March 2. Vati's is on May
21. When does Mormor have hers??? We were happy with your
pictures and Mormor's; pity that Birger can't be seen better in
the third. I guess Mormor was already shivering in the cold and
blurred the picture?! If you're good you too are getting a lovely
picture of all of us soon, that is, if it turns out well: because
Tommy always makes such faces that one cannot take a picture
of him.

In the meantime it has become afternoon; I don't have the time
to calmly complete a letter. Hanušku, my darling, I think of you with
great longing but nevertheless not a day goes by that I don't say, "Dear
God, I thank you my child is not here!" May God protect you further.
I'm always with you in my thoughts and with my heart and I love you
very very much! It is my greatest wish that we all will be able to be together again. Pray too, so that this wish may be soon fulfilled.

Kissing you, your
Mutti

January 1942

Dearest Aunt Gertrude!

I plan to go to the post office today therefore must quickly
complete a letter to you. I was so happy yesterday with your letters
the entire morning seemed to be steeped with sun; unfortunately
the afternoon was awful, but that's just the way it is. Life consists
not only of sun! It is such a wonderful feeling for me to know the
boy is in such good hands! It would be nice if I only knew for sure
that he now and then rewards you with a joyful hour. He is a good
boy and, except for his poor eating, he has never annoyed us; he
was never ill-mannered or disobedient. Tommy is the complete

opposite and with a wild temperament. It's impossible to describe what this means today, especially now during the school holidays when the child is confined mainly to the narrow four walls of our "apartment." It is sheer luck that the doctors love him and that he spends more time with them than with us. He is their favorite and they look at his pranks as true miracles, which in return makes his education more difficult for *me;* but on the other hand I am so unnerved and impatient that I perhaps am severe when one could easily laugh a bit and be forgiving. May God grant your good wishes! Otherwise I can't imagine that I will see my child again. Last night I was so desperate that I seriously suggested Willi to end it all and rather commit suicide with me and Tommy. Luckily, Willi is a rational, calm man and knows how to handle me. Fact is that mentally I simply can't go on.

You probably can tell me if you heard anything from the Fischers. I haven't received any more mail from them but the day before yesterday I sent them some money. Let me know if they write to Herr Carl. I'm mainly interested to know if they have received the food. Can Herr Carl also send them some money? Is it at all possible now? There is a chance that we will visit them. Has Frau Coutinho written? Herr Carl's friend will let you know in case we depart. We are very happy with the pictures. You look lovely in the picture with Hanuš. No, unfortunately I didn't get back the portfolio with the pictures (the pictures I had are *all* gone) and I am still mourning over them. Just today I want to duplicate the picture of Hanuš that I love so much, the one that Willi's received a copy of. Please give warm regards to Herr Haglund for me; I thank him for being good to Hanuš! Were you happy with Hanuš' report card? Does he really cope with school by himself and need no assistance? You know, his principal once told me he never had such a good student as Hanuš: whenever he looked up he met his attentive eyes. But that could have changed. Now there are no longer letters from Uncle Max, nor to him; but that too we have to accept! I'm getting little mail now anyway; this week perhaps a couple of letters for my birthday if anyone will still be able to think about it. I don't like birthdays anymore. Already so many bad and lost years. Was Hanuš happy with the book? Next he is

getting a calendar and that'll do for a while. Does he have enough
space for all the stuff that he owns?!

Well, unfortunately, I have to conclude here. Think of us, you
two, and keep your fingers crossed that everything will turn out
well for us, and all those unfortunates! My joint rheumatism has
been recently plaguing me again, just when I have no time to be
sick! I can perform all the chores but am incapable of doing the
washing because my joints are so painful.

My regards to Uncle and his wife!

All the love and goodness for you!

Your Ilse

January 19, 1942

Dearest Aunt Gertrude!

Today I'm writing once outside our normal correspondence
routine; I feel so desperate and helpless that I simply must talk
to someone. I received no mail from you this week; only Babička
received a small letter. Hanuš should be ashamed for writing such
letters full of mistakes and lacking in content! But Babi was nevertheless happy. And that is the main thing. When I burnt some
correspondence today some letters from the World War fell into
my hands that all evoked bleak memories!

[5 illegible words] . . . from Carl's brother-in-law, who at the
time didn't write for such a long time and had us so worried; finally, it turned out his silence was due to the fact that he and his
wife were quarantined and thus not allowed to write. (But you still
remember, right?) And Estela's friend stood there without clothes
and underwear: all she possessed was stolen from her; and she
herself, with husband and child, was waiting for her deportation
at any hour. Those poor ones! What they went through! Now the
letters have turned into ashes. But I'm so down with my nerves
that I don't know what to do about it. And I do stupid things out
of desperation. So today, for example, I had someone read my future in the cards. Since there were terrible things I am even more
depressed, despite the fact that as an "intelligent" person I should
laugh about it. Pray for the war to end—

I'm no longer in a state to even picture a reunion with my child. But how beautiful could it be if we could be together in Steninge in the summer: you, we, Lil, her Mama, her children. This is a dream—

Forgive the bad writing. Does Frau Lion have news? We don't.
Farewell, keep on protecting my child for me!
Sincerely,
Your Ilse
Hanušku, stay good and healthy!

Royal Department of Foreign Affairs-Inheritance and
Compensation Office
Re. Forwarding message from Ilse Weber

R 20 Ec/II 2.3.1942
The Royal Foreign Office is honored to bring to your knowledge the content of a letter received from the Swedish Consulate in Prague:
"Frau Ilse Weber requested me to inform her son, Hanuš Weber, who is with Frau Löwenadler, Strandvägen 19, Stockholm, that she is being evacuated these days. Frau Weber was unable to leave a new address. The son should send letters either to his grandmother, Salvatorstrasse 2, or to Dr. Erich Steiger, Prienstrasse 8, Prague."

Royal Swedish Consulate Prague
To the Royal Foreign Ministry, Stockholm   *R 20 Ec/II*

Prague, June 22, 1942
With reference to previous correspondence regarding Frau Ilse Weber, I am thereby informing Frau Löwenadler, Strandvägen 19, Stockholm, who fosters Frau Weber's son, that Frau Weber is still in Theresienstadt, where she works as a nurse at a children's hospital. Her husband will also work in Theresienstadt after recovering

*Obscured (mostly likely censored) in the original text.

from a long illness. Son Thomas was accommodated in a children's
home in the same town. According to the present information
Frau Weber is healthy, and she likes her work.

Gustaf Löwenhard

[9 months passed from the time the Swedish consulate reported on
Ilse's evacuation, until Gertrude received word from Ilse]

Ilse Weber   *To Hans Weber*
Theresienstadt (Bohemia)   *c/o Frau v. Löwenadler*
                                      Stockholm, Strandvägen 19 ö.g.

Theresienstadt, 28. XII. 42

My Dearest Ones!

For the turn of the year we are wishing you all the best and
sending the birthday child special heartfelt wishes. We are all
healthy and looking forward to receiving news from you soon; all
sorts of mail are allowed. I see Aunt Clara every day. Write by airmail: it is faster.

With love, your Mutti

Ilse Weber

[6 months between correspondences]

Theresienstadt, June 12, 1943

Dearest Grandmother, Beloved Boy!

We painfully miss news from you all the more since letters and
parcels from Sweden do arrive here. Please do write regularly even
if we don't answer immediately, as we're worried about your health.
Hannerle, do you go to school and what grade? Where will you
spend the summer? Are the grandchildren making progress? Vati,
Tommy, Clara and I are healthy. The children whom I take care of
here are good and sweet and love me very much because they feel
that I see my own child in them. Tommy is studying very little; he

prefers to play football. Vati thinks that as a football player he has a future. Dearest Grandmother, hopefully you had a good winter and your old catarrh didn't plague you much. We think of you with infinite love and longing and hope to receive many letters from you soon: Clara too.

    Your Mutti Ilse and Vati Willi

Weber Thomas	*To Hanuš R. Weber*
Theresienstadt	*Tullgarnhemmet*
Rathausstrasse 19	*Upsala, Sweden*

Theresienstadt, 15. VIII. 43

Dear Hanuš!

    We were very happy with your greetings. I live in a boys' home with many boys; we have lots of fun and I play football a lot and some other games. Will you wear a high-school cap? Send us then a picture of you, all right? The photos of the little ones in Steninge were pretty. Vati is healthy, works, and sends you a kiss; Mutti, who is industrious, another one; and I am sending the third. Regards from all of us. [And] Grandmother.

    Thomas

Theresienstadt, 3. XI. 1943

Dearest Gertrude!

    It's true there is nothing new to report but you would surely like to hear again that the three of us are healthy. We think often with love and longing about you. Just stay really healthy and don't forget us! How is the child doing in school? Does he manage well? Please, please, write once a week! And now I have one more request: couldn't you provide me the address of Erich Bier, previously Copenhagen?

    I'm kissing you as well as the child, and remain for ever
    Your Mutti

Wolf Weber   *Herrn*
Theresienstadt   *Hans-Rafael Weber*
Jägerstrasse 11   *c/o Löwenadler*
                                                        Stockholm
                                          Strandvägen 19 ö.g.

13 XI 1943

My Dearest Ones!

The little brother is pleased too with the "student" brother; as far as he's concerned, he's not so keen on studying and reading, and prefers to play football. Not long ago he scored the only goal in a match. Your grandchildren are sweet; we had their pictures enlarged by an artist acquaintance of ours and they smile at me from the wall when I'm sad. The little boy is the embodiment of sunshine and the little girl has such a sweet, musing face. How is their Mutti? What about Hanni's confirmation? Please answer this question. Much Love, and all the best,

Vati Wolf Weber

Theresienstadt 1943,
No specific date

My Dearest Aunt Gertrude, my Dearest Boy!

We are yearning greatly for you and your letters. Uncle Willi, his wife and the little brother are well. Everybody is industrious. Hannerle's Mutti looks after sick children and thinks of each as her own. Therefore she is twice as loving to the poor souls and for that they love her so much. When she's on night duty, just like today, she tells them stories before they go to sleep and sings lullabies. The little brother grows fast and is always hungry. We're all healthy and put our trust in God, who guides us best. Don't forget us, and keep us in your hearts!

To aunt Gertrude special greetings and thanks from my husband and me!

Your Lilli[140]

Read with pleasure your letters to Babi. There's no reason to assume that Carl's relatives will establish contact. Hannerle should not tell only about eating and drinking but also about his studies: what interests him apart from soldiers and Indians. His brother is going through a tremendous transformation now. Much love! L.

To the two of you, as always, really, really many warm regards and kisses,

    Willi

7.1.1944

Dear Hanuš!

I thank you for your letter with the picture, Mutti and Vatti for the cards. I am almost as big as you but I don't have a student cap yet. I am in a children's home as well. Are you still with the Scouts? Do you play football? Are you doing sports at all or still sitting with the books at home?

We all send warmest regards to you and Mormor really whole-heartedly. Write back soon.

    Your brother, Tommy
    Regards to Uncle Max

January 18, 1944

My Dearest Aunt Gertrude!

Since I was sick I didn't receive your card and learned of the sad news only yesterday from a third party. I don't need to tell you how deeply affected I was by the death of your dear daughter, my selfless, altruistic friend. It is as though I became very very poor, as if a piece of my own self was snatched away from me. You know best how unique our friendship was. I can't bring myself to think at all about the sweet children. May God grant that I will be able to repay my debt of gratitude through them, for I was deeply

indebted to your daughter. Since yesterday I can't think of anything else but the hard blow that hit us all and, in particular, you.
Please write to me as often and with as many details as you can.
I already feel better. Kiss my boy and let me kiss your hands with
sympathy and gratitude.

Your Ilse

Weber Wolf	*(sent to)*	
Theresienstadt	*Hans R. Weber*	
Jägerstrasse 11/16	~~*c.o. Löwenadler*~~	*Tullgarn 1C*
	~~*StockholmStranvägen 19 ö.g.*~~	*Upsala*

30. VI. 44

Dearest Hanuš!

I was astonished as there was no letter of congratulations from
you on my birthday table. *Why do you write so seldom?* We get the
small packets regularly. They make us happy and taste good. We
three are healthy and work industriously. Tommy grows up and has
many opportunities to play. I received his first poem for my birthday. How are you and Mormor? *Please do write more often and in
detail.* Stay healthy. Warm regards from us all and a hug from me.

Willi

Mormor hälsar (Grandmother greets)

Theresienstadt, (no date)

My Most Precious Child!

A long time with no news from you. T. G[141] we are healthy;
hope and wish to hear the same from you. Don't get a cold, wear
only warm underwear and clothes. I am very anxious for you my
golden child. The main thing: you stay healthy.

May God watch over you and protect you, heartfelt regards,

Your Mama

DEAREST AUNT!
    RECIEVED TWO CARDS. REPORT ABOUT HANS
MAKES US VERY HAPPY. WHY DOESN'T HE WRITE HIM-
SELF? WHERE IS GRANDMOTHER? DID SHE WRITE TO
YOU? WE ARE HEALTHY.
    MUCH LOVE ILSE
    (29.?) IX. 44

THE WORLD OF THERESIENSTADT

Ruth Bondy

The life of Ilse Weber in the Theresienstadt ghetto between 1942–1944, as reflected in the poems she left behind (and also in the few letters she was able to send from there), provides a unique glimpse into the lives of its tens of thousands of Jewish inhabitants, their suffering, and the special ways they found to cope with the harsh reality during the war.

The Theresienstadt ghetto (or Terezin in Czech) was the only ghetto located in central Europe that was erected in a town without a pre-existing Jewish community. It was deemed a ghetto, but resembled a concentration camp in certain respects: it featured separate living quarters for men and women, received regular food supplies (though meager and of poor quality), and was governed by a centralized administration under the control of the SS command. Most of the Jews incarcerated in Theresienstadt were eventually sent to death camps, but the ghetto was not destroyed, liquidated, or set afire until the end of the war. Consequently, a relatively large proportion of documentation concerning the ghetto remains. During the three and a half years of its existence, over 150,000 prisoners from the Protectorate of Bohemia and Moravia, the German Reich, including Austria, Holland, Denmark, Slovakia, and small numbers from other countries, passed through the gates of the Theresienstadt ghetto. Of them, about 34,000 perished in the ghetto itself and close to 87,000 were sent to extermination camps in sixty-three transports. Of these, only a few thousands survived. In the final months of the war the number of prisoners living in the ghetto grew to approximately 30,000 as survivors of the death marches made their way there during its final days.

Theresienstadt was a fortress city surrounded by walls, ramparts, and trenches; it had only a few gates that could be easily guarded; inside were eleven barracks suitable for mass accommodation. In November and December 1941 two construction units of engineers, technicians, artisans, and workers were sent from Prague to Theresienstadt to prepare the city for its new purpose. The preparations were not completed before the mass transports containing 1,000 people each began to arrive. Moreover, instead of living in planned family-style housing, the men were separated from the women and children. All ghetto prisoners aged fifteen to sixty-five (and, as of October 1944, younger inmates as well) were required to work. Hospitals and nursing homes were established and, most importantly, the water and sewage plumbing system (it was designed for a much smaller population) was expanded, largely owing to the professional skills of Jewish engineers and technicians incarcerated in the ghetto.

While all of the synagogues in the Protectorate were shut down even before the ghetto was established, improvised prayer rooms were set up in most of the barracks, a small synagogue operated in one of the houses, and prayer corners were organized in venues that hosted both plays and lectures. There was no dearth of rabbis and cantors in the ghetto to lead the services. The rabbis prepared boys for their bar mitzvah, conducted wedding ceremonies and recited the Kaddish prayer for the dead. Children's rooms were set up in the men's and women's barracks and the Jewish leadership allocated the best buildings—the school and town hall—as houses for children aged ten to fifteen, with girls and boys housed separately. Parents were not required to transfer their children to the children's houses but many did so for the children's benefit. The children received slightly more food, and, most importantly, were under the supervision of teachers and counselors. The children held competitions, published single-copy newspapers, painted, and drew. They participated in plays for children that were performed dozens of times in the ghetto, the most popular of which was the children's opera *Brundibar*. Ilse Weber herself was a counselor for young children, volunteered in the children's hospital, and sang and played the guitar for them. Cultural events were held at the prisoners' initiative separately in the men's and women's barracks, featuring poetry readings, improvised humorous sketches, and scenes from theatrical plays that former actors among the prisoners remembered by heart. Musical accompaniment to these productions was provided by harmonicas and tin bowls that served as drums, since the possession of musical instruments was forbidden. Over time, various instruments were smuggled into the ghetto—such as Ilse's guitar—and a broken piano was found in an attic. Secret concerts were held as well.

Theresienstadt also served as a ghetto for the elderly and the disabled veterans of World War I from the Reich and Austria. Their arrival changed the demographic structure of the Theresienstadt ghetto dramatically. For lack of room, the elderly people were housed in the attics of the barracks or within the walls of the city, in dark, dank cellars. By the thousands, these elderly people began to die of exhaustion, diarrhea, and lack of desire to live. Early on, the dead of the Theresienstadt ghetto were buried in cemeteries outside the wall. However, in order to contend with the mounting death rate, a crematorium was built and started to operate in the summer of 1942. Toward the end of the war the ashes of over 30,000 that were preserved in numbered cardboard boxes, were thrown into the river in order to destroy the evidence.

The idea of the Theresienstadt ghetto as a "model Jewish city" was conceived in early 1943 after the world media published in December 1942, for the first time, authoritative news reports about the mass extermination of Jews in occupied Europe. In October 1943, 466 Danish Jews were brought to the ghetto and the Danish Red Cross, through the International Red Cross in Geneva, requested a visit that naturally required meticulous planning on the part of the Germans. A beautification campaign was thus launched in the fall of 1943: the streets of the ghetto, until then marked only with letters, were given poetic names; a bank was established, and special ghetto money was printed; dummy shops were created, with barely any stock; and a "café" with a resident jazz band was opened. Theresienstadt was no longer known as a ghetto, but rather a "Jewish settlement area." In order to alleviate the overcrowding in the ghetto during the last months before the delegation's visit, thousands of Jews were sent to Auschwitz-Birkenau. The hoax succeeded beyond expectation: The representative of the International Red Cross from Geneva wrote a report that very evening characterizing Theresienstadt as a "city like all other cities," whose residents even benefited from larger food rations than the general population, and lacked nothing, with the exception of alcoholic drinks and cigarettes. The delegation viewed Theresienstadt as a "final destination" and did not inquire after the whereabouts of the tens of thousands of Jews who had passed through the ghetto on their way east. Before the scenery for the large-scale deception in the Theresienstadt ghetto itself was dismantled, a propaganda film was recorded, entitled *Theresienstadt, the Jewish Settlement Area.* The prisoners cynically referred to it as "The Führer Gives the Jews a City." The film was never screened before the general public because the Reich fell before it could be completed.

Following the Red Cross's report, thousands of the ghetto prisoners were sent to Auschwitz. Within a single month, from September 28 to October 28, 1944, 18,500 Jews were deported, among them Willi Weber and, later, his wife Ilse Weber along with their younger son Tommy. Towards the end of the war approximately 11,000 prisoners remained in the ghetto: a few men fit for work, women who worked in a factory and farming, the privileged prisoners, the Danish Jews, and a few elderly people and children. In February 1945, sealed rooms that could be used to asphyxiate prisoners with gas began to be built within the ghetto walls, and a huge pit was dug. These preparations indicate that the SS command intended to liquidate the remaining ghetto inhabitants. The tumultuous events unfolding in advance of the defeat of the Nazi regime precluded these plans. In February 1945 a deal between Heinrich Himmler and the Swiss authorities enabled a transport of 1,200 people to reach Switzerland. On April 15, 1945, the Danish prisoners were transferred to Sweden by Swedish Red Cross buses. The surviving residents of Theresienstadt definitively learned about the exterminations on April 20, 1945, when emaciated survivors of the death marches began to arrive. Only then did the Theresienstadt residents realized the full extent of the atrocities that their loved ones had met in the "east." The death march survivors were infected with epidemic typhus, which took the lives of hundreds of victims. The first units of the Red Army entered Theresienstadt on May 8, 1945, after the members of the SS command had fled. Following the gradual return of the liberated prisoners to their native countries, the ghetto officially ceased to exist on August 15, 1945. Among the emaciated survivors was Willi Weber, Ilse's husband. Immediately upon liberation of Theresienstadt, he succeeded in entering the ghetto during the typhus epidemic and retrieved some 60 poems written by his wife. By concealing this treasure prior to his and Ilse's deportation to Auschwitz, he preserved an important part of Ilse Weber's legacy.

Based on Ruth Bondy, "Theresienstadt" in: *The Yad Vashem Encyclopedia of the Ghettos During the Holocaust* (Yad Vashem, Jerusalem: 2009), pp. 821–831. Ruth Bondy, is a writer and translator. She was born in Prague, was incarcerated in the Theresienstadt ghetto and deported to Auschwitz-Birkenau. She was an inmate of a number of forced labor camps. Following liberation she returned to Prague, joined the overseas recruitment organization "Gahal" and immigrated to Israel in 1948. One of the founders of *Beit Terezin* (Theresienstadt Martyrs Remembrance Association) she published historical studies and won numerous awards. Her books on the Holocaust include *Elder of the Jews: Jakob Edelstein of Theresienstadt* (1989) and *Trapped: Essays on the History of the Czech Jews, 1939–1943* (2008).

POEMS FROM
THERESIENSTADT

Most of Ilse Weber's poems, buried by her husband Willi Weber in Theresienstadt, were retrieved after the liberation. In many cases they included notes of melodies (mostly originated as guitar improvisations). After 1945, Willi Weber made some typed copies. Between 1949 to 1951, during house searches in Willi and Hanuš Weber's Prague apartment, as a result of suspected "activities hostile to the state," some of the original papers were confiscated. While this led to the loss of part of the scoring, the texts themselves are preserved in the transcripts. Later, Willi and Hanuš received further poems from survivors. One of these was a version in German of "The Hills," translated from a Czech translation, Ilse's German original having been lost.[1] Ilse's son, Hanuš Weber, owns the transcripts of the poems. They appear here in chronological order, as far as possible. Ilse's surviving musical compositions to the Theresienstadt poems are:

I Wander Through Theresienstadt   Emigrants' Song

And the Rain Runs   Goodbye Comrade

Little Lullaby   Wiegala

Ukolébavka/Lullaby   Modlitba/Prayer

Theresienstadt developed its own dialect, conditioned by the hardship and herding together of people from different origins. Ilse incorporated some of Theresienstadt's idioms in her poems. This is explained in footnotes based on reports by Jiří (George) Lauscher and Herbert Thomas Mandl.

Bedřich Fritta: *A Transport Arrives*

The Way to Theresienstadt[2]

This is the way to Theresienstadt
that many thousands have trod,
each one suffering the same lot,
injustice endured.

With unseeing eyes and heads bent low,
the six-pointed star on each heart,
trudging in dust, pace funeral slow,
footsore, weary, lives torn apart.

Heavy baggage chafes their hands,
they're hurried along, harsh voices goad
with an urgency no one understands,
thirsty on the sun-scorched road.

This is the way to Theresienstadt,
which drinks our hearts' blood,
where those so weary and bereaved
are dying on the stony road.

A way of horror and wretchedness,
tears flowing from dawn to dawn,
of children, of mothers' distress,
helpless, forsaken, forlorn.

Scrawny legs fail, uncertain eyes glance,
the two-legged herd lashed and prod,
forward and back is the nature of dance,
ending 'neath merciful sod.

Speeding also on this road,
the loud roaring wagons pass by
relentless with their groaning loads,
carrying those destined to die.

This is the way to Theresienstadt,
of suffering beyond any scale.
By none of those who witnessed that
the memory will ever pale.

Hamburg Barracks

A brown block building, fair from afar,
home and prison, Hamburg barracks,
with a proper, orderly façade.
The thick walls unite us all,
surround a women's realm so small,
a petty world set apart.

Once were soldiers here, and only later
did we move in, seventy centimeters[3]
calculated for our *lebensraum*.
A thousand soldiers once. That time is long gone.
In the barracks we are five thousand,
and one tree blooms for us all.

A Satchel Speaks[4]

I'm a small satchel from Frankfurt am Main,
where's my master? Will we be united again?
An old blind man with a yellow star,
he held me like a child in his care.
His Travelling Companion, he gave me that name;
his hand's touch was gentle, always the same.
My vulcanized fiber could be seen
in our better days, all shiny and clean.
I accompanied him in all kinds of weather,
right to the last we were always together.
Blind now, and old, he's somewhere alone.
Who's taken him from me, and where has he gone?
I'm left abandoned in this empty square,
but look, on my strap his name still appears.
I'm filthy and dank and my lock is kaput.
I'm spoiled and plundered, companion forgot,
I still hold his towel, his cup dented and bent,
small blind man's slate, for wherever we went.
All else is gone, the medicine, the bread.
He seeks me, I know, with increasing dread.
How difficult for one who cannot see
in all this piled baggage to look for little me,
and it's hard for me to figure out
why on earth I'm left useless, going to pot.
I am a small satchel from Frankfurt am Main.
My master needs me, shall I ever see him again?

A Small Picture[5]

Dark hearse coming, is there more
the passerby can see?
Count them, silver pillars, four
holding fancy canopy.

That gloomy carriage moves
now a different load.
Dark bread, a hundred loaves,
along that well-worn road.

Soft the way, with fallen snow,
wind whistling through the square,
no harnessed horse makes it go;
harnessed children, pair by pair.

Children together in the traces,
steps confined, unsteady,
sweat dripping from their faces.
Is this load too heavy?

Their manner childishly grave,
young cheeks frozen red,
such responsibility to have,
to earn their sparse black bread.

The title of this picture?
See for yourself. Stare.
Large letters on the wagon,
Youth Welfare.

Evening Comes

Evening comes and laughter fills the room
and noisy quarrels as always, shadows loom.
A little boy opens the door,
and peeps: "Is Mother here?"

Oh yes, there she sits, her glance greets the boy
with the boundlessness of maternal joy.
"Mommy," he says, with glowing pride,
"I have coals and wood for you tonight.

"Tomorrow morning you can make a fire
and cook soup." The mother, laughing, inquires,
"That's nice. Where did you get the coal and wood?"
He whispers, "I took it from the outside yard,

"I sneaked it out. What is that funny look?
You're angry? You're not pleased with what I took?"
She looks into his eyes, so wide, without guile,
takes the boy in her lap, and says with a smile,

"My darling, heed me this once with care,
the pain you cause is as much as I can bear,
I have just you, you alone, my dear,
and I shall not forever be with you here.

"Never forget what I'm about to impart,
if you ever do, you'll break mother's heart.
Always cherish what to another belongs,
to touch what is not yours is terribly wrong.

"Not even may you take a crust, not the smallest grain,
not even with empty belly pang,
to sneak is to steal, to be a thief. Were
you dishonest, I couldn't hold you dear."

"But Mommy, the others, about them who cares?"
She holds his small face, her hands on his ears.
"As long as you live, despair will not win
if you keep your conscience wakeful and clean.

"We're taking back now the wood and the coal,
I want to keep nothing at all that you stole,
then your hands we'll thoroughly scrub
and you'll once again be my good little cub."

He examines her closely, now a serious lad,
"I did not know I did something bad,
but now," she hears his little heart beat,
"I must tell the other boys in the street."

Little Tommy's Evening Prayer

Dear God above, make me *fromm*;
I'd like the chicken pox to come,
so I can stay in the children's ward,
and do not count my sins, dear Lord,
let me be happy if you will,
safe from the seriously ill.
Put me someplace where you may
be sure I won't be in the way,
but it's so hard to find a bed,[6]
so let me stay in the children ward.[7]
I'm still little, my heart is pure,
make it chicken pox for sure,
mumps and measles I've already seen,
and scarlet fever leads to quarantine.
Send a disease that doesn't ache.
Nurse Mizzi is great, but doesn't bake
like nurse Emma and her tasty bits.
Here I can be jolly, with laughing fits.
Forgive all my misdeeds,
our dear physician tends our needs.
I lie here in a real bed, with a plump pillow,
how about if I turn jaundice yellow?
Oh, dear God, please make me ill
so the doctor during his morning call
will with a serious face declare,
"This boy can't go anywhere,
he must stay for observation, yes."
And at night, will you let my fever rise?
Don't be mad I ask so much, please,
but my room fills me with unease,
crowded with people so horribly.
Make a good boy out of me.
Spruce up my morning, no bellyache,

then at noon I'll take
chopped liver and potatoes, my favorite fare.
Keep Mommy in your care,
and Daddy, in the Sudeten barracks,
and look after those I love,
the lady who gave us sugar today,
and the nurses
and the doctor.
Amen.

For Aunt Ilse Heaven

Ukolébavka[8]

Hajej, dadej, maličký,
slunéčko už dávno spí,
žádný ptáček už nezpívá,
měsíček se z nebe dívá,
vše na světě je tiché—
tichounké.

Lullaby

Sleep, sleep, my little one,
the sun slumbers long,
the last birdsong has gone,
the moon looks down,
the world is still—
quite still.

Little Lullaby[9]

Night is creeping through the ghetto,
silent, profound.
Sleep, forget what's all around,
rest your little head on my arm,
with mother you'll sleep safe and warm.

Sleep, much can happen during night,
while asleep your worries may flee.
A new day comes and you shall see,
everything's been made anew,
peace and sunshine just for you.

Whooping Cough Children

Thirty children are allowed
to wander through the meadow,
the others all watch wistfully,
wishing to be in their place.

Thirty happy under trees,
holding flowers in their hands,
they escaped the musty walls,
gloomy hallways of the camp.

Balmy grass gently receives
little limbs so tired,
a bright sun kisses pallid cheeks,
each ray so much desired.

The others watching those outside
wish they too were frail,
ill enough to be with those
wandering on the grass.

Blue Hour at the Children's Ward

In the west it's getting dark,
twilight creeps into the ward.
Dusk rests on red fevered cheeks,
on ailing children's beds.
It's the blue hour of storytelling
and the children whisper to each other.

"Today," a little boy with a head bandage says,
"I dreamt I lived under a tree. I was
in cloud-cuckoo-land that
offered nothing to do but eat."
"What did you eat?" asks a girl with round eyes.
"Cakes, sausages and all kinds of pies,
all in cloud-cuckoo-land, all to enjoy."
"Cakes!" grumbles a yellow-jaundiced boy
whose hungry hopes have just been dashed,
"What I want is potatoes, mashed."
"And I," calls out a shrill wee voice,
"a scrambled egg would be my choice."
Young voices echo through the hall:
"An egg! Just this once! Eggs for all!
For ten months not one egg eaten,
and how it tastes we've long forgotten."
A hoarse voice rises jovially:
"At home we had an apple tree,
if I could have an apple, just one..."
Then from a dim corner a wail's begun,
Heinzi, tubercular and lame,
his cheeks, pale, white as snow, says "Home...
if I could only . . . how I wish . . .
to have what I left on my dish.
I ate no soup, no potatoes, no meat.

They yelled at me each time I didn't eat,
now mother is sick and father is dead,
and all I want is a piece of dry bread."
"My uncle once," Evi says, laughing, vain,
"brought me a pig of marzipan."
Peterle looks dreamily into space:
"Chocolate's the thing you can't replace."
"Oh chocolate and marzipan!"
His neighbor resents his élan,
"I want to eat lentils, beans, yellow peas,
in really big quantities."
"Yes," interrupts our little Liese,
"vegetables, nothing better than these,
spinach, kohlrabi and carrots, slaw,
how I love to eat them, even raw . . ."

I hear all this, and my heart is heavy,
what's for supper? Just thin black coffee.
I turn on the switch, the lights blaze bright
the children's drawn faces drain the light,
faces marked by hunger and privation,
the black charcoal traces of malnutrition.

You innocent victims of a blind power,
may help come to you in a timely hour,
to heal and save, take you far away
from this foul sickly swamp of decay.

Oh, I wish you will be children again,
with the right to love, to feel shining sun,
to the joy each child can claim at birth,
round cheeks and glances bright with mirth,
the chance to eat some this, some that,
you poor children of *Theresienstadt*.

Theresienstadt Lullaby

Hush-a-bye, children, sleep, don't pine,
boy from Bohemia, girl from the Rhine.
Though you arrived here sadly shorn,
wrenched from the land where you were born,
now you sleep side by side, endowed
with dreams where laughter is allowed.
Far from all suffering, yours and mine,
hush-a-bye, children, sleep, don't pine.

What do you see behind your eyes,
you serious boy, little Viennese?
Your father lost in the camp, now dead
each night sat at the side of your bed.
You are still young, you must let go.
We try to be kind to you, and so
to help you bear it, give your grief ease,
sleep, serious boy, little Viennese.

Sleep you little ones, blonde or brunette,
from Bohemia, Moravia, try to forget
your exile, from all over Deutschland snatched
away, sick, hungry, until you reached
this place of misery, shared our woe,
God willing, you shall live and grow.
Now we are wavering, troubled, forlorn,
but every night is followed by dawn.

Hush-a-bye, children, it will end,
this nightmare gloom. New world, new friend,
will greet us, manacles fall away,
hardship forgotten on that day
when you're made whole, diseases cured,
hunger appeased, your life restored.
You'll struggle forward hand in hand,
and for home and heritage take your stand.

Earth: Probably presented to Ilse by the same child who drew "For Aunt Ilse Heaven." See page 191.

Glance into Freedom

At last each gate wide-open lies,
like children, into freedom we burst.
The lindens bloom in dark green hurst
and all is soaked in their bouquet
beneath the sun this shining day.
The summer watches with a thousand eyes.

Berries ripen, it's the roses time,
the earth can barely wait to yield
its harvest. A herd trails a shepherd,
geese, let loose, all honks and hoots
gobble up green tender shoots,
and all rests quiet, sublime.

We look around, amazed, awry,
confined all winter in stale air.
Now spring has fled and summer's here,
how many days before it too goes?
These confining walls let nothing grow,
resent each sunbeam. Why?

Our longing strays to a far horizon.
Why are these others so cruel?
The Earth was given to us all,
are you still ours, blue horizon?
The barracks gates are locked,
and silently we return to prison.

Family Life

He's in the Sudeten barracks,
and I'm in the Hamburg here.
One child away so far,
the other is not near.

Surrounded by so many others,
each indifferent, cut from his life,
children severed from mothers,
husband from child and wife.

The child no longer can recall
how living at home feels.
He carries and cleans his own food bowl,
and by himself gets his meals.

He doesn't come to me to cry,
he makes his bed alone.
It often seems to me,
I no longer have a son.

When he comes to my barracks cot,
he keeps staring at my bread.
I give it to him, my so distant tot.
I'd give him more and remain unfed.

Some days I come across
my husband in the street,
pulling the battered hearse.
Mute smiles the way we greet.

Two hours visit at day's end.
It's eight. It's time to fly.
Not a minute, husband, friend,
for even a kiss good-bye.

Once more upon us night descends,
my bunk I barely see.
How I wish that husband and child
were again with me.

To Go Home[10]

"I want to go home!" I first heard this cry
full of misery and agony
in the Fair Hall, just before leaving Prague.
It was winter, the snow lay in big
drifts, heaped high on house, tree, bush,
and near the Hall, turned to dirty slush.
No stove gave heat, the doors didn't shut,
shivering, one tried to rest, but
the floor was wet, sopping,
seemed the commotion was stopping
and, now in the lull, came a cry
from the furthest corner of that room,
expressing clearly our misery, out of the gloom,
from the mouth of an innocent, "I want to go home."

One year has passed, a year of pain,
the ghetto's invisible walls lock us in,
days but links in a chain of grief,
each bringing newly contrived mischief.
Starved, bullied, treated with scorn,
a thousand such trials borne.
Looted, humiliated, and to our disgust
what we believed in turned to dust.
It often seems so frightfully hard
to get support from beliefs we shared,
yet this prayer, soaring from horror and gloom,
engages our hearts, "I want to go home."

Letter to My Child

My dear son, it is three years today
since you traveled, all alone, far away.
I can still see you in the Prague station, on that train,
in the compartment, shy and tear-stained,
your curly-haired head leaning toward me,
how you begged, "Let me stay with you, Mommy."
That we sent you away seemed to you cruel,
you were eight years old, small and frail,
and as we walk home without you, each step I take
is harder, it feels as if my heart will break.
I have cried so often, believe me dear,
despite that I'm happy you are not here.
The unknown woman who took you in,
she will surely be rewarded in heaven,
I bless her with my every breath,
however much you love her, is not enough.
It's become so bleak for us here,
they took everything away, we have nothing anymore.
Our house, our home, not a corner is left.
Of even one scrap of what we loved, we're bereft.
They took your toy train and all its gear of course,
and even your brother's small rocking horse.
Even robbed of our names by these cheats,
marked like cattle, we go through the streets,
numbers on our necks. I'd bear this disgrace
if only your father were with me in this place,
and, if you please, also the little one.
My life has never been so alone.
Small as you are, how do I explain
so many crammed in one room still feels strange.
Body against body, we share each other's distress,
feeling painfully each one's loneliness.
Are you healthy, my boy and learning a lot?

Someone sings you to sleep each night? I fear not.
Sometimes, at night's quieter shore,
I think I feel you at my side once more.
Imagine when we meet some day,
you won't understand a word I say.
In Sweden, you'll lose our German tongue.
If I spoke one Swedish word, I'd be wrong.
Strangest of all to meet again
a grown-up person who's my son.
Do you still play games with your tin
soldiers? A real barracks is what I'm in,
with cold rooms and the darkest walls,
with no trees, no leaves, no sunlight at all.
Nursing children I'm of some use
easing their pain, I even choose,
at times, to stay with them all night,
a shadow in the small lamp's light.
I sit in silence, protect their sleep,
and each is the "you" I cannot keep.
In my thoughts and dreams I hold you near
and yet it's a blessing to me you're not here.
Life has taken so much away,
all my joy gone since you left that day.
Oh yes, the burden is hard to bear,
but at least I know that you are spared.
A thousand torments to be endured,
if your happy childhood is ensured.
It's getting late and I must lie down.
If I could rest eyes on you again!
Dear son, no matter how strong my need,
I can only write letters you'll never read.

Eldertransport[11]

A line of weary elders goes through town,
heavy laden, backs bent,
heading for the train.

Eyes blind with tears,
feet aching and sore,
each step, brings pain.

Torn from kin, on their way to new trials,
robbed of possessions, nascent exiles,
in silence they proceed.

In hearts overwhelmed with horror,
they repeatedly ask the Almighty Name,
why? Please explain.

They trudge along under autumnal skies,
behind closed windows hidden eyes
won't let them go.

Oh, do still say something loving to them,
to somehow ease their burdens,
hoping in vain.

For no, we're forbidden to extend our arms,
to those who always extended theirs, relieving
our sorrow and pain.

Forbidden to approach, much less embrace.
We must abandon these aged friends,
to their solitude.

Goodbye Mother

I have always loved you
since I was a child.
Such good friends we were
I feel it now more than ever.
Yet I let you go today
without extending a hand,
in your distress all alone
for the first time in your life.

I saw you from among the crowd,
a bundle on your back,
stunned and ill at ease,
searching for my face.
Of course I knew you looked for me,
still I remained away,
and with not a single word
of goodbye for your departure.

From the distance I could
hug you only with my eyes,
too cowardly to run to you
to slip by your side.
I saw you and the others
pass through the barracks gate
tormented and without a home,
off to an unknown fate.

I didn't say goodbye to you,
and you may never know
that even as I deserted you
I never felt so close.

Remembrance

I often meet old women
as along the streets I tread,
I breathe in their air of sorrow,
of a lonely life, and hollow.
My heart fills with anxiety and dread.

So also my mother goes
along strange ghetto lanes,
hunched by age and duress,
eyes blank with loneliness,
of all she loved, nought remains.

Bedřich Fritta: *Roll Call*

The Magdeburg Barracks Gate

There is a tale from long ago
of a princess reduced by toil and woe
who met a peculiar fate.
Returning to her royal abode
torn and dirty from the road
she'd say to a mare's head over the gate,
 "Oh Fallada, 'tis you hang there."[12]

Like the poor princess, it's my fate
to stride, worn out, through the old gate
of the barracks of Magdeburg,
where hangs a weathered horse's head.
I pass it, and my joy has fled.
For it seems from afar I hear this dirge,
"Tis you; pass under, Princess fair."

You old gate of Theresienstadt,
as I enter ill and weary and hot,
bruised by the path I strode,
wounded by rocks, my feet so sore
my heart bleeds, each beat a sharp tug,
and often, so often I hear from afar,
"If your mother only knew,
Her heart would surely break in two."

The Seven[13]

Dismal clouds over the land,
seven wander hand in hand,
does the Lord see everything?
Guards sharpen bayonets.
In this misery, under threat,
one of the seven begins to sing.

And he sings to far corners of the earth,
of his friends marching to their death,
defiance rises in his song
nor falters at his grave.
Dark the clouds that cloak the brave,
loud winds of approaching storm.

Heads high, brothers, ahead you'll see
the day when everyone is free,
despite the pain we've faced.
Never whine, my friend, nor moan,
our fate must be proudly borne,
our early deaths embraced.

They break our bones, grind us down,
hark, they will not stay immune,
from their evil deeds.
Curses, groans, it all evens out.
A sea of tears will sprout
from their dragon seeds.

Seven candles for the dead
in barracks dark and cold.
Seven lights for the dead,
seven David's stars of gold.
Hour by hour through this awful night,
seven watch the lights.

Look how these lights have blazed,
Lord, exterminate the crazed
license of this age so crude.
When will you lend surcease
from all this wickedness,
avenging innocent blood?

Our people must not vanish, behold,
in heaven above gleaming gold,
once more David's star.
And just as in the past,
we'll all be free. At last
tasting what now seems so far.

The Sheep from Lidice[14]

Sheep walk the empty street, their wool off-white,
while shepherd girls sing in the day's last light:
a peaceful picture. Yet, hanging in the air
a breath of death. Stop and stare.
Dim woolly sheep so far off from their fold,
sheepcotes in ashes, shepherds' bodies cold.

The village men were murdered row by row,
the small Bohemian village empty now.
The women who tended ram and ewe
seized and transported, the children too.
In ashes, each little house where peace once dwelled,
a village laid to waste, the livestock spared.

These Lidice sheep belong right here in this place.
Homeless humans, homeless sheep embrace.
The same terrible chance confines us without home or hearth,
the world's most tortured people and the saddest flock on earth.
The sun went down, its last ray disappeared,
and somewhere in the barracks, a Jewish tune is heard.

Evening Song

Golden stars and moon, aloof
high above our barracks roof.
Of the whole wide world
only the heavens are mine.

Golden moon and golden stars
how I love you, you are far.
Yet for all my yearning
the heavens are too small.

Dawn[15]

The physician has just silently left,
what he knows I have long guessed,
death's shadow lies on your cheeks,
and breath barely heaves your pale breast.

I enclose your little hand in mine
and feel your pulse so weak.
The clock ticks loud, unremitting;
through shutters comes daybreak.

Soon the sun will beam from heaven's height,
covering our world with its glow.
Little girl, you will no more see that light;
all ends for you, everything shall go.

Once you possessed woods, flowers, trees,
gamboling like a fawn.
Ah why can't you go on with your dreams?
Why does life have to pain you so?

Past, your child's joy, your merry play,
for our great distress you are too small,
an hour more and you'll be on your way,
and your parents will be quite alone.

Your pulse stops, your breath is gone.
Your eyes are open, dark and empty,
death has kissed your pale cheek,
and leads you fondly in eternity.

A Data Card

My father serves in the *Wehrmacht*,
why was I sent to Theresienstadt?
On the way here, Mommy passed away,
so now I have no family.

About being Jewish I'm a dunce,
I blessed baby Jesus, had a Christmas tree once,
I played with Christian children, all their games,
and thought all children were the same.

Papa, does he know what's happened to us?
Perhaps I will never see him again,
and once home, he'll find it hard to bear,
that neither Mommy nor I are there.

I am not going back to Germany,
a Jew they made me, a Jew I will be,
and after so much injustice done to us,
can a man forget such prejudice?

I have found many new friends here.
They treat me well. I hold them dear.
My new friends won't abandon me,
and in their homeland I'll be free.

Musica Prohibita

I wander through Theresienstadt.
A policemen's glance makes my flesh crawl,
the lute[16] I found is concealed, held tight,
wrapped like an infant in a shawl.

My heart beats fast, my cheeks are hot,
I dread his probing eyes.
If he discovers what I've got
they'll take the lute I prize.

In this place we are all condemned,
a shamed, despairing crowd.
All instruments are contraband,
no music is allowed.

Want and cruelty we endure,
every torment they devise.
Let them try our spirits more,
from the dust we shall arise.

We must be strong within ourselves,
lest in despair and dread we drown.
Must sing until the song dissolves
these walls, and our joy tears them down.

Music lights up a poet's words,
from our plight brings release,
even the sparest songs of birds
bear moments of blessed peace.

And when again we lose our nerve
drowning, drowning in despair,
the boundless beauty of the world
wafts resuscitating air.

Music is a beatitude,
it is there salvation lies.
Fearlessly, I tote my lute
beneath the policeman's eyes.

Malva Schalek: *Ilse Weber sings with a guitar, 1942*

Died During Transport

I do not know you, dead man,
I pass your bier by chance.
'Neath spare white hairs, I can
just spy your empty glance.

Your name is to me unknown.
Around your neck a dirty
band, whereupon is shown
transport number, 830.

You've been stripped completely bare
of name, of home, of past.
Your corpse is here, your heart afar,
this place is your last.

I cannot resist the urge
to take your hand right now.
Your stiff fingers and my soft ones merge,
I stroke your icy brow.

Through your last hard hours,
driven from your home,
your death was lonely, sour,
so far from all you loved.

In this wide world, where can they be?
At home you might have mended.
Dead nameless brother, sleep,
death has been your friend.

For those far away, who wait and grieve,
your death is even harder
than it is for you, reprieved
in this silent boneyard.

I touch you gently once again,
no one can hurt you now.
Rest peacefully, unknown dead man,
I'll often think of you.

A Stranger's Cradle[17]

By a strange child's cradle I linger,
often, in evening's glow,
her little fingers
nestled in my hand.
The wide-open eyes of this
unknown child look at me.
Eyes trusting and angelic,
as only a child's can be.
With hardship and dreariness
I'm then overcome.
I feel such love,
as if she were my child.
Her dear starry eyes,
not yet bleak from suffering—
perhaps, far away,
someone loves my child!

Modlitba[18]

Dobrý den nám, Bože, dej,
všechny lidi požehnej,
abychom se rádi měli,
všeho zlého zapomněli.
Dobrý den nám, Bože, dej,
všechny lidi požehnej.

Prayer

Good morning to you, God,
bless all the people, everyone.
Let them love their neighbors,
shun injustice and wrongdoing.
Good morning to you, God,
bless all the people, everyone.

Before Falling Asleep

Sleep, my little Slovenly Peter,[19]
a seventy-five centimeter
space[20] we share.
High above our bastion
stand moon and stars, the heavens.
They are still here.

Neither push me with your knees, nor
forget, little one, your life before.
Your bed was painted white.
Dream of its bright green bars,
not rough like this cot of ours,
of splintered slabs that bite.

Where do you linger in your dream?
Thirty of us in this one room,
not easy to bear.
Above us beds are crackling,
beneath, two girls are cackling,
and damp is the air.

Good-night, wiggle, I need space too,
I've saved one more kiss for you,
little rascal mine.
The dark night will soon be gone,
the sun's light the world will crown,
and all will be fine.

And the Rain Runs

And the rain runs and the rain runs.
In the dark I think of you, little one.
High are the mountains, deep is the sea,
my weary heart yearns for thee.
And the rain runs, and the rain runs.
Why are you far away, little one?

And the rain runs and the rain runs,
God himself parted us, little one.
You aren't meant to see hardship and woe,
nor to get lost in a stony alley.
And the rain runs and the rain runs.
You've not forgotten me, little one?

Bedřich Fritta: *Hearse*[21]

Theresienstadt Nursery Rhyme

Rira, riraearse,
we're riding in the hearse,
rira, riraearse
we're riding in the hearse.
We stand there, we stand here,
riding fast, cold corpses near,
riraearse
we're riding in the hearse.

Rira, rirarollen,
all we had has been stolen,
rira, rirarollen,
all long gone, all stolen.
Happiness, home, all disappears,
the last baggage gone, remain just fears,
rirarollen,
the hearse keeps rolling.

Rira, riraearse,
they hitched us to the hearse,
rira, riraearse,
they hitched us to the hearse.
Loaded with our pain,
we'll never take a step again,
riraearse
so heavy will be the hearse.

A Little Piece of Freedom

There, where the guard stands his watch
at the green open meadow,
where streets lead on to Bauschowitz,[22]
there ends our ghetto.

The bastion's brick wall shuts everything in,
outside the path to humanity lies open.
So happy we could have been
with them to breathe and to hope.

The wall surrounds us, and the guard
stands unmoving by the bridge.
We go as beggars, poor and sad,
our glances hungry and demanding.

We know precisely: in yonder world
we no longer own our lives.
We still have a weed-strewn field,
yes, that they have graciously given.

We are released, we're free at last,
we no more lack possessions and home.
Even the guard lets us pass
as we're carried to our grave.

The One from the O.D.[23]

I lean against the wall, I never laugh,
the band on my arm says *O.D.*
The job's not hard, I get time off,
rest for my anxiety.

In the evening I see in the mirror
a young woman's face impassioned,
her eyes grave, lips tight with terror,
her hair already ashen.

I never speak of what my job required,
don't seek friends, remain alone,
many take this path, and each mired
in misery of her own.

I often may seem bitter and tough,
my tears never ease my pain.
For what I've seen can't be years enough
to make me whole again.

Theresienstadt, Theresienstadt

Theresienstadt, Theresienstadt,
I'm tired of this and sick of that.
If only I could get away
from all your walled-in pain and woe,
the shrill of sorrow, the moaning low,
that haunts your streets each day.

While spring has come and warmed us twice,
we're still bound tightly in your vise,
hungry and yearning, immured in sadness.
We crave for that glorious day
when we'll be free to fly away,
our tears exchanged for gladness.

A Conversation in the Alley

My window overlooks a narrow way,
where women gather long hours each day
to gossip with each other.
And from each one the theme recurs,
a tale of the splendor that once was hers.
Ah, telling with such pleasure
a tale of childhood's happy peace,
former days of wealth and ease,
that ends in this old fort.
And as each past becomes so bright,
present pain assumes its weight.
They once had rank and worth.
Gone from running a business, a going concern
to peeling spuds, waiting your turn
for the toilet, or sweeping stairs.
Frau Doctor, Frau Counsel, Frau Engineer,
one laughs at the title or bursts into tears.
Titles don't pass through the processing gate,
the *Schleuse*[24] took your wealth, sad to relate,
your past is of no use to you here.
Worth nothing now, your chauffeured car,
the villa with its park, no longer yours,
and the jewelry that you once wore.
We're prisoners here, only numbers,
the same hassle and woe encumbers
all. What you were before erased.
Your vanity undressed.
What each of us in actuality is
in our community will be obvious.
Nothing blinds like wealth and rank,
here, name and title just clank clank clank,
and inner worth is best.

Someone with a sympathetic heart
for others' sorrow, tears and hurt,
who possesses to the full
determination, who can hide her fear:
this is what is needed here,
essential to survival.
I cannot pity those who lack
these qualities, who keep looking back,
who to their fancied pasts succumb.
They are clueless who think this way.
Here only inner value holds sway,
our only asset in days to come.

Be Kind To One Another

Is it so hard to show you care,
to offer another a kind word,
to share a little of their burden?
Is your heart an empty void?

In our suffering we're all alike,
once we've gone down this vale.
He alone will prosper and be happy
who spreads good will and love,

who gives a broken piece of his bread,
when his neighbor's eyes beseech,
who doesn't refuse to help
when others cannot go it alone.

Be kind to one another in word and deed,
otherwise these times will knock us down.
All must be friends, comrades in need,
we're all by the same fate bound.

This Already Happened

It's already happened more than once,
you've been spurned once again,
someone who was once your friend
suddenly passes by,
a stranger, looking the other way.

Hard to bear, so much pain,
but I've learned to let it pass.
One cannot expect people
to renounce their safety,
for the sake of friendship.

Can any friendship reach that far?
Unconditional love from a friend?
You might like to give your all,
but you cannot expect
love to be reciprocated.

The Ration Card[25]

I have earned a ration card,
I have my pick of stuff,
seized from helpless dead
and living, more here than enough.

Each object gives its origin,
a name and an address.
I read the words and no harm's done
in studying them, I guess.

This small shirt came from Hamburg,
these pants from Frankfurt am Main.
This warm dress, is it my style?
It comes from Neuwied am Rhein.

These shoes, I've needed, how
badly! My leather soles are frayed.
This pair shod a white-toed Frau
from Kiel. Filched when she arrived.

The sewing bag travelled from Wien.
It's gray, the lining pink.
Just like . . . my mother's . . . last seen . . .
One doesn't know what to think.

But best of all the ration card
down at the grocery store.
I'll buy stock cubes, fake eggs and lard,
they won't make me sick.

Such a lovely thermos flask,
they took my own from
me. Contraband, no, don't ask,
best play deaf and dumb.

Living in Theresienstadt,
what you thought you were has faded.
A ration card is what you've got,
and a conscience slightly jaded.

Prominent Figures[26]

Some people here still wear a hat,
some are no longer kind.
They dine with knife and fork that
gleam, but left their hearts behind.

Our jailers call them 'prominent,'
and those so called agree,
so comfortably dominant,
above indignity.

Observe the fear-filled nightmares
of those camped on the floor.
The prominent are free from cares,
their beds are warm, secure.

What hurts the most, what we resent:
our lives are threatened without pause
while they are immune. They're prominent,
ruled by different laws.

How beneficent they could be,
if they our lot would share,
our common humanity,
and keep us from despair.

They sow hatred and envy,
and just as these walls divide,
as they favored their own safety,
our sense of kinship died.

In the Hamburg Barracks

In the Hamburg barracks,
Oh boy! There's lots of girls.
For one of them I'm making tracks,
got to give her a whirl.
Valerie, Valera, I'm special, I'm AK.[27]
Sweetheart, my sweetheart, you know it, yeah.

Her eyes like stars,
when they meet mine,
they fill the barracks
with bright sunshine.
Valerie, Valera, I'm special, I'm AK.
Sweetheart, my sweetheart, you know it, yeah.

Caressing her is so cozy
while evading the patrols.
It's like a thousand roses
bloomed all around the walls.
Valerie, Valera, I'm special, I'm AK.
Sweetheart, my sweetheart, you know it, yeah.

Once they open the fortress,
good-bye Theresienstadt.
I'll bring home the very best
the whole globe ever had.
Valerie, Valera, I'm special, I'm AK.
Sweetheart, my sweetheart, you know it, yeah.

The Dungeon

Beyond the ambulance chaos,
       by chance, I came upon
a sinister detention room
       that never sees the sun.
Hidden doors within the wall,
       rusty hinges screeched.
It was as if the world was lost,
       the silence never breached.

The ceiling hatch above me
       was black with ancient grime.
On gray walls around me, were
       lines from another time.
In this dungeon dark and narrow,
       walls spoke of remorseful tears,
of defiance and harsh rule,
       of long and lonely years,

of yearning for companionship,
       the living world out there,
the beating pulse of others,
       the shackled wish to share.
Outside, a symphony of life;
       here, the silence of the grave.
I turn and give another glance
       before I take my leave.

To what that prisoner was denied,
       I have been long restored.
Yet amidst the barrack's whirr and stir
       I hear a dissonant chord.
It interrupts my tumultuous days,
       my fragmented dreams at night,
the dark, deserted dungeon
       lingers in my mind.

I'll never forget you, prisoner,
       your unremitting pain,
somehow I burn with longing,
       to visit there again.

Bedřich Fritta: *Arrival*

Evening[28]

In evening when we've finished chores,
no gleaming lamps welcome us home.
We stay in this alley out of doors,
dismayed by the darkness of our room.

They turned our lights off weeks ago
because someone did something wrong.
What happened? We shall never know,
in darkness all month long.

So now we stand in an alley's arcade,
gazing at gleaming stars,
long evenings of late parade,
dull barrack voices in our ears.

It took this trial for us to learn,
the wonders of night's sky.
Anyway, let us return
and sleep, so we don't cry.

A Meadow in the Bastion

The sky is blue, the far hills green,
the evening is quite warm enough.
The bastion meadow delightful, seen
from the border patrol's flat roof.

How strange it looks from up here,
not like the lawns back home I know.
May is still truly May, but it's queer
to see pipes sprout in a meadow.

Back home, the words entrance,
forgetting would make them less real.
And maybe then we'd be happy for once,
it's nice here, but for ghastly meals.

Like candles on the chestnut row
a thousand flowers bloom.
The hawthorn's purple fire glows,
opposing evening's gloom.

A breeze grazes, gentle, cool,
half eight says the town hall's bell.
Back to the barracks, my heart is full,
I'll endure this life for a spell.

Barracks' Yard Ration[29]

They arrived by the hundreds,
       from miles of mire and mud,
and now they wait patiently,
       facing the cooks and the tubs.

Frail, elderly, ill
       they stand, tormented, forlorn.
Greed, repulsion, and shame
       color expressions careworn.

Bowls in the manner of beggars
       extended by trembling hands.
Embarrassed by their hunger,
       how much anguish can they stand?

They grab rotten potatoes
       poking in puddles of slime.
Old, beat, exhausted;
       starving retreating in shame.

They lunge at the empty tubs,
       a greedy, sickly pack,
leaving as hungry as before,
       to sleep in a makeshift shack.

The Hungry

They plod along, weighed down by care.
Hunger, hunger, always there,
it digs into guts, wears out every bone
and turns faces into stone.

Whatever makes people noble and good,
hunger, hunger, lack of food
destroys. Away with honor and trust.
Consciences sold for old dry crust.

Tyranny, force, cannot tame
hunger, hunger's incessant claim.
Hauteur, pride and arrogance
melt as snow at sun's ascent.

Envy and hatred sprout like weeds.
We grow blind and deaf to others' needs.
Others exist no longer
for those consumed by hunger.

So many beggars, so near,
along every road, it's hard to bear.
Disgraceful that some shun those in need,
smug with their own ample feed.

The Potato Peeler

I peel potatoes all day long,
with a hundred other women,
from the very crack of dawn
in this musty shed again.

I sit without heeding
a word others say,
for while my hands are peeling,
my thoughts are far away.

Amidst sly jokes and laughter,
a carelessness I can't share,
I think with unease of my daughter,
missing in Poland somewhere.

The brown potatoes come and go,
baskets are piled high.
They sent my son to Dachau,
why did God let him die?

An hour trickles, another is gone,
my hands are hard and raw.
Typhus took my grandson,
Oh, when will my life end?

Potatoes, potatoes, potatoes
I've been peeling forever, it seems.
I'm becoming a potato:
they've even invaded my dreams.

Peelings have me in their toils,
hissing coldly serpentine,
constricting me in python coils
that mercilessly entwine.

And now a new day comes along
I peel in the shed again,
from crack of dawn
with a hundred other women.

The Engineer's Barracks[30]

Outside the Engineer's barracks
          the air itself seems to sigh.
There lie the very old,
          lost in days gone by.

They lie on wooden plank beds,
          among them, anguish reigns,
their inward-turning eyes redeem,
          what of the past remains.

The DreamGod reproduces
          a beautiful, tender day.
They doze off, forgetful
          of the present's disarray.

Each one back with home and children,
          the things that brought content,
recent years forgotten,
          the torments underwent.

Through the Engineer's barracks
          death silently creeps,
and with great compassion
          collects elders in their sleep.

Bedřich Fritta: *Sickward*

A Shed

A shed: men, women, children, the old,
just names and numbers, lying in rows.
One shroud covers all, all are blessed
by one God who takes, who bestows.

The crowd shudders when, crudely,
the wagons are hurriedly filled.
And as the caskets crash and collide,
those watching twitch and duck.

Sometimes, as if the dead want
to press their case one last time,
the lids gape open to present
scrawny limbs, rags and grime.

Tired horses drag with tired steps,
followed to torn and gaping sod,
the bonds of slavery fall away,
released as the coffins descend.

Burial

Thirty coffins in the field,
          soon to be piled in a heap.
In front of the first in the line,
          I stand and try to weep.

I plucked a leafy branch,
          passing a tree on the way,
I laid it on the coarse white plank
          hoping my tribute would stay.

I read your name on the lid,
          over and over. A spell
it became. A strange refrain,
          not the name I knew so well.

I seek your image in my mind,
          tell me where it has gone.
I remain silent and tearless,
          my chest all but frozen.

I hear your children pleading,
          "Shield mother when we're away."
Distant, they've no idea
          of the hardship you faced each day.

Thirty caskets wait in the field,
          thirty more in the dray,
pall bearers too tired to live,
          bearing more bodies away.

Worn out by hardship,
      more by what we see,
the ailing feebly falling,
      death lacking dignity.

I could not protect you from
      your hunger and privation.
Illness found you helpless;
      death was your salvation.

Your coffin has been carried off.
      Oh to feel grief, to even sigh.
Dead inside,
      I've forgotten how to cry.

Transport to Poland

The transport to Poland is announced,[31]
a nightmare, deadly pall.
The Council Elders[32] snoop here and there,
their indifference doesn't fool us at all.

We shrink from their glances, fear in our eyes.
"Can it be me?" we shudder in dread.
One wishes to get far away
and leave the fateful paper unread.

Calamity stalks the fort
on quiet muffled paws,
we have such a fear of Poland
without really knowing the cause.

If misery or death is there,
no one will attest.
Going to Poland is worse than death;
at least the dead have rest.

A neighbor goes today, your turn tomorrow.
Stripped of rights, of anything to lose,
we're Ahasuerus'[33] kin,
eternal wandering Jews.

Bedřich Fritta: *East Transport*

A Transport is Called up[34]

Five thousand are leaving tomorrow
on a huge Polandtransport.
Five thousand people, family, friends,
companions of every sort
who shared our misery,
whose torment, we hope, soon ends.

It feels so wrong to stay behind,
what they go to nobody knows.
They pack their bundles, faces tight,
the abyss between us is wide
Only chance has let us stay,
tomorrow we'll share their plight?

What keeps us here, moaning, complaining?
Is it to a homeland we cling?
The world outside is a pitiless waste.
We dare not look in our friend's eyes.
Will he understand and forgive
us for remaining when he leaves?

Now he's joining the other line,
we stay, irresolute and shamed:
we're not noble or significant,
we cling to our petty survival.
The train of the banished has just left,
we already begin to forget.

I Wander through Theresienstadt

I wander through Theresienstadt,
my heart weighed down with pain,
suddenly I come to a halt,
just there at the bastion.

I linger on the bridge and gaze
beyond the vale below:
I long to flee, to run away,
I long to go back home!

"Home!" a word so wonderful,
you make my heart so sad.
They took my home, took my all,
I've nowhere to hang my head.

I turn around, distraught and sad,
dejected to the core.
Theresienstadt, Theresienstadt,
when will the suffering end?
When shall we be free again?

Five Years

Sometimes, as I take a stroll
to escape the bastion's bustle,
I see children and recall
I too have children, in a far off land.

An unknown girl, with eyes that shine,
brings bittersweet memories.
And over there, a boy just like mine
makes me stop and gaze for awhile.

Five years ago we sent them on
to live with strangers in a foreign land.
We remain here, deceived, forlorn,
we remain here, by hardship bound.

Can't believe five years have gone by,
I'm now very tired and gray.
Elsewhere a boy perhaps tall as I,
my little girl a Frau.

Will I ever, ever see those two?
For this joy, my life's on hold,
meanwhile I'm weary through and through,
five years out in the cold.

Farewell, My Comrade

Farewell, my comrade,
our ways diverge,
tomorrow I must go far.
I part from thee,
driven away from here,
I board the Polandtransport.

You often encouraged me
with kindness and loyalty,
always ready to help.
A touch of your hand
eased the worries
we shared about our fate.

Farewell, comrade,
it's too bad that we part,
separating is very hard.
Don't lose your courage,
we were such good friends.
We'll never meet again.

Farewell

One day when all will be over,
every heartache and woe,
then we'll put out our hands
and bid each other adieu.

The gates will open for us,
we'll return to our former lives.
Without a word we'll go our ways,
just look in each other's eyes.

We are no longer confined,
a bright future has appeared.
The suffering has passed
and with it the closeness we shared.

I can no longer take your hand,
which often helped me endure,
for we go separate ways,
each to a different future.

For a last pressure of your hands
not one word could I summon.
Yes, every suffering comes to an end,
but you, but you, are gone.

Barren of Earthly Possessions[35]

Everything we had they took,
little things held dear.
They stripped us of earthly goods
when we arrived here.

We suffered hunger and want,
on hard beds lying,
hoary, gaunt
battling woe, and bitter dying.

Yet thousands of candles together
shone with grit and contempt,
preserving our sacred treasure,
in our hearts, holy writ.

Ah, we may be tortured,
threatened with Polandtransport,
but our starving souls are nurtured
with a poet's eternal words.

We hear of faraway places,
of lives free of fear.
We return then to the barracks,
hearts kindled with modest cheer.

Emigrant Song[36]

Swallow your tears, bite your grief,
let your will be strong as steel.
Ignore the insults and offense,
to overcome this trial.

> Everything will be all right, everything will be all right,
> you do not wait in vain.
> Believe in the future, keep up the fight:
> the world will be a garden again!

Discord, hate and greed are over,
and all the suffering ends.
Your enemy will call you "brother,"
and shamefaced, reach out his hand.

> Everything will be all right, everything will be all right,
> you do not wait in vain.
> Believe in the future, keep up the fight:
> the world will be a garden again!

No longer to be ostracized
when others are laughing, carefree.
For you the birds awaken! Arise!
The sun also rises for thee.

> Everything will be all right, everything will be all right,
> you do not wait in vain.
> Believe in the future, keep up the fight:
> the world will be a garden again!

For you the tree bears fruit, the sun is bright,
you find homeland and family.
Evil vanishes like a bad dream,
and life once more is happy.

Everything will be all right, everything will be all right,
you do not wait in vain.
Believe in the future, keep up the fight:
the world will be a garden again!

Confession

Since my early childhood days,
as far as I remember,
my Judaism was not a gift:
but a persistent mental ember.

A grey cloud of anxiety
shading light wherever found,
bitter absinthe in life's cup,
an infinitely open wound.

And when I found some happiness,
a promise of some bliss,
it cruelly drained this happiness,
stealing my quiet and peace.

I tried first to defend myself,
argued to the last,
was always overwhelmed,
hated and harassed.

Bit by bit it snatched from me
everything my heart held dear.
And yet today I recognize:
my Jewishness is me.

I do not have a way with words,
does my feeling have a name?
I burn for my Jewish people,
a firebrand, heart aflame.

And if I'm forced to chose today,
I will not hesitate.
I'll stand with my people,
willingly share their fate.

Lullaby from the Poland Transport

Sleep little friend, the night is long.
The engine hums a monotonous song,
as night creeps over the land.
You are still little, you can rest,
sleep, little friend, sleep your best,
we are on our way to Poland.

Sleep little one, we have come far,
our home has vanished in the dark,
stolen a long time ago.
We loved it dearly, it is no more.
We sit in silence we find no words,
we're going all the way to Poland.

Sleep little friend, I'm keeping watch.
Your sweet sleep helps me catch
some rest. I'll no longer be blue,
it eases my worries, our way is sure.
The stars are shining bright and pure,
God is in Poland, too.

Wiegala (Lullaby)[37]

Wiegala, wiegala, weier,
the wind plays on the lyre,
blows green music, sweet and strong.
The nightingale sings his song.
Wiegala, wiegala, weier,
the wind plays on the lyre.

Wiegala, wiegala, werne,
the moon is a lantern,
it sails along the heavens dark,
gazing down at our earthly ark.
Wiegala, wiegala, werne,
the moon is a lantern.

Wiegala, wiegala, wille,
why is the world so still?
No sound upsets your sleep so sweet.
Sleep, my child, sleep, sleep.
Wiegala, wiegala, wille,
why is the world so still?

Wiegala

Alternate translation

Rockaby

Rockaby, rockaby, fire,
the wind sings on the lyre,
blows green music, sweet and strong,
the nightingale singing his song.
Rockaby, rockaby fire,
the wind plays on the lyre.

Rockaby, rockaby, stone,
the moon shines all alone,
it sails along the heavens dark,
gazing down at our earthly ark.
Rockaby, rockaby stone,
the moon shines all alone.

Rockaby, field and hill,
why is the world so still?
Your breath, my child, so sweet so deep,
sleep, my child, sleep, sleep.
Rockaby, field and hill,
why is the world so still?

Afterword: Against Forgetting

by Ulrike Migdal

Theresienstadt, an Austro-Hungarian garrison town north of Prague, which had been converted during World War II to a concentration camp, became a graveyard for poems.

Presumably, there are many such "graves" never discovered because the people who had buried the poems were murdered. Fortunately, one "grave" was recovered by a prisoner who had worked as a gardener and had hidden a collection of poems, written by his wife, before he was deported to Auschwitz.

In Theresienstadt, whoever found his name on a transport list had to fear the worst. The words "east-transport" had an aura of horror. The prisoners, lacking knowledge about the exact destination, suspected they posed a more terrible threat than Theresienstadt.

Those caught by the mass extermination industry had hardly a chance to salvage from Auschwitz, Sobibór or Treblinka any form of written material: letters, poems, notes, sketches. These were places where any possibility of recording artistic production was nonexistent. A prisoner, in case he escaped the gas chamber, could save only memories. After the liberation, some survivors transformed memories into literary testimonies for future generations.

At Yad Vashem, Jerusalem, in the early 1980s, I spent weeks leafing through papers in the memorial archive to find literary voices from the Theresienstadt ghetto. I discovered many documents that bore witness to the suffering and torture, and to the prisoners' artistic and literary creativity. Among the documents, which, unlike their authors, escaped destruction, was a poem titled "Letter to My

Child." No signature or any other clue gave an indication of its author. I published it in 1986 as by an unknown author, together with other poems, chansons, satires and reports from Theresienstadt, in a collection called *And the Music Plays Along . . .*

The following spring I received a letter from Stockholm. The writer had just read my book and disclosed what Yad Vashem had been unaware of: "The author of the poem 'Letter to My Child' is my mother, Ilse Weber, who was murdered in Auschwitz. And I am Hanuš, the child the poem addresses."

Hanuš Weber, a long-time correspondent for Swedish television, described to me the Odyssey of that "letter," never sent because the Theresienstadt censorship would have never allowed it to pass.

The Swedish writer Amelie Posse had met regularly with survivors who, after their liberation from the concentration camps in the spring of 1945, were brought to Sweden by Red Cross "White Busses." Some of them showed her things they had salvaged from the camps: drawings, sketches and poems by fellow sufferers not lucky enough to have survived. A woman liberated from the Ravensbruck camp, Margarete Waern, gave Posse the poem "Letter to My Child," which she translated and published in one of the biggest Swedish daily newspapers. This legacy of a desperate mother to her unreachable son had thus reached its addressee, Hanuš, in May 1945, forty two years before he wrote to me.

Six years earlier, in May 1939, Ilse Weber had sent her eight-year-old first-born son to a friend in England. Ilse's friend Lilian, a Swedish diplomat's daughter, took Hanuš from England to her homeland, Sweden, where he spent the war years in safety with her mother, Gertrude von Löwenadler.

That Hanuš and more than six hundred Czech children had been able to reach England on the eve of the second World War was due to the singular efforts of Nicholas George Winton,[1] a young British stockbroker who learned, from the friend with whom he was planning a skiing vacation, about efforts to help persecuted people to emigrate. Winton, learning of the desperate situation of Jews in the occupied Sudetenland, developed a plan for rescuing Jewish children, negotiating with countries to accept them from Czechoslovakia.

He found that only Britain would cooperate. Immigration permits would be granted to Jewish children no older than 17 years with a sponsor or a foster family. In addition, fifty pounds had to be deposited for each child to cover travel expenses for a possible return home.

Winton directed his rescue operation from a hotel room in Prague, coordinating inquiries from desperate parents with his London office's efforts to find foster families and sponsors. Between March 14 and August 2, 1939, eight transport trains left Prague, bringing 669 children to England. In instances when departure documents were not completed on time, Winton issued forgeries. The Nazis tolerated his work at the time.

The last large transport was planned for September 1. The children sat on a train, but it never left because emigration was suddenly prohibited due to the outbreak of the war. To our knowledge, not one of those 250 survived. Nicholas Winton kept silent about his rescue operation for five decades (except for one occasion in the mid 1950s in an election campaign). The story came to public attention only in 1988, when Winton's wife found in their attic documents, including many children's photographs, letters of appeal and telegrams, which she gave to Dr. Elisabeth Maxwell, a researcher of the Holocaust and wife of newspaper magnate Robert Maxwell.[2] In February 1988, Dr. Maxwell published Winton's story in the *Sunday Mirror*, and that same night it featured on the BBC program *That's Life*, in which Winton was reunited with many of the "children" he had saved.[3]

Hanuš had written to me in the spring of 1987. A year or so later we met in Stockholm, and the story gradually unfolded. Hanuš was fourteen when, in May 1945, he read "Letter to My Child" in the newspaper *Dagens Nyheter*. At that time there was nothing he hoped for more than to see his beloved Maminka again. A few weeks later came a message from his father: "At home again best greetings father vilem weber. Datum 13/6/1945."[4]

A day later came another telegram: "Month at home send you both best greetings. Cable if news from ilse. Vilem Weber."[5] Gertrude von Löwenadler telegraphed back: "Received letter. Answered through legation. All well here, much love. Hanuš and Mormor."[6] Hanuš was confused. Why did Maminka not write? Where was she?

Three weeks later, Gertrude von Löwenadler received a letter from Willi Weber, dated July 1, 1945, in which he reported about the separation of the family in Theresienstadt and the stations in his odyssey through the concentration camps.

Dearest Aunt Gertrude,

Until September 44 Ilse, Tommy and I, with some relatives of mine, were still together in Theresienstadt. Ilse's life revolved around her profession as a children's nurse and she achieved a lot considering the conditions there. She was also extremely productive with her literary work, and her poems and songs have become with time the common property of thousands of people. (. . .)

We hoped to survive this terrible war in Theresienstadt, then in September last year the Germans ordered the [Jewish] ghetto administration to assemble 5,000 men aged 16 to 50, for "excavation work" in the area of Dresden.

I, who otherwise fought any transport by all available means, did nothing this time. (. . . .) Because they had promised those who went on the transport that their families would stay in Theresienstadt and that all of them would continue to have the possibility to write and receive replies.

How great was our surprise when on the second night of our journey (in cattle cars) we arrived at the extermination camp Oświęcim, Poland. Only on the next day did we find out details about this camp. In this camp, we were first robbed of all our things, put into rags that Gypsies would hardly wear today, and left for two days with no food. This was the German (bestial) system.

We also found out at the camp that a selection took place with

*each new transport. The old, the sick, women with children up to age
10 and 14 were lined up and killed in some German way. The usual
procedure was to send those "selected" persons to the gas chambers,
where they were relieved of their torment within half an hour. There
were however exceptions. Almost half of my transport, around 2,500
persons, perished.*

*I do not want this time to lose myself in details, since I assume you
are updated by newspapers, the radio, etc. It should suffice if I tell you
that in many, many years a person cannot experience so much horror
as in a few days in Oświęcim or other German concentration camps.*

*I grabbed at the first given opportunity and went with a few hun-
dred men as assistant metalworker to the Gleiwitz concentration camp.
The conditions there were even worse than in Oświęcim but, most importantly, there were no gas chambers and no crematoriums so that one
did not have to fear selections.*

*In Gleiwitz we worked daily with no exception for twelve hours
under extremely unfavorable and inhuman conditions, so that by mid-
January 1945, almost all of us were only wrecks (called 'Muselmen').*

*The Red Army liberated us—almost at the last moment—in
January 1945.*

*During the last months, I had one wish, that everyone who stayed
back in Theresienstadt was spared the transport to Oświęcim—but the
first familiar person I met in Prague, a nurse who had worked with
Ilse, took away my illusion and told me that after the departure of the
5,000 men, another 15,000 persons were sent away. Ilse was in one of
these transports.*

Willi spared his son descriptions of the horrors, leaving him
with an optimistic view of the future:

July 2 1945

My Dearest Big Boy!
*We often spoke with Mutti about you, and during our last con-
versation we agreed that should this terrible war finally once come to*

*an end and we would return safely home, our first journey would be
to you and Mormor. I hope that Mutti and Tommy will come soon to
Prague, and then we'll visit you to learn how and where you lived all
those years, and we'll make up for all the years that life has withheld
from us.*

*I can no longer imagine you. When you went away you were a boy
soooo little (you reached a little over my knee) and today . . . until we
meet again, will I not have to look up at you? I am already so curious!*

*First, I will have to be content with a detailed letter from you so
that I can at least make a mental picture of you. I am interested in everything that concerns you and Mormor. Are you both healthy? You do
not have any difficulties at school (aren't there already holidays?) and
there are no difficulties regarding your stay in Sweden? Hanuš, please
give Mormor a heartfelt kiss from me and be kissed many many times
by me and warmly greeted by your Vatti, Willi.*

The words of the nurse, who Willi had accidentally met among
the many uprooted in Prague, did not deter him from continuing the
search for his wife and younger son Tommy. "Ilse went to Auschwitz,"
the nurse had said. "I know that. The entire children's infirmary with
all its little patients was put in a deportation transport beginning of
October 1944. Ilse did not want to abandon them so she voluntarily
registered in order to accompany the sick children to Auschwitz."

Other survivors confirmed that wife and son had been "added to
a transport." Such meager information left room for the possibility
that Ilse and Tommy had survived and landed in one of the Allies' DP-Camps. And other voices claimed Ilse and Tommy had not
been transported. Surviving relatives appeared. Willi encountered
familiar faces. Ilse and Tommy were not among them.

Looking for an apartment posed no problem. Wilhelm Weber was
allocated a few rooms in a modern quarter of Prague, where German
occupiers had lived. Here he was able to offer the family a place to stay.

Meanwhile, in Stockholm, Hanuš prepared himself for seeing
his father. Frau von Löwenadler, the lovable so-called "Mormor"
(grandmother in Swedish), shared her foster son's joy and at the

same time was relieved. Hanuš was 14. His puberty had begun and high school exams had not yet taken place. In retrospect, Hanuš realized that, sad as Mormor was to let him go, she felt relieved from the responsibility.

Hanuš looked upon the journey back as an adventure; but eager as he was for Prague and family, he had to wait. Not until the autumn of 1945, three months after the first sign his father was alive, did the journey from Stockholm begin.

Once he had decided to stay in Czechoslovakia Willi had taken all measures to expedite his son's return. Hanuš arrived in Prague in mid-November. A few months later he recounted details of his return journey to his Uncle Oscar, who had immigrated to Palestine in 1933. In awkward German he wrote:

The journey to Prague was very slow. 16 days. First, we were on the way three days with the boat to Lübeck, and then we stayed one week in Lübeck itself, and 4 other days on the ship, and the rest of the days in a camp in Sweden.

The boat journey was the worst. I was not especially seasick; I puked only 3 times. The weather was very bad, and we had to lie in the middle of the sea because we did not want to come across a (possibly) German mine. It was fun in Lübeck; we had nothing to do, only to pick up food three times a day, and I went every day out to town and practiced my English with English soldiers. The journey with the train was nothing special either. There were in our wagon, which was one of the best, 22 people, 3 of them babies, luggage and bicycles. The train went very slowly; it was a long train of cattle wagons, and we had to sit and sleep on the floor, but we saw very well.

Around 30 people were lost during the journey because, when the train stopped, many got off and came back too late. At the first station 20 people got off and did not return on time. For that they might be stuck in Germany for at least ½ year. There was nothing warm to eat but I befriended the English escort and got hot tea. Nights were the worst, and the toilets, because there were none. Pigs were pure compared to us.

Re-united with his son, Willi Weber was torn between joy and horror. He described to the foster mother in Stockholm his first impression:

On Wednesday evening I turned on the radio and by coincidence heard the announcement that the train with the Swedish and Danish repatriates arrives in Prague on Thursday at 7 o'clock in the morning.

Thursday, early morning, I was on my way to the train station, which is on the outskirts of Prague. It took a few hours until the train came in. Yet even then we were not allowed to approach the train because it had been surrounded by police who proceeded to thoroughly examine the repatriates. Allegedly, former SS and SA men have arrived with the foreigners' transports lately, and the authorities tried to catch them at the first opportunity.

I nevertheless found a way to sneak closer to the train, saw from afar a few relatives who had reached Sweden via Theresienstadt and Germany, and who called for the boy for me.

If I want to be completely honest I must admit that I truly did not recognize Hanuš at first sight. I still lived in the time of 7 years ago where Hanuš set out into the world as a little boy with brown curls. Suddenly a big, straight young man with black hair stood before me, and he did not recognize me either. We examined each other, and slowly, slowly I found similarities with that earlier Hanuš . . .

We stayed silent during our ride with the streetcar as one does not dare to use the German language in public over here now.

Hanuš will have told you about his journey home. I must only emphasize that I was more than horrified when the people arrived here in cattle cars. Coming home, Hanuš had to first get into the bathtub, and thereby the chapter of journeying found its conclusion (. . .) It is just so terrible that Ilse could no longer experience this moment. During the last years she had lived solely for that moment when she could be re-united with the boy again. And how exceedingly happy she would have been to see him again just as he is . . .

Ilse's prediction "to suddenly have a grown-up son" had been experienced by Willi. And another prophecy from "Letter to My Child" had materialized: "Imagine when we meet some day, / you won't understand a word I say." Hanuš had forgotten his Czech and his German was poor.

Little by little, people from Hanuš' childhood reappeared. Some he remembered personally, others he recognized from childhood photographs. One of Willi Weber's eight siblings had escaped to England immediately after the occupation. Two brothers, together with their families, were murdered in the concentration camps. Two others, like Willi, had survived the camps and three had served in the Czech army in exile. As for Ilse's family, her mother and two half-sisters, Herta and Mutzi (Bettina), were murdered in the camps. Her two brothers, Oscar and Ernst, survived the war as soldiers: Ernst had fled to Poland directly after German troops invaded Czechoslovakia. He joined the Czech Exile Army, and fought in Poland, France, the Soviet Union, Africa and the Middle East. Oscar, who immigrated to Palestine in 1933, served in the Royal Air Force in Northern Africa.

The returnees were drawn to the center of Prague on Revoluční Street. This daily meeting point was not only frequented by family members, but also by leading communists, who knew the returnees from the Soviet Union. Heated debates ensued. All faced the problem of building a new existence in Czechoslovakia or having to prepare for a new exodus. Despite painful injuries, Willi Weber, half a year after the war's end, was still spending most of his time searching for his wife and younger son. In early 1946 the spinal injuries from whippings in Auschwitz were treated surgically. He survived the complicated operation but only regained mobility after several months of rehabilitation. By mid 1946 he was supporting himself and Hanuš by selling American cigarettes that his brother Max sent him from England.

Hanuš, struggling with grave language problems, could discuss with his father nothing that expressed, even remotely, the emotions that troubled them both in different ways. The father may have perceived this situation as oppressive, while Hanuš, as he acknowledges in retrospect, was happy that the silence kept the horror in abeyance.

After more than a year of private Czech lessons, Hanuš was admitted to high school. With the language hurdle halfway overcome, he and Willi expressed renewed hope for the return of Ilse and Tommy. About their experiences after 1939, they remained silent.

Willi Weber asked every survivor from Auschwitz he met about the fate of his wife and child. An acquaintance from their hometown who had carried bodies to the crematoriums denied having seen the two. Yet statements of other former inmates left no more doubt. At the end of 1946, Willi Weber decided to have Ilse and Tommy pronounced dead. The official declaration of death issued by the Civil District Court in Prague, dated January 9, 1947, stated: "Elsa Weber, born Herlinger, born in Vítkovice as daughter to the parents Moritz and Theresia Herlinger on January 11, 1903, Jewish religion, as a result of racial persecution, went missing on 4.10.1944, at that time she was deported from Terezin (Theresienstadt) to Auschwitz, and was in direct life-threatening situation." The death declaration of Tomáš Weber repeated the formula.

After he had to abandon all hope, Willi Weber tried to talk about the events and horror of the camp; but the son refused to listen.

Yet Hanuš recollects fragments from his father's stories. Willi told him that when she made her decision to go, Ilse was aware of the transport's destination. In late 1943 a man had surfaced at the camp with terrible news. This prisoner, wearing an SS officer uniform, had escaped from Auschwitz and smuggled himself into Theresienstadt. He told the Jewish council of elders about the unprecedented crimes he had witnessed. No one wanted to believe Vítězslav Lederer, the "bearer of bad tidings."

Willi Weber, working at the outer perimeters of the camp, close to the rampart, suspected that Lederer told the truth. On the day of his transport he pleaded with his wife to "under no circumstances" volunteer for any transport. She promised.

Ilse Weber's Theresienstadt songs and poems were concealed by Willi when he received his transport order in September 1944. He revealed to his son the hazardous circumstances of this self-imposed "task," and recalled the dreadful moment when he found his name on the list of five thousand men destined for transport to the east, allegedly, according to the SS, a work contingent for Eastern Germany.

In the little time left, Willi filled an old sack with poems and songs that his wife had composed in the camp, as well as several drawings.[7] He then dug a hole in the ground in one of the farthest tool sheds to which he had access as a camp gardener. He buried the bundle in and covered it with a layer of clay so that the hiding place would not look suspicious. Two or three days later the transport left, and, after a seemingly endless train ride in cattle cars, arrived at a camp that, ironically, bore the name of the hometown of Willi's ancestors: Oświęcim.

Hanuš learned about the cruel, emaciating labor in Auschwitz and Gleiwitz, that the father, reduced to a skeleton by malnutrition, survived. Willi's story of liberation and home-coming seemed a fantasy. As the Red Army approached Gleiwitz, the SS sent the prisoners on a death march towards the German border. The gravely ill Willi had no chance of survival; whoever could not drag himself further was shot and thrown in a ditch. A family friend, the young physician Dr. Jindřich Flusser, a fellow prisoner, concealed the exhausted, pain-wracked Willi under a pile of rotten potatoes. Willi crawled out of the stinking pile only when he could no longer hear any human sound. In the empty camp were hundreds of corpses. During his lonely escape Willi lived on field crops and food that he found in the ghost towns the Wehrmacht had left in haste. His one objective was to regain the strength to return to Theresienstadt, to reunite with his wife and son. For weeks he wandered through woods in the border area between Poland and Slovakia, unaware of his exact location, dreading the Wehrmacht's appearance.

One morning he heard voices close by: men who spoke Czech. Leaving his hiding place, Willi encountered members of a Czech Army company. When a sergeant asked for his name, it turned out that fate had brought him to his brother Sigmund, an officer in that

unit. Present also were his sister Emily and her children, Felix, a lieu-
tenant in the army corps, and his sister Ruth, whose husband, Otto
Heller, a high officer in the "Svoboda-Army"[8] had served against the
Germans on the Russian front. Willi Weber joined the soldiers and
arrived with them on May 14 to liberated Prague.

Willi asked Major Heller to accompany him to Theresienstadt,
at the time ravaged by a typhus epidemic. With the quarantine cir-
cumvented by the Major's uniform, Willi entered the camp. None
of those he addressed had news of his wife and son.

Willi returned to the shed where he had buried his wife's songs
and poems. In light of the camp's horrifying condition, he feared
that the Russian liberators would burn it. He recovered the precious
sack, and so Ilse Weber's Theresienstadt heritage was smuggled out
beneath Major Heller's uniform.

Repeatedly, Willi Weber returned to Theresienstadt for annual
commemorations. Important as the visits were for his father, Hanuš
increasingly dreaded them as he sought to avoid confronting the
unspeakable past.

During those early post-war years Willi and Hanuš were sent
verses of Ilse's, some of which were not part of the trove Willi
concealed. Some, who had survived the camps, described in their
letters how Ilse Weber's poems had helped them keep their will
to live.

One of these poems was triggered by a retaliatory reaction on
the part of the terror masters. On May 27, 1942, following the assassination of Reinhard Heydrich, the head of the RSHA and the
"Reich Protector of Bohemia and Moravia," the entire Czech village
of Lidice[9] was liquidated: the men shot, the women were taken to
concentration camps; the children were deported to Łódź, a handful
were selected to be "Germanized" (because of their "Aryan" appearance), and the rest sent to Chełmno and gassed. To the victims, Ilse
Weber dedicated a poem, "The Sheep from Lidice," in which she
called the massacre by name.[10]

According to Jiří Lauscher, who was in Theresienstadt at the time, Ilse's Lidice poem, smuggled out of the camp, brought Gestapo interrogations aimed at identifying the author. None of the prisoners identified Ilse and the refusal to denounce one of their own, despite threats and torture, heartened the prisoners.

The poems were as important to the prisoners as the scarce daily bread. Ilse, working in Theresienstadt as a children's nurse, was often asked to recite her poems. Judith Flusser, who as young Judith Birn had been Hanuš' nanny, wrote many verses from memory after her liberation. Even today, 85 years old, she knows more than a dozen by heart.

Other prisoners from Theresienstadt attended recitations that often featured Ilse's poems. The *Freizeitgestaltung*[11] was a Theresienstadt initiative which enabled the prisoners to communicate with their fellow sufferers through the arts. After a merciless day of work they could attend musical performances, lectures and recitations.

Later, Ilse Weber's poems helped many to find their way in their new lives, while somehow recollecting and facing the horrors they had experienced. Years later Willi Weber continued to receive letters from survivors, telling about the effects the poems had on them. To some of the letters, the senders attached those verses that had comforted them in the camp and during later trials. One of these poems that was translated back from its Czech version into its original German is,

The Hills

So near, as if a barrier
blocks the way to town,
the chain of hills is stretching
mutely watching
the ghetto's need and sorrow,
coffins and death's harvest
the transport's gloomy round dance.

In the summer the summits wore green garments
and shadows hovered over the slopes,
now they glitter in the snow and sun scald.
When I'm walking the narrow streets here,
I turn my glance toward them,
in the dread of the world around me
preserving myself a little fleeting bliss.

From these hills I would look down,
until the ghetto walls founder in rubble,
then with the world's light I will beacon my blessing.
I will again stride toward a goal,
high above me heaven's splendor,
Oh fully aware of the bliss that calls on us, the freedom,
which hateful violence has long ago killed in us.

My hand tears the yellow star from my chest.
My Jewishness needs no badge,
I am already scarred with centuries-long agony,
I am free!

Despite his relatives' gloomy prophecies, Willi Weber gradually began to believe in a future in Czechoslovakia for him and his son. Income from employment at the Israeli embassy provided for the two of them. This position ended in 1967 when the "Six-Day War" terminated diplomatic relations between Israel and Czechoslovakia.

Hanuš, who admits to not having been a diligent student, still made the effort to complete high school. In addition, he pursued piano lessons provided by two famous pianists: Edith Steiner-Krauss and Alice Herz-Sommer, whose performances had often consoled their fellow prisoners at Theresienstadt. Hanuš' keyboard career ended when Edith Steiner-Krauss and, a little later, Alice Herz-Sommer, immigrated to Israel.

The year 1948 brought the liberated "home comers" a scary

vision. Antisemitism, by no means in remission, became virulent after the communist takeover of Czechoslovakia. In an autobiographical outline, Hanuš notes: "our pessimists were right and the Communists gained the upper hand. The biggest part of the Weber family came to the obvious conclusions and left Prague for England, France or the USA."

Unlike most of his relatives, Willi Weber stayed with his son in Prague. "Vati and I are good friends," Hanuš wrote in 1950 to his uncle Oscar in Israel. However, as well as they understood each other, silence continued to cover the parents' time at the concentration camps. To finish his exams, have friends, take up an interesting job: these were young Hanuš' goals. In 1951, he completed high school and soon after became involved in political adventures that would qualify him for his future job in TV news.

Through his knowledge of languages and accidental acquaintances, Hanuš became a member of the Socialist Youth Organization.[12] Promoted to the international department of the Organization's central committee, he met, as he later wrote, that "young Swedish student leader whom later on I'd continue to meet owing to the course of my career, the future Swedish Prime Minister, Olof Palme." His acquaintances at the time also included Erich Honecker, chairman of the Free German Youth and later the Chairman of the State Council of the German Democratic Republic, Alexander Scheljepin, Secretary-General of the Komsomol and later head of the KGB in the Soviet Union, as well as a number of other future significant communist leaders.

After two years of blue-collar employment, Hanuš applied for political studies at Prague University. His application was rejected and he was sent for two years of army service. This luckily shielded him from reprisal and prosecution when an intensive antisemitism campaign broke out, reaching its height with the Stalinist-style Slánský show trial. Hanuš, although a close friend of the son of the later executed Rudolf Slánský, was protected in the army.

Hanuš noted in his diary[13] "I came back to Prague as a three times demoted soldier and, after a short period as penicillin producer, I started at the Swedish desk of Radio Prague. I was an absolute exception among the editors, who were all party members; but they didn't know Swedish and so Sweden not only saved my life but also gave me my career."

Beginning in 1955, Hanuš worked for the Czech broadcasting service. Although a media person, he was allowed to leave the territory of the ČSSR[14] only for travelling to Poland, GDR and the Soviet Union. As he did not belong to the communist party, he was considered "politically unreliable." It wasn't until 1961 that he received permission to travel to the West, as a functionary of the Czechoslovakian Ice Hockey Association, to the world championship in Switzerland. By 1963, his travels had taken him back to Sweden. Four years earlier, in 1959, when Jaroslav Heyrovský, a Czech chemist, received the Nobel Prize, the Swedish media had employed Hanuš, as the only Swedish-speaking Czech in Prague. Their cooperation soon extended to sports reporting and, from 1967–1968, to politics (the Prague Spring). From 1967 onward, he worked for Sveriges, the Swedish national public radio and television broadcaster.[15] At the same time, Hanuš invested a great deal of time helping to prepare for the "Prague Spring." As a correspondent for the *Expressen*,[16] he had many opportunities to place reports in the West. As translator for the president and first party secretary Antonin Novotný, Hanuš had little to fear. By the second half of the 1960s, as the political thaw in the ČSSR began, Willi Weber and Hanuš had begun looking more confidentially toward the future until, as Hanuš ironically noted, "in August 1968 our Russian 'friends' invaded in order to help us."

The week after the Soviet invasion, Hanuš left the country illegally, escaping through Austria to Sweden. His speeches there against the Russian occupation brought an invitation to return to the ČSSR. Alexander Dubček asked him and other expatriate journalists to support further the democratization in threatened Czechoslovakia. Hanuš, despite warnings, followed the call and went back. From the end of 1968, Hanuš was back at his desk at Swedish Media in Prague. Dubček had been unable to deliver on his promise of democratization and, in April 1969, was forced to resign. The day before the Iron Curtain descended over the land, banning citizens from leaving, Hanuš and his Swedish wife left Czechoslovakia. Hanuš built a new existence in Sweden as a television journalist.

In 1973, Hanuš asked his father for further details about his experience in the concentration camp. After three decades, he was prepared to hear about the events that took place in the years between his departure from Prague in 1939 and his return in 1945. Denial of his parents' history ended when Hanuš began to work on a film about the culture of the concentration camps. He would show this television film to Willi on his next visit to Sweden, planned for summer 1974.

Hanuš carefully prepared an interview during which he would probe his father for details of his camp experience. A camera team of the Swedish television stood by. Hanuš was waiting at Arlanda airport in Stockholm for his father's arrival when a call from the Copenhagen airport informed him that shortly before changing to his flight to Stockholm, Willi Weber suffered a heart attack and died. The opportunity to discover details of his parents' time in Theresienstadt seemed to have been lost forever. Then, almost three years later, a man he hardly remembered resurfaced in Hanuš' life: James Treen, the widowed husband of Ilse's friend Lilian. Mr. Treen, planning to remarry, was clearing out his London house preparatory to moving. In the attic he had found a box of letters from Ilse to Lilian. He asked Hanuš' advice. Hanuš asked him to bring the correspondence on his next visit to Sweden.

Sooner than expected, on January 4, 1977, as Hanuš and his wife Eva celebrated the birth of their son, Tommy, James Treen arrived with a trunk full of Ilse's letters to Lilian, dated from 1933 to 1944. Hanuš left the letters in the trunk, unread, fearful of the darkness of those years.

A dozen years passed. In 1989, Hanuš' uncle in Israel asked

him to write his life story. Ilse's brother, Oscar Mareni,[17] intended to assemble the Herlinger family chronicle in order to preserve the origins and fates of the individual family members for those who survived and for future generations. Only then did Hanuš begin to immerse himself in the world of Ilse's childhood and youth.

The story of his mother began in Vítkovice, which was a significant border town in the region of Bohemia and Moravia until it was incorporated as a neighborhood of Ostrava (formerly Mährisch-Ostrau) in 1924. Today Vítkovice is a district of Ostrava.

Before Czechoslovakia's birth in 1918, the regions of Bohemia and Moravia were provinces of the Austro-Hungarian Empire. Ostrava was multilingual. Czechs, Poles, Germans, Gypsies and Jews lived in relative harmony.

The Rothschild family had developed the Vítkovice Iron Works into central Europe's biggest mining and iron works enterprise. Toward the end of the 19th century, the construction of a railway line from Vienna to Poland and further into Russia led to a rapid development of the town. Members of the Herlinger family held influential positions in the municipal administration and contributed substantially to the development of the cultural life of Vítkovice.

A typical industrial town, Vítkovice possessed exemplary facilities: "The asphalt streets, the gas, the electricity, the hospital, the big Peter-and-Paul Church, the cloister, the kindergarten, the schools, day-care center, as well as an asylum for old people, etc., have all been financed by the Iron Works."[18]

As a Rothschild enterprise, the company was controlled by Jewish directors and Jews occupied work categories from day laborers to engineers. "The Ironworks surveyed everything; its administration knew everything and looked after everything." Therefore, it is not surprising that the Jews, in fact especially the German speaking Jews, set the social and cultural "tone" in Vítkovice.

In the days of the Habsburg Empire, each national group in each region led a separate cultural life: "Czechs, Poles and Germans lived more next to each other than with each other," as Oscar Mareni notes in his family history. The Germans had their own town theater and later their theater at the German house, the Czechs in turn had their theater in the *Český dům* and in the *Národní dům*, while the Poles saw the *Dom Polski* as their social and cultural center. The Jews were involved mainly with the German cultural events "that would not have existed without them."

Ilse Herlinger was born on January 11, 1903 into this climate of cultural demarcation and intellectual-artistic riches of Jewish-German theater and music. Oscar remembered that already as a child Ilse spent many hours reading. It was also from Oscar that Hanuš learned that Ilse had been only ten years old when her father, in financial difficulties and hoping to salvage his family's material situation, committed suicide. Following this, Ilse and her two brothers, Oscar and Ernst, helped their mother to run the tavern she had leased. With books as her refuge, Ilse devoured literature and immersed herself into two language worlds. Attending a German girls' school, she considered German her mother tongue, but also mastered Czech.

Young Ilse loved fairy tales and, as a teenager, devoted herself increasingly to typical young girls' literature. With her brothers, she read the weekly-published installments of *Princess High Spirits* and the monthly magazine *Das Kränzchen*[19] to which she subscribed.

When Ilse was thirteen, she put an ad in *Das Kränzchen* seeking pen pals. She received a number of answers and established a correspondence network. From the very beginning, Ilse felt a spiritual kinship with one correspondent, a young Scandinavian, Lilian von Löwenadler, whose father served at the time as Swedish consul in Hamburg. Both had been born in 1903. A lively correspondence ensued.

Ilse began to write poems and poetical stories and they were first published on the pages of the *Kränzchen*. She also wrote little plays for children that were produced and published, and translated Czech poems into German, as well as German poems and songs into

Czech. They were aired by the local broadcasting services, first in Ostrava and later in Prague.

Ilse's library became so extensive that the family's bookcase could no longer contain it, so Ilse stuffed books in the family's linen cupboard and in a glass case in which her grandfather had exhibited his products at the world exhibition in Paris.

When a call for Ilse was left unanswered, her family knew she would be immersed in a book. As Oscar put it in his family chronicle, "Mama muttered in such cases: 'Ilse prays again to her holy bookcase!'"

Oscar recollects that Ilse became dangerous when she decided that the furniture had to be taken outside and dusted thoroughly. The furniture was dragged down into the yard and Ilse, without asking the help of a maid, but decorated picturesquely with a headscarf, began her work. So far so good! However, as soon as she took a break from her work, everything was over and the "catastrophe" started. She sat on the plush armchair that had been brought outside and started to read a book—and the *Erbrichterei*,[20] the world, the cleaning and everything connected, was forgotten! In the end, all the furniture had to be dragged again upstairs after it had been cleaned hastily.

Ilse beamed with vivacity and was extraordinarily generous. Oscar remembered how every year a group of Gypsies set up their winter camp in the large garden that belonged to the Herlingers' inn. In the spring of 1917, shortly before the family had to move on, a young woman died during childbirth despite the efforts of the house physician who had been called there. The barely fourteen-year-old Ilse, who had just completed a course for child-care, promised the widower to care for the newborn. Upon his return after a year, the overjoyed father took the healthy one-year-old in his arms. As token of his gratitude, he presented Ilse with a balalaika. Since Gypsies were generally despised as common criminals at the time, the Herlingers showed extraordinary courage in accommodating them and taking one of their children into their family.

Ilse Weber in the *Erbrichterei*, 1927

Ilse's spirit of enterprise was proverbial. In his report on the Erbrichterei or *Fojtstvi*,[21] the Czech name for the house the Herlingers lived in for generations, Oscar Mareni sums up: "Ilse was always full of ideas."

When Ilse was seventeen she arranged a trip to Italy for a group of young people. In a very short period she learned Italian in a Berlitz course, imparting it to the young tourists who, full with admiration for her linguistic talents, willingly paid for their lessons. In this way Ilse financed her trip. Overcoming bureaucratic hurdles, she exhibited astonishing organizational skills.

With the same method, she learned to play an instrument by teaching others to play. On the day after each guitar lesson, she passed on her newly acquired skills to students for a fee. In this way Ilse mastered the guitar and the mandolin, astonishing her friends with her musical skills.

At mask balls, wrapped with texts as "newspaper," or singing, accompanied by a concertina, she solicited contributions for the Jewish National Fund, acknowledging donations with spontaneous verses.

Around this time, as her brother recalls, "which must have been at the time of the *Kapp-Putsch*"[22] Ilse travelled to Hamburg in order to "finally meet there her long time pen pal from the *Kränzchen*."

Lilian von Löwenadler became Ilse's best friend. She visited the Herlingers repeatedly for weeks at a time and, according to Ilse's brother Oscar, "was already regarded by us a family member."

Oscar and Ilse were "good comrades." He often chaperoned her with her suitors, often admirers with academic degrees. He also accompanied her to gymnastics at the Maccabi Club and on her lengthy bicycle tours in the Vítkovice area. Afternoons they sang, with Ilse playing "the piano, the guitar, the lute, the mandolin, the balalaika or the concertina—depending on her mood." She played classical music and operettas, and passages out of anthologies titled *Musical Gems*. A big part of this collection belonged to Ilse's mother, who had been trained as a singer at the Vienna conservatorium, but later abandoned her career to start a family.

Still a teenager, Ilse, with her circle of companions, discussed a broad variety of topics. They would argue for hours on Strindberg and Shaw, socialism, communism and other themes. Oscar recalled the idealistic enthusiasm the group devoted to big goals. "It was after the First World War and therefore plans were forged how to ensure eternal peace and create paradise on earth."

Inspired by these meetings, Ilse initiated a sort of a cultural club for which she had high educational goals. Together with her friends, she founded the *G.I.F.T*[23]: Spirit, Intelligence, Friendship and Loyalty. Its goal was to familiarize members with modern music and literature, each member contributing according to his possibilities and abilities.

The basis for literary discussions was a newspaper, *Die Fackel*,[24] published by the language and culture critic Karl Krauss.

Presiding over G.I.F.T with Ilse were Alfred Wechsler, and a young man named Neugeboren. After he finished high-school, Alfred Wechsler worked as a miner in order to disseminate communist ideas below ground. He later became a journalist and editor of *Die Rote Fahne*[25] in Berlin. By the time of Hitler's takeover, he had already become disillusioned with communism and immigrated to Palestine, where he died young. Neugeboren's uncompromising Strindbergian philosophy led him, as the jazzy 1920s decade frittered away, to shoot himself on the grave of Heinrich Heine in the Montmartre cemetery in Paris.

While collecting a remarkable library, the focus of the group was musical and literary events; but in the social climate of growing antisemitism, they increasingly turned to heated political debate.

The Jewish youth in Ostrava was divided into two political camps: one was convinced that a socialist revolution would defeat antisemitism; the other saw salvation in Zionism. As Communist Party officials after WWII, some former G.I.F.T. members played important roles in socialist Czechoslovakia. Many of them were executed in the aftermath of the Slánský affair.

Ilse did not regard herself an activist. She distanced herself from heated debate, from political or religious zeal. Her elderly brother (in 2007 he celebrated his 100th birthday[26]) spoke in retrospect of Ilse's moderate engagement in several areas. Oscar remembered that in her early twenties she had been the vice president of the International Women's League for Peace and Freedom after having, as a teenager, led a Zionist girls' circle, a gymnastics group that also met once a week for talks.

From an early age Ilse was familiar with the issues of religious life. Her mother took her often "to the temple" as it was called by the family. The adolescent Ilse observed with great interest how the children related to what they saw and heard during the services. Inspired by the aura of the Shabbat services, Ilse wrote stories. Her *Jüdische Kindermärchen* (Jewish Children's Tales), published in 1928 by the Dr. Robert Färber publishing company in Mährisch-Ostrau, dedicated to her mother, was praised as an enrichment of Jewish children's literature.

"These tales turned out really Jewish" wrote *Die Wahrheit*[27] in Vienna. "The tone of the tales certainly strikes as a special Jewish tale." "Knowledge of Judaism, love for Judaism as well as Palestine, with the affective art, tone and mysterious atmosphere of old folktales," was the judgment of the *Jüdische Zeitung*[28] from Breslau. The monthly journal of B'nai Brith recommended the book to all parents, Jewish schools and youth associations, and declared it well suited for "educational transmission of moral values." The *Mährisch-Ostrauer Morgenzeitung*[29] referred to the "deeply experienced ethic" conveyed by the tales, and then emphasized "the poetic form the authoress gives [the tales] elevates them from being simple stories with ethical intentions to highly enjoyable artworks for mature people." To the *Selbstwehr*[30] of Prague, the tales were " . . . A collection of wonderfully simple stories with crystal clear lyric" in which the child is led sensitively and emphatically through all human and Jewish spheres of experience. "The contrast between egoism and altruism, good and evil, rise and fall, courage and despair, is presented with simple explanations, and not once is the educational strength of the book doubtful, it consistently leads the child to choose the beautiful and the good. I see this book as a reminder to all the Jewish parents: take me and put me in your child's hand, you will be giving him a key to himself, assisting the growth and the inner peace of his character," stated the *Jüdische Pressezentrale Zürich* (Jewish Press Central Zürich).

The book moved into many Jewish houses and saw numerous editions. The same applied to another book, *Das Trittroller-Wettrennen* (The Scooter Race), that appeared in many new editions until 1930. Ilse Weber's third children's book, titled *Mendel Rosenbusch*, published in 1929 and "dedicated to my little friends Bubi, Hans and Gyuszi," also was a big success. The storyline was once again deeply embedded in the customs and values of Jewish religion and tradition, weaving them, in child-friendly language, into tales of a magical, wise old man.

At the age of 26, Ilse Weber could look back on three published children's books, a whole series of audio plays for the radio, and numerous publications of poems and articles in newspapers and magazines. However, her mother was worried about the personal happiness of her 26-year-old daughter, for whom there was no groom in sight.

Oscar Mareni describes the mother-daughter dialogue on the day Ilse announced she had decided to marry.

"Who is it, lawyer A or doctor B?" The mother asked.

"Neither the one nor the other. I will marry Willi Weber!"

Whereupon the mother's answer followed promptly: "Does Willi Weber know about this?"

Ilse answered: "Actually no. But I will tell him, it's a promise."

She kept her promise, the groom-to-be had no objections to the plan, and the wedding took place in 1930. The previous year, ill with malaria, Willi had returned to Czechoslovakia from Palestine. He had worked for nine years in a kibbutz, committed to Zionism. Declining opportunities to study law or to take over his father's restaurant, he trained as a farmer and gardener in order to be as useful as possible in the development of Palestine.

Ilse and Willi knew each other from childhood. Willi was born in Ostrava in 1901. While Ilse's family had lived in Moravia for hundreds of years, Willi's parents originated from the Polish town of Oświęcim (Auschwitz). At the end of the 19th century they had moved to Ostrava where Willi's father opened a kosher restaurant. Willi and his eight siblings all became skillful cooks, much to Ilse's satisfaction as a wife not too interested in cooking.

The two were reunited after Willi's return to Czechoslovakia. He had returned literarily empty-handed, while Ilse had become a respected authoress. When they married, Willi opened a small collection agency. His business flourished until the Germans invaded northern Czechoslovakia. (Sudetenland, as they called it—a gift by England and France at Munich). The resulting loss of a large share of its original market threatened the viability of Willi's company.

Ilse had become, as she noted, not without irony, a "quite normal housewife," who found her literary ambition to write a big novel buried under domestic "slavery." Her first son Hanuš was born on New Year's night in 1931. His brother Tommy, named after the first president of the Czech Republic, Tomáš Masaryk, arrived in 1934.

Hanuš Weber has often been asked how he remembers his mother. He resignedly admits to recalling just a few isolated pictures. He finds it impossible to distinguish between his own impressions and what issued from his mother's pen, or the stories of friends and relatives. Through her letters however, he knows more about her than most children do about their parents. And the letters to Lilian tell him even more. They give insight into a microcosm of terror. Ilse described precisely how antisemitism poisoned people's lives. The threat of the National Socialist regime was also the dominant theme of the letters that Ilse exchanged with the eminent writer Karel Čapek until his untimely death in 1938. The entire correspondence has been lost but, according to Willi Weber's recollection, they focused on Hitler's verbal attacks against Czechoslovakia and its leading politicians.

Hanuš reconstructs Ilse's life from her letters, poems, stories and notes. The earliest note was a questionnaire in a pack of yellowing notes written with thin pencil in Sütterlin script, which Hanuš could not decipher. It was in papers his father had given him that had remained untouched for years, remnants of the Herlingers' property, saved by a friend from Ostrava.

The questionnaire was prepared for subscribers of the *Kränzchen* magazine and sixteen-year-old Ilse filled it in carefully. Her entries convey her approach to life, her inclinations and wishes, as a teenager.

Motto:
"Who trusts in God has a strong abode."[31]
Highest wish: to be able to write poetry! And unity in the family.
Favorite poets, writers or composers:
Schiller, Paul Keller,[32] Schubert, Heine.
Favorite flowers: violet, myrtle.
Favorite dish:
Bread and butter or bread with goose liver and hashed gooseneck.
Little passion: children.
Big antipathy: against falsehood and liars.
Favorite book: *Das Letzte Märchen* by Paul Keller.[33]

Favorite poem: "Die Glocke" and "Frau Sorge" by Suder-
mann.[34]
Favorite color: blue, white, red.
Favorite drink: water.
Favorite occupation: write letters, stories and poems.

When Isle Herlinger wrote this, she had already written a number of romantic nature poems that were later published in *Kränzchen*
and other magazines. A few of the manuscripts resurfaced after the
war in a small binder that, along with 90 neckties, constituted the
only remnants of the entire Herlinger household. They were restored to Willi and Hanuš by a friend from Ostrava.

A questionnaire sixteen-year-old Ilse filled for subscribing
to the *Kränzchen* magazine.

Spring

Frau Sunshine casts a golden web,
and it bedazzles every view,
the world a heavenly bunch of flowers
blossoming anew.

Go then, misgiving, suffering, pain,
you should disappear
as the thick snow melts
when spring is here.
The world is brimming with delight,
the world will give us all,
we are still young and full of life
why would we think of fall?

Sun!

Night fades,
the sun lofty and golden,
rises, illuminates:
the door of heaven.

All glows with light,
shadows depart,
if clouds draw near,
take courage, heart.

Joy's hour is now,
put by concern,
the hour past
will not return.

When the Evening Comes

So beautiful going through a spacious field,
the evening's silence, accompaniment of a harp.
The wind's cozy, crazy prowl
letting loose a tremulous chord.

I'm at the edge, eavesdropping, subdued.
How softly the cricket chirps his ditty.
And the sweet richness of a nightingale's song,
implores and woos from under a nearby bush.

Oh blessed to get used to this sky,
Oh magic of this great solitude
that all our earthly pain occludes!
So beautiful going through a spacious field!

Eveningsmood

In soft twilight, the last of day fades.
Up on the hill, a gray haze clings.
Along the hedge race rapacious shades,
and night unfolds its broad wings.

Through dark clouds knifes a last beam,
the wind strikes harshly through the tall reeds.
Deep in the valley a hidden stream
sings sweet lullabies.

Still the Days Are Full of Light

Still the days are full of light,
not yet the heavy-hanging blight.
But the fog's smothering gray,
lurking in forest and field,
brings to this sundrenched weald
a gloomy prophecy.

Are late sunflowers, various
asters multifarious,
all that summers do?
Never the world so bright,
the sun such mild delight,
and never sky so blue.

Yet in this radiant, rainbow place,
too much will not suffice,
is not enough for my greedy eye.
Alarm invades heart's veins.
Such splendor beauty only attains,
just before it goes away.

Late Summer

A field, riot of color, nature's loom,
a thousand flowers aglow, in bloom,
aloft, sparrow song, heavenly guide.
What joy to stride a narrow line,
ripened corn waving on either side,
cheeks warm in bountiful summer sunshine!

Then reapers pass through the field,
and step by fatal step they wield
the sharp-edged curving scythe, and slash
the standing corn, each flower stem's crown
cut off, its radiance a trash
of blossom as the sun goes down.

Twilight

Upon a field twilight's feathered
    pinions brood.
Beyond, silent stance of dark walls
    of distant wood.

Bells chime through the air, the herds turn
    toward their home.
Intoxicating fragrance wafts
    from the tilled loam.

I stride into the sunset, dreaming,
    near unseeing;
feeling every color, a soft
    tingle shakes my being.

The Sun Already Sleeps

The shepherd comes home
from pasture with the sheep,
and behind the distant hills
the sun has already gone to sleep.

The mother protects
the chick asleep in the nest,
till the golden day-break
wakes it to happiness.

A brook ripples softly,
languorous through the night,
its long journey
has taught it not to halt.

It murmurs to me a lullaby,
murmurs all is well,
I sit on its bank
listening, in its spell.

Autumn

Pitilessly the scythes slash
           through the golden wheat,
soon the wind will be roaring
           over empty fields.

How long yet, before the leaves
           fall down to the ground,
how long before the melodies
           will be gone?

With a pale mouth the sun kisses
          forest and lea,
how long still, and everything
          will disappear . . .

In The Pustevna[35]

Trees on the hill,
their many branches declare
a silent cathedral,
hovering in air.

A thousand crystals shimmer,
candles of sparkling ice,
flakes fall aglimmer,
slow, faint, precise.

Let adoration reign,
sky bows to Earth's dim allure,
so faith once again
is festive and pure.

Wintermood in the Mountains

Trees silently pray!
Gently you must tread
in this sanctuary,
humbly, uttering no word.

White branches
dispel any hint of scorn,
in deep silence,
our God reborn.

A number of children's poems, included in the letters to Lilian, were found in the trunk that Lilian's husband brought to Stockholm.

Toward the end, it appears, not all the letters to Lilian were received, some intercepted by the German censorship, others allowed through after passages had been blackened.

With her frequent letters to Hanuš, Ilse sought to help him retain his mother tongue. In the first weeks after his departure, she wrote almost daily, never failing to encourage him to answer quickly and in detail. First in multi-page notebooks, then big writing paper, the young boy had to report in detail about all his experiences. Despite the high number of letters received from Ilse, Hanuš' willingness to write in detail eroded more and more.

Reading these letters pains Hanuš: "Although after five decades as a journalist I have little time for sentimental feelings, I want to cry when I read Ilse's letters with all the questions that I never answered, and her hidden reproaches for my pathetic and unimaginative writing style. Ilse could not know at the time that my old principal's fear came true. My Czech had practically disappeared, while my Swedish was perfect." The many exhortations irritated the child who naturally did not read between the lines the longing and despair that gave rise to Ilse's breathless questions and pleas.

An abyss opened when Lilian left nine-year-old Hanuš, as well as her own children, in Sweden in order to return alone to her husband in England. What Ilse experienced as a deep shock seemed to Hanuš as a relatively minor change in his young life.

Lilian had planned to spend the summer in Sweden with her daughter and foster-son, Hanuš, until after the birth of her second child, but in 1939, with Sweden's storms commencing early and ferocious, she postponed her return to England. A flight to London with a stopover in Oslo was booked for April 10, 1940 for her, her children and Hanuš. However, the Wehrmacht's raids on Norway on April 9 foiled the journey. Ignoring warnings, Lilian boarded alone a ship destined for Great Britain. The children remained with her mother in Sweden while, her ship dodging German submarines, Lilian spent nearly six months at sea, anchoring at the USA, Africa, the Soviet Union and Portugal.

In England, Lilian joined a volunteer organization for national defense. After a short training, she began her service as an air observer. Her health was compromised by her strenuous sea voyage, and ice cold nights at the watch tower brought on a dangerous pleurisy which, after an operation, led to her early death. A photograph of her in uniform, sent through Stockholm to Prague, was her last greeting to Ilse, a greeting that, for whatever reason, was not intercepted by the censorship. Ilse's oldest friend, the person who had promised to look after her son, was gone. Ilse's fear for Hanuš' wellbeing subsided only after Lilian's mother took the boy in.

Ilse's "dearest Hannerle" coped well with the change. Much better than she had thought possible. From an unheated little house in the fishermen's village of Steninge and a daily six kilometers walk to school, he had moved to Frau von Löwenadler's warm city apartment. Ilse now wrote to "dear Aunt Gertrude" and, almost every day, to her "dearest Hannerle."

What a contradiction between the pessimistic letters to the old woman, in which Ilse spoke bluntly about the growing threats in her homeland, and those to "little Hannerle," in which she simulated normalcy and cheer: humorous, as if they were written in a different time; full of funny accounts of Tommy's struggles to accommodate both football and violin.

Ilse first wrote from Vítkovice, later, after December 1940, when the circumstances for Jews in Mährisch-Ostrau had turned life-threatening, from Prague, where the family had resettled. At the beginning of February 1942, the chain of letters broke off. Weeks went by. On March 2, 1942, an official letter of the Royal Swedish Foreign Ministry arrived to the von Löwenadler's house. It informed the recipients: "Frau Ilse Weber is being evacuated these days. She could not leave an address."[36]

Weeks later, an odd letter arrived from Ilse's mother, Therese. Dated March 25, 1942 it reads:

Dear Frau Löwenadler! As I was about to post an Easter card it was brought to my attention that this is not allowed. Therefore, I am taking advantage of the moment as I am admitted to send a letter and wish you the best and most pleasant Easter. I received your letter on 22.3.42 and am happy, again and again, with the reports; yes, Hanuš has a really good life when I consider how poor Tommy is doing. His mother works as a children's nurse in a children's home. Her working hours are from 8 o'clock in the evening until 9 o'clock in the morning. I think that this is too strenuous for her, but she's happy with this occupation—she writes seldom, but it satisfies me—at least I find out from her that she's healthy. Her husband is also occupied and since 2 other brothers and a sister together with a 14-year old son and a sister-in-law live not so far from them, they see each other and speak quite often. My niece, who at first was with them, has journeyed on, which grieves Ilse and me endlessly. It may be there is a journey in store for me too, but that is postponed until the weather improves. For the time being, I hope to receive a great many letters from you! I am kissing my grandchild in my thoughts and greeting you warmly. Your Th. Herlinger.

Therese's time in Prague was limited. Six weeks after she sent this letter she was sent on her own journey to the East.

Dear Frau v. Löwenadler! I must suspend our correspondence, but maybe not for long. I am going away on Saturday the 9/5 42 and my journey will bring me to Ilse. She is T.G[37], well, she is very much loved by the little patients. They wanted to move her to another institution, but her patients wrote, without her knowledge, and likely with the physicians' assistance, such a splendid letter to the authorities, that they abandoned the idea. She is even allowed to keep her child with her. —I was most happy with the news from Lilian and am asking you to thank her on my behalf and greet her warmly for me. She must be anxious for her little children, whom she has not seen for so long. The time will come that will allow a reunion. I still have many errands so I must conclude, want only also to say that a friend of my daughter, Frau Grete Meller, Prague XIII, Strášnice 5/1 1436 would be happy to hear from time to time something about Hanuš. Will you be so kind? With all of my heart, I wish you a speedy and full recovery, thank you again for all the good you do for Hanuš. I will conclude by expressing my deepest appreciation, your Therese Herlinger.

Hanuš and his foster mother received postcards from Theresienstadt, mostly with preprinted texts or with handwritten lines of stereotypical formulations, everybody healthy, as well as questions concerning the receivers' condition.

Hanuš remembers that the educators at the Jewish youth center[38] in Uppsala, where he was accommodated, tried not to worry the children. During the week he studied at the oldest educational institute in Sweden, the *Katedralskolan*, where, following an old family tradition, all of the von Löwenadler children went.

On weekends he stayed with Gertrude, "Mormor," who shielded him from the gloomy news of his parents. Neither Hanuš nor "Mormor" could know what was hiding behind the name Theresienstadt—let alone imagine life in this concentration camp. Neither could those who, as the Webers, received overnight a transport order. According to euphemistic protocol, the "old-age ghetto" was to concentrate all the Jews from "the protectorate of Bohemia and Moravia" as well as Jews over the age of 65 from Germany, Austria and all West Europe, including war veterans with high distinctions and prominent persons.

There are numerous stories of Jews from Berlin and Wien who traded their entire fortunes for a supposedly "age resting" place in the "Theresienbad" (Terezin Spa), pictured in Nazi propaganda as a nice town and an adequate place of residence for old people.

It was forbidden to send letters from Theresienstadt to the "outside" world. The SS- commandant's censor passed only standardized postcards with a limited number of words, as well as preprinted confirmations for small packages sent to the inmates. Hanuš in

distant Sweden, had no idea what his family was going through in
its new residence, which had a normal place name on cards and
normal sounding streets with house numbers.[39] He was puzzled that
his little brother wrote "Thomas," instead of "Tommy," that his father signed as "Wolf," and that he, Hanuš, was always called on the
postcards "Hans Raphael."

Before her own "journey" on May 6, 1942, Grandmother
Therese had given Hanuš a nice picture of Theresienstadt.

*Hanuš my dearest child, I am going to your dear Mama, am very happy
to see her. The town has supposedly beautiful scenery and the air so re-
freshing, that one is always hungry. Tommy wants to eat the whole day.
Learn this from him—but not always just tasty food!! Continue to be
good; learn diligently in order to bring dear Mormor much joy. Kissing
you with whole my heart. Your Babička.*

Four long decades would pass before Hanuš gained insight into
the lives of mother, father and brother in Theresienstadt, and their
preceding time in Prague during his absence.

Working on his family chronicles, Oscar Mareni found by
chance a letter Willi Weber had sent him in the autumn of 1945,
describing in detail the experience of persecution and deportation
up to the war's end:

Dear Oskar,[40]

*I obtained today through the Jewish community in Mährisch-Os-
trau your letter to the Witkowitzer Coal Mines of June 23, 1945.
A few days after having inquired, I received your address from my
brother in London, so you will be getting this letter and today's telegram from me for sure. (. . .)*

*It can be gathered from your short report that you are reunited with
your wife, and I take it also your children, and hopefully, you are doing
well. I want to try to report to you all important details in chronological order, especially the information regarding family members.*

*In the fall of 1939 Mama received from the Vítk. administration
a notice for the end of the year. A correction was sent just a few hours*

later and it declared that she had to leave the Erbrichterei already on the next day and without any compensation. (I should have the original letter somewhere, so that you or Ernst can sue Vítkovice for compensation.) Attached to the letter was a Gestapo order to report there in person immediately and, during her visit, it was disclosed to her that she would have to report in the evening with a small suitcase at the Gestapo building since she would be transferred to Poland.

Due to a large number of interventions, even with the Gestapo, I managed to cancel the transport. On the next day however, Mama received another notification to once again report to the Gestapo building in the evening in order to settle small formalities. Ilse and I accompanied Mama there and despite all our efforts, she was put in a car and driven off. It was one of the worst nights we have experienced. Ilse did nothing but quarrel with God. To describe it in all its details would be pointless. You will have to make do with the brief description of the facts. On the next morning, Mama appeared at our home with thoroughly soaked shoes, soaked clothes and told us the following: She had been taken to a place near Orlau on the Polish border where the accompanying policeman showed her the way that she had to take to Poland, drew her attention to the high voltage wires and minefields and—vanished. Mama wandered around for hours until, following a gleam of light, she arrived at a provisional bakery. The Polish owner and his wife treated her very decently. On the next day a child of this family brought her in a roundabout way to Ostrau-Karwin streetcar with which she then returned home. In light of the fact that she had been expelled from Ostrava by Gestapo decree, I decided to bring her and Mutzi to Prague on the following day and booked her a room in a guesthouse, where the two recovered within a few weeks.

The situation in Mährisch-Ostrau became more and more dangerous; one had to fear for one's life in the streets. The war broke out and an extremely eager Gestapo man organized several raids in Ostrava, so I decided to move with Ilse and the children to Prague on the next day. In Prague, I rented a 3 room apartment for us and Mama. Mutzi had returned in the meantime to Ostrava, where she took over the management of a Jewish old people's home. Until the middle of 1942, we stayed here, and had many beautiful months, because while in the province Jews hardly dared to breathe, Jews in Prague were confronted with very few restrictions.

In the course of 1940 and 1941 much changed to the disfavor of Jews. In several districts Jews had to give up their apartments and to move in with other Jews' apartments in districts 1 and 5; businesses were taken away, houses and other properties were confiscated, bank accounts were closed, jewelry, furs, pianos, ski boots, warm clothes, and so on, all had to be handed over, ration cards were marked with "Jew," and one received much less than the others, could only go shopping on specific hours, one wasn't allowed at all to use certain streets, and in September 1941, every Jew had to wear a 10 cm yellow Star of Zion with the inscription "Jew." In October 1941, the transports started: the first targeted group was the people who received support from the Jewish Community, then the wealthy, lawyers, as well as the entire Jewish intelligentsia. The reports from the various Polish ghettos were terrible and we did everything here to help our people by sending food packs and money. For us who remained here, the option of leaving the country had disappeared in 1940. I applied for my Palestine certificate already in 1938, and it was granted; then the Palestine Office in Prague was notified by our government that the available certificates should first be given to the Sudeten-German Jews, and I, among others, had to resign my option for 1938. However, I was assured by my friend and by the head of the P.O.,[41] *Oskar Karpe and Jankef Edelstein,*[42] *that with the next certificates, in March 1939, I and Erwin Sternlicht, with whom I wanted to go to Erez, would receive the certificates automatically. At the beginning of March 1939, Sternlicht and I deposited 120,000 Kč for the certificate that we were supposed to receive on March 15. On 15.3.1939, you know this date as well, Adolf's hordes arrived, the entire P.O. apart for a few exceptions went to Erez Israel, and we stayed here. Some weeks later, a few certificates did arrive, but the price had climbed to 450.000 Kč, which neither Erwin nor I could afford, and in light of those circumstances we had to stay here.*

The ghetto in Theresienstadt, where—apart from a few exceptions—all remaining Jews in the Protectorate and some more from

Germany, Holland, France and Denmark went, was established on
November 1941. 150,000 people, ultimately destined for Poland,
were sent to Theresienstadt that previously had housed only 4000
inhabitants. At some point, 65,000 people lived in Theresienstadt,
around 30,000 died there, around 110,000 went to the East and
10,000 people survived this difficult time there. In the beginning of
February 1942, Ilse, Tommy and I received a transport notification.
Ilse had worked before at the social welfare of the community, in the
kindergarten, Tommy, who developed splendidly, went to the Jewish
elementary school, learned to play the violin, at which he made excellent progress, which was not surprising in light of his absolute pitch.
I worked for a while in a nursery near Prague, and I still anticipated
emigration, as I had permits to go to Argentine and San Domingo.

Theresienstadt had its own Jewish administration, although the
leading people were appointed by the Germans, and everything was run
only according to German orders. The Judenälteste [Eldest of the Jews:
head of the Jewish administration] was Jankef Edelstein, members of
the Council of Elders included engineer Zucker, engineer Schliesser etc.
Not one of the leaders lived to see the liberation. At the beginning the
situation in Theresienstadt was very bad since the Aryan population still
lived there and Jews were squeezed into the remaining barracks. Men
were housed separately from women and children. At the beginning one
had to lie on straw, after that on mattresses and later three storey-high
wooden bunks were installed almost everywhere. Each one was entitled
to 80 cm of Lebensraum only. The rations were awful: early in the morning some kind of black brew, at noon rotten potatoes with hedge nettle
and another unidentifiable brew in the evenings; little bread; everything
else only minimally or not at all. At the beginning men would not see
or speak to their wives in weeks since everyone was locked up in the
barracks and unable to move freely. Later the Aryans had to leave Theresienstadt and the whole town was transformed into a ghetto. People had
more freedom of movement but the rations stayed just as awful as before
and most of the 30,000 who perished died of starvation. Most of the
dead were old people; the young always figured out how to help themselves in some way, and those who worked received bigger rations. Many
succeeded in establishing contact with the outer world and to smuggle in

packages. In the ghetto itself, theft was common: moral concepts had generally been completely altered. It was the time for roughnecks with sharp elbows. Only those kind of people could manage to survive.

The most terrible thing during this time were the transports that arrived daily from the aforementioned countries, and, even worse, the departing deportations. We had no idea where the transports went, neither did we know what happened to the people who left, but we had an instinctive fear of the unknown and everyone struggled to stay off the transport list. Almost no one was successful because the Germans made sure that only people with essential jobs remained. On Yom Kippur 1942, 10,000 old people went away without any luggage. Edelstein called this one, and all other transports, "cold pogroms." The transports continued until October 1944.

In 1944, the situation of the ghetto improved since the Red Cross appeared to have contacted the Germans over Theresienstadt and announced the appointment of commissions. They worked months long for the embellishment of the townscape and now and again erected "Potemkin villages" overnight. At this time the Germans also approved of leisure activities that engaged all sorts of artists, with whom they carried out the most beautiful concerts, opera performances, theater performances, cabarets, sports events, etc. Many a time one visited those events with empty stomach, but they were at least as important as food.

Bedřich Fritta: *Film and Reality*

The double face of Theresienstadt was very visible to the inmates: on the one hand transports left for Treblinka and Auschwitz (which the inmates knew only as "the east"), on the other hand the SS established a fake town to deceive the world. From the spring of 1944 Theresienstadt appears in Nazi propaganda as a Jewish "model ghetto."

As a "model ghetto," concealing the cruel reality of smoking crematoriums, Theresienstadt demonstrated: "See, the Jews in Hitler's Reich live so peacefully—despite all the atrocious news stories." Holocaust-denial was born in the midst of the Holocaust.

When the Red Cross inspectors visited the camp, they were shown "marvelous life with good food and comfortable accommodation." Before being murdered, the artists in Theresienstadt were forced to sing, joke and dance, all according to a carefully planned script. This absurd spectacle was filmed as *Theresienstadt: Ein Dokumentarfilm aus dem Jüdischen Siedlungsgebiet* (Theresienstadt: A Documentary Film from the Jewish Settlement Area), commonly known by the misleading title "Der Führer schenkt den Juden eine Stadt" (The Führer presents the Jews with a City).

In his letter, Willi Weber describes how Ilse's mood was affected by the situation around her:

During our last year in Prague Ilse was a nervous wreck since life was more than difficult, the work unsatisfactory, and the prospect of a better calmer life practically non-existent. On the day we received the notification for the transport she underwent a transformation that continued until our last shared days. The certainty to be able to assist at the ghetto made her so confident and strong that she overcame all the difficulties with ease. Already during our arrival to Theresienstadt she reported as a nurse and started to run a children's infirmary. At first she was given a room with eight broken beds, no mattresses or bed linens, without any equipment, as nothing was actually available. It was only later that she managed to receive a bigger hall with 26 beds for her infirmary. Wherever it was possible, Ilse scrounged or she organized things by means of "schleusen"—a Theresienstadt term for, nicely said, taking—everything possible that contributed to the adornment of the sickbay. The hall was decorated by an academic painter with the most splendid fairy tale themes; she did everything in her power to make the sick children's stay at the infirmary as pleasant as possible. Children have been always her special preference, and here she had quite great opportunities to work with them. She also succeeded, despite a prohibition, to organize a guitar, and that was really the most important treatment. At her infirmary, against all regulations, songs were sung and music was played from early morning until evening.

I believe that Theresienstadt was also the peak of Ilse's career as a writer. With simple words she recorded our life and experience in poetic form, which over time has become the common property of thousands of people. Her Theresienstadt folksongs were sung by the children with increasing enthusiasm. Almost every evening, after 12 working hours, Ilse went to visit a variety of infirmaries, barracks, etc; with notes and her guitar and with her songs and poems, she gave people new hope for a better tomorrow. Enclosed, I am sending you some poems that perhaps tell more than my entire long letter.

Ruth Elias,[43] whose space in Theresienstadt was right next to Ilse Weber's, had witnessed the creation of many of her poems. Ruth had been deported to Theresienstadt as a 16 year-old girl and was added to an Auschwitz transport in December 1943. At the selection the pregnant young woman was chosen by the camp physician, Dr. Josef Mengele, for a brutal experiment: the baby to which she gave birth at the infirmary in the women's block was subject to testing how long a "newly born" could survive without nourishment. Unwilling to witness the experiment's end, the young mother killed her child. In her book *Triumph of Hope* Ruth Elias recalls her friend and companion Ilse Weber.

When I came to Theresienstadt in April 1942, I was assigned accommodation in a little room in the Hamburg barracks. It was like all barracks, a building with two big inner courtyards, which had served as a parade ground for the k.u.k.[44] soldiers and were surrounded by arcades. At that time the regular soldiers were housed in big dormitories; the of-

ficers, however, were accommodated in small apartments that contained an anteroom with a kitchen, a large living room and a tiny room for the "Putzfleck," the officer's servant. I was assigned a place in the kitchen anteroom of the officer's apartment, which already housed a mother with her daughter. One could reach two rooms from this anteroom: the living room of the officer's family, where around twenty women were now living, and a small chamber where Ilse Weber had been put with her sister-in-law Erna (Taub). Anyone who came in or went out had to pass by my bed, and that is how I met Ilse Weber.

Ilse Weber's husband had been brought to the Magdeburg barracks, her son Tommy into the "children's home." During the first months, the entrance of women to the men's barracks, and vice versa, was strictly forbidden. Many newcomers, isolated from their beloved and in the middle of masses of mostly sad strangers, slid into a deep depression.

Ilse had a special personality. She worked as a nurse in a children's ward. When she went to work, she wore a pristine white nurse apron with wide shoulder straps and a white nurse cap on the head. It was always a mystery to me how she succeeded to keep her clothes so clean as there were no hot water nor soap for washing in Theresienstadt. Ilse's indescribable sense of duty for her family and children-patients never let her rest.

She allowed herself only little sleep. She took advantage of every free moment to draw images with words that captured everyday life in Theresienstadt. In a simple and clear language her verses reproduced the camp's life, suffering and privation. She wrote during her night watch but also at home after work. Even today I can see Ilse's little room—we called it in Theresienstadt dialect "kumbalek"—that she fixed comfortably despite the shortage of space. Out of the altogether four mattresses that she and her sister-in-law had at their disposal (each inmate received two mattresses which were so short that only children could stretch out on them), and the two suitcases they brought along, which were used as pillows at night, Ilse built a seating corner, where we could sit together and where she could write when she wasn't with her patients.

A place of honor on the wall of her "kumbalek" was given to a lute [the name Ruth Elias gave to Ilse's guitar] that a Czech police officer had "sluiced" i.e. smuggled, for her. Musical instruments of any sort were confiscated as "contraband" during the first ghetto year, their possession was strictly forbidden. However, Ilse was lucky that her "kumbalek" was never checked by the SS because if the lute would have been discovered she would have been immediately ordered onto an east-transport. Ilse engaged "her" Theresienstadt children, at least those who were not seriously sick, the whole day with music, singing and playing. That was her own therapy, which together with the physician's and nurses work, worked real wonders. Under her guidance the little patients wrote poems, songs and little plays that were even recited and performed in front of an audience, especially on holidays. There were seldom unhappier children than the healthy ones who had to leave the infirmary. Out of the flock of sick and the children dismissed from the hospital, "Nurse Ilse," as she was known in Theresienstadt, formed a choir that played a part in the inmates' free-time activities.

It may sound paradoxical, but we spent unforgettable hours in Ilse's "kumbalek," during which she sang songs with the lute. Ilse was not only a poet, but also an excellent musician, who set to music some of her poems herself. I found it incomprehensible how she managed during this terrible time to see so much ugliness, but sometimes also beauty, and describe it so expressively in her verses. An almost complete image of the ghetto life emerged in this way.

When Ilse wrote poems, she read them to us or sang them with the lute, and so I became witness to her creation. Many of her verses originated at first not on paper but while she was improvising with the lute. To her son Hanuš she wrote a letter that she was not allowed to send, and as she read it to us, it touched us so much that we all had to cry.

Ilse Weber spoke often of Hanuš and how much she pined for him. She often doubted whether she acted rightly to have robbed this child of motherly love and sent him to strangers. At the same time she was happy to have saved him from the privations and humiliations of the ghetto-life. Ilse literally threw herself into her work with the sick children because in each child she saw her own son, her Hanuš.

Her heartbreaking poem, "Letter to My Child," testifies to the deep love, longing, hope and desperation of the mother. Despite the suffering and humiliation Ilse experienced with her family in Theresienstadt, her love, pride and loyalty to her people, to Judaism, find their deep expression in the poem "Confession."

Willi enclosed this poem and some others in his autumn 1945 letter to Oscar as sample of Ilse's creativity in Theresienstadt. About himself and Tommy, he wrote:

I arrived to Theresienstadt with serious sciatica and therefore could be active only in the office of "social welfare" during my first year. Later I was assigned to all kinds of jobs, and in the last year I was brought in as a gardener for the town embellishment. During the last year (1944) I worked as a guard in the nicest park of Theresienstadt, with the most marvelous children's playground—swing boats, merry-go-round, sandbanks, snug berths, wading pools with hot and cold water etc.— naturally everything only for the announced committee.

Tommy was overjoyed when he could help me with impaling paper scraps, the diverse clearing work, planting flowerbeds, and was particularly proud when early in the morning he could take a bunch of flowers hidden under the coat—it was also forbidden at the ghetto to own flowers—for his children's home.

The children were precisely aware of our situation and their hatred of Germans was boundless. Unfortunately, we had to encourage them to things that were contrary to all moral stands and often we spoke with Ilse about the possibility to amend for that at a later point in time. Sadly, that was completely unnecessary because, as you perhaps know from the reports, of around 10,000 deported protectorate children, only around 30 came back.

Regarding Ilse and Oscar's mother Therese, Willi Weber's letter says:

Mama stayed in Prague until 1942, but was then overjoyed to come to Theresienstadt where, despite all of the circumstances, she was able to lead a relatively calm life. On 18.10 she went with a 5000 transport to Poland and just like with the others, we have never heard anything from her again. Mutzi arrived to Theresienstadt in July 1942, together with all the people from Ostrava, around 5000 in number. She remained here only for a few weeks and was sent to Poland, together with almost 98% of the Ostrava people.

Uncle Gustav was sent to Poland already in autumn 1939, during the Ostrauer Sonderaktion [Ostrava Special Action]⁴⁵ and during his transfer he perished and was buried near Przemyśl. His wife, his brother and wife, the Frommowitsches, Immerglücks, the old Mr. Weiss with his son Julka, who was married to an Aryan, stayed in Ostrava; Aunt Johanna had passed away there in the meantime. Many others came to Theresienstadt and were immediately transported further on to Poland, just like all the others. I am prepared to answer to your specific questions in a more detailed manner. (. . .)

It is peculiar that when people are struck by the hard blows of fate they tend to be seeking life and not death. Life just goes on. Today, after some months have already passed and all the hardship and harshness has faded, I still have only one wish, that in Auschwitz, Ilse went, together with the child, directly from the train to the gas chamber. It would have spared her a great deal of suffering because Ilse would have hardly been able to bear this miserable existence.

Almost twenty-five years after Willi's death Hanuš heard from a family friend that his father's wish for a quick death for Ilse and Tommy was fulfilled.

Unexpectedly, Hanuš met a friend from Ostrava during a visit to Germany. From him, he learned the following:

I was in Theresienstadt together with your parents, but I was deported to Auschwitz with an earlier transport than your father. In autumn 1945 I came back to Prague and one of the first people I met was Willi. He asked me how I succeeded to survive. As I told him that I had been in Auschwitz for a long time before I was sent on a death march, your father asked me if I had not seen Ilse and Tommy. My answer was no, and I have regretted this every day until today. Willi always hoped that Ilse and Tommy were still alive, and I did not have the heart to destroy his hopes. I knew exactly what had happened. When we arrived in Auschwitz, we underwent a "selection" and most of my fellow inmates from Theresienstadt were sent directly to the gas chamber. I was a good athlete and still had some muscles so I was transferred to the group classified as "fit-for-work." My work was dreadful. I ended up in the "Leichen-trägerkommando" [corpse carrier commando], *a group of inmates who pulled out the corpses from the gas chambers and transported them to the crematorium. There was only one group that had it worse, and it was the one tasked with breaking the gold out of the deads' jaws and tearing off the prostheses. I wanted to survive, but now I believe that the price for it was too high. I feel that I survived at the expense of the dead.*

The most terrible moments were those when I recognized my old friends who were standing in line outside the gas chamber. Sometime in autumn 1944 I noticed a group of ten or fifteen children that had arrived with a transport. Ilse stood in their middle trying to comfort the little ones. Next to her stood a boy who was bigger than the rest of the children. I think that this big boy was Tommy, but I am not sure. We were not allowed under any circumstances to make contact with those who were waiting outside the gas chamber, but as the nearest guardsmen were positioned quite far away I went over to Ilse, who immediately recognized me.

"Is it true that we can take a shower after the journey?" she asked. I did not want to lie and so I answered: "No, that is no shower room, it is a gas chamber, and I will give you a piece of advice now. I have often heard you singing in the infirmary. Go as quickly as possible into the chamber. Sit with the children on the floor and start singing. Sing what you always sing with them. That way you will inhale the gas quicker. Otherwise you would be trampled to death when panic breaks out.

Ilse's reaction was strange. She laughed, somehow absently, hugged one of the children and said: "So we will not be taking a shower—"

Ulrika Migdal studied philosophy, literature and music and received her PhD in philosophy in 1979. She lectured and held research positions in Germany and New York, and published essays, radio features, poems and theater pieces, as well as the book *And the Music Plays Along. Chansons and Satires from Theresienstadt.*

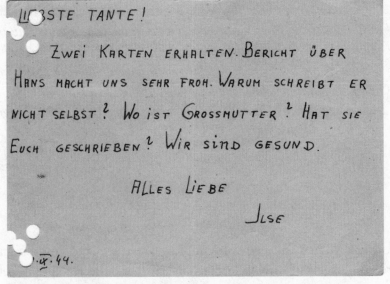

Two sides of postcard sent by Ilse to Gertrude Von Löwenadler from
Theresienstadt, dated September 1944 and postmarked November 14.

THE DRAWINGS

There were different artists in Theresienstadt who risked their lives in order to portray life behind the façade of the "model ghetto." Those who were employed by the Technical Drawing Office of the Jewish Self Administration had access to drawing materials and more freedom of movement around the ghetto. They were ordered by the camp's management to draw technical construction-plans, as well as street and building maps, and to illustrate the SS-reports. Aside from these official tasks they worked secretly on drawings depicting the misery and brutality of the camp's everyday life.

Bedřich Fritta, who supervised the drawing-studio in the technical-graphic department of the Jewish self-administration, was born as Fritz Taussig in 1906 in Višňová u Frýdlantu in northern Bohemia (he later changed his name for assimilation reasons). Up to his deportation to Theresienstadt (December 4, 1941, as part of the second Aufbaukommando), he worked in Prague as graphic designer and illustrator of political caricatures, among others, for the satirical magazine *Simplicissimus*.[46] In Theresienstadt, Fritta created a collection of around 170 drawings, mostly by ink, that are today in the possession of his son, Thomas Fritta-Haas.

Drawings the Theresienstadt artists managed to smuggle outside the ghetto were sent abroad and provided evidence against the NS propaganda's claims. The spread of what the Nazis called "horror propaganda," and Fritta's and other artists' refusal to take part in the "ghetto's embellishment," led to their arrest a few weeks after the ghetto was inspected by the Red Cross delegation. On July 17 1944, on orders of the ghetto commander, the artists from the technical-office were incarcerated in the small, dark Gestapo jail cells in

the Small Fortress. End of October they were transported to Auschwitz. Fritta was imprisoned together with his wife and three-year-
old son. He was tortured and died of blood poisoning a week after
his arrival to Auschwitz. His close friend, Leo Haas, born in 1901
in Opava (Troppau), created around 500 drawings in Theresienstadt, and, as Fritta and the other painters, was arrested for dissemi-
nating "horror propaganda." He was transferred from Auschwitz to
Sachsenhausen camp where he was assigned to the counterfeiting
team.[47] In February 1945 the team was transferred to Mauthausen
and finally to Ebensee, where they were liberated. Haas returned to
Theresienstadt and found his entire art collection, as well as many
works by Fritta, hidden under the floorboards in the attic of the
Magdeburg barracks. He adopted Fritta's young son and settled in
Prague, where he continued to work as an illustrator and painter. In
1955, he moved to Eastern Germany and later became a university
art professor in East Berlin. He died in 1983.

   Malva Schalek (Malvina Shalková) was born in 1882 in Prague.
After finishing art school she worked for a while as a court sketch artist, and one of her assignments was the proceedings against the clairvoyant and conjurer Erik Jan Hanussen, also known as Hermann
(Herschel) Chaim Steinschneider, in 1933.[48] She drew numerous
portraits in Theresienstadt, many of which depict imprisoned artists. She was murdered in Auschwitz in 1944.

Ulrike Migdal

NOTES

ILSE WEBER AND HER CULTURAL MILIEU

1 See Ulrike Migdal, Afterword, pp.279-80.

2 From 1940 up to her deportation to Theresienstadt on February 6, 1942, Ilse lived in Prague. During this time, as a Jew, she was barred from taking part in any cultural or intellectual activities.

3 *Die Weltbühne*, 28-2, 1932, p.104; 20, 1933, p.296.

4 *Jüdische Rundschau*, Berlin, Heft [Issue] 38, 12, V. 1933.

5 Hindenburg, president of the Weimar Republic from 1925 to 1934, played an important role in the rise of the Nazi party to power.

6 Mirjam Zadoff, *Next Year in Marienbad. The Lost World of Jewish Spa Culture.* Trans. William Templer, Pennsylvania: University of Pennsylvania Press, 2012, pp.205-207.

7 *Reichstag fire*: The arson attack on the Berlin parliament building on February 27, 1933, that prompted the Reichstag Fire Decree, suspending most of the civil liberties in Germany.

8 As Antonioni wrote: "We have no hesitation in saying that if this is propaganda, then we welcome propaganda. It is a powerful, incisive, extremely effective film . . . The episode in which Süss violates the young girl is done with astonishing skill." See: Susan Tegel, *Jud Süss, Life, Legend, Fiction, Film.* N.Y: Continuum International Publishing Group, 2011, p.12.

9 See Ruth Bondy, The World of Theresienstadt, p.175.

10 Ilse Weber, *Wann Wohl das Leid ein Ende hat. Briefe und Gedichte aus Theresienstadt, Herausgegeben von Ulrike Migdal,* München: Carl Hanser Verlag, 2008.

11 Andrés Nader, *Traumatic Verses*, Rochester, N.Y: Camden House, 2007, p.18.

12 Indeed, in recent years some of Ilse's poems, which she had set to music, have been publicly performed by such artists as Anne Sofie von Otter, Bente Kahan and Ute Lemper.

13 Most famous is the philosopher and cultural critic Theodor Adorno's dictum that writing poetry after Auschwitz is barbaric. It is interesting to follow the debate between Theodor Adorno and H.G Adler, a camp survivor who wrote poems while in Theresienstadt. After the war, Adler continued to write scholarly and literary works on the Holocaust and his experience. See Ruth Franklin, "A Long View. A rediscovered master of Holocaust writing," in: *The New Yorker*, January 31, 2011.

14 The National Socialist abuse, vulgarization and manipulation of the German language was recorded by Victor Klemperer in his 1947 work: *LTI-Lingua Tertii Imperii: Notizbuch eines Philologen*, Berlin: Aufbau Verlag, trans. Martin Brady, *The Language of the Third Reich: LTI, Lingua Tertii Imperii, A Philologist's Notebook*, London and New Brunswick, Athlone Press, 2000.

15 As Nader points out, Ilse's poem is an adaptation of a traditional folk song "Die goldene Kutsche," (The Golden Coach). See Nader, p.118.

16 Terrence Des Pres, *The Survivor. An Anatomy of Life in the Death Camps*, Oxford: Oxford University Press, 1976, p.99.

17 Jean Améry, *Radical Humanism*. Selected Essays, trans. Sidney and Stella P. Rosenfeld. Bloomington: Indiana University Press, 1984, p.33.

18 The poet and writer Ruth Klüger, a camp survivor, notes she recited and composed poems while in Theresienstadt as a means of mental survival; See Ruth Klüger, *Still Alive: A Holocaust Girlhood Remembered*, N.Y.: Feminist Press at CUNY, 2001.

19 See Yad Vashem Website:
http://www.yadvashem.org/odot_PDF?Mcrosoft%20word%20-%201154.pdf

20 Améry, p.29.

LETTERS

1 *Ostrawitz*: mountain village in the Beskids Mountains in the Carpathians, where the Herlingers liked to go for vacation.

2 *lkmj*: typed by Hanuš.

3 *Lilian's mother*: Gertrude von Löwenadler, married to a diplomat who was the Swedish consul in Hamburg in the early 1920s.

4 *Lo*: Lotte Hannesen, Lilian's friend from Berlin. Publisher and editor of a magazine with stories, articles, riddles, etc. The magazine was a supplement to about 40 German-language children's magazines, which were published in Europe and some South American countries. Ilse published in this magazine under her maiden name, Herlinger, a series of tales, little narratives, and articles. After her visit to the Löwenadler family in Hamburg in 1921, on her way back to Ostrava, Ilse stopped in Berlin to meet Lotte Hannesen.

5 *Hässelby-Villastad*: westernmost and biggest district of Stockholm. MS

6 *"Nedělejte komedie!"*: literally, don't make a comedy. MS

7 *Felix*: Ilse's nephew, son of the Willi Weber's oldest sister, Emily (Milli).

8 *Gre*: Grete Edelstein, illustrator and close friend of Ilse; lived in Berlin with her husband, a physician, Dr. Edelstein, and son Hans. She illustrated Ilse Herlinger's children's book *Tales for Jewish Children*, which was published in 1928 by the publisher Dr. Robert Färber, in Moravia-Ostrava.

9 *Ernst Immerglück*: Ilse's cousin, "wholesaler and retail dealer," directed a food company with several branches and played the piano professionally; was little Hanuš' first piano teacher.

10 *Ernst*: Ilse's older brother. Ilse Weber had five siblings: three half-siblings from her father's first marriage: Herta (b. 1898); Bettina (Mutzi, b. 1891); and Erwin (b. 1895); and from her father's marriage with Therese: Ernst (in Czech Arnošt, b. 1900); Ilse (b. 1903), and Oskar (b. 1907; "Oscar" from 1933 on).

11 *Wilma Gross*: Ilse's school friend; mutual friend of Ilse, Oskar and Lilian.

12 *Die Gefährten* (The Companions, 1932): A novel by Anna Seghers (1900-1983), one of the most important German women writers of the 20th century. Born to a Jewish family, she fled to Mexico in 1941, where she founded an anti-Fascist club. "The Companions," an account of the international Communist movement after the Russian Revolution with emphasis on the fate of individuals and their sacrifices for the cause, is her most avant-garde work. In 1939, Seghers wrote the novel *The Seventh Cross*, which was set in 1936 and described the escape of seven prisoners from a concentration camp. The novel was published in the USA in 1942 and made into a movie in 1944, one of the few depictions of Nazi concentration camps during World War II. MS

13 *Der Scharlatan* (The Charlatan, 1932): A novel by Herman Kesten, a German-Jewish writer and publisher (1900–1996). His pre-war novels depict the moral chaos at the end of the Weimar Republic. In 1940, he emigrated to New York where he continued to write, and together with Klaus Mann, edited an anthology of European creative writing. After the war, he received many prizes and was highly regarded, especially by the German Group 47 of writers and critics. MS

14 *Die Weltbühne* (The World Stage): A German weekly magazine founded in 1905, it focused on politics, arts and business, and was a main forum for leftists and socialist intellectuals. The Nazis banned it after the Reichstag fire and its last edition appeared on March 7, 1933. It was published in exile as *The New World Stage*, and after the war, it continued to appear in East Berlin until 1993. MS.

15 *Aufruf* (The Call): a political newspaper with socialistic orientation during the Weimar Republic. MS

16 *Neue Wahrheit* (New Truth): Social-Democratic newspaper. MS

17 *Vorwärts* (Forward), was established in 1876 as the official newspaper of German
    Social Democratic Workers' Party and, from 1890, the Social Democratic Party of
    Germany. (Friedrich Engels published in it in 1877–1878 a series of articles, later
    published as the *Anti-Dühring*, considered as one of the most significant works of
    Marxism). The newspaper was banned by the Nazis in 1933 and the last issue ap-
    peared on February 28, 1933. The paper moved to Prague and after Nazi pressure
    went to Paris until 1940. MS

18 *Theodor Lessing* (1872–1933): German-Jewish philosopher of culture, writer and po-
    litical journalist, stood for pragmatic socialism, equal rights for women, and inter-
    national understanding. On August 30–31, 1933, he was assassinated by national
    socialists in Marienbad.

19 *"Watschengefries"*: a stupid face that cries out for a slap. MS

20 The mention here of a mother-in-law is surprising because it implies that Lilian was
    married. Yet were she indeed married (at least living with her husband), one would
    expect Ilse to have been referring to the husband Curt in her letters to Lilian. Since
    Ilse refers to Lilian as single, it would seem that she and Curt were seperated. We
    can only speculate about why, as mentioned here, Lilian is visiting Hamburg, where
    it seems, Curt and his mother lived. We do know from Lilian's planned marriage to
    James Treen (letter from March 17, 1936 et seq) that Lilian must have divorced Curt.
    See also letter of Christmas morning 1935 in which Ilse dreams that Lilian would not
    go back to Curt. MS.

21 *Glückliche Menschen*: (Happy People, 1931) and *Der Scharlatan* (The Charalatan
    1932): novels by the German-Jewish writer and publisher Hermann Kesten (1900–
    1996). See footnote number 13. MS

22 *L'Isle d'Adam*: Philippe Auguste de Villiers de L'Isle-Adam (1838–1889), French poet
    from the late Romantic era, influenced by E.A. Poe; known for his narrative incli-
    nation toward the mystical-fantastic; among his works, *Sardonic Tales* (1883) and
    Tomorrow's Eve (1886).

23 *Hedwig Courths-Mahler* (1867–1950): popular German writer of romantic novels.
    MS

24 *Braunbuch*: Braunbuch über Reichstagsbrand und Hitlerterror. The first *Brown Book*,
    1933, titled *Brown Book of the Hitler Terror and the Reichstag Fire*, appeared in Paris, and
    was presented on August 1 at a press conference. The background was the Reichstag fire
    trial, the main defendant was Van der Lubbe, the other defendants were three Bulgarian
    communists, Dimitroff, Popov, and Tanev. The book was edited by Alexander Abusch
    (together with Albert Norden). Willi Münzenberg, leader of the Workers International
    Relief, was in charge of the edition. Münzenberg was the propagandist of the Comint-
    ern (international communist organization), and founded the Edition du Carrefour,
    which published the *Brown Book*. Among his co-workers was a group of commu-
    nist authors and journalists: Alfred Kantorowicz, Gustav Regler, Arthur Koestler, and

Bruno Frei. John Heartfield designed the book. The cover featured a blood–smeared Göring with an executioner's axe in front of the burning Reichstag. The *Brown Book* was translated into seventeen languages and sold several million copies.

25 *Friedl*: Friedl Thorš, a girl from the nearby town Ostrava, whom Ilse befriended and who belonged to the outer circle of Ilse's cultural club. This external circle, which met only on weekends, also included Gretel Schott and Olga Meitner (mentioned in the letter from January 5, 1935).

26 *Liese Tittor*: A young girl from the neighborhood. Ilse conscientiously looked after her for years (she also took care of her training as photographer).

27 English in the original version of the letters. Subsequent English in the original will be **in bold fonts as here.**

28 *Milli*: Ilse's sister-in-law, Willi's oldest sister. Willi Weber had eight siblings: Emily (Milli b. 1893); Sigmund (b. 1896); Karl (b.1899); Erna (b. 1903); Manek (b. 1904) Max (b. 1895); Berta (Bertl, b. 1907, hundred-years-old, lives in New York); and Selma (b. 1908); Willi was born in 1901 and died in 1974.

29 *Our president*: Tomáš Garrigue Masaryk (1859–1937), sociologist, philosopher, and politician. First president of the 1918–established Czechoslovakia; resigned for reasons of age in 1935. Among his works: *Suicide and the Meaning of Civilization* (1881).

30 *AIZ* (The Workers Pictorail Newspaper): Founded in 1921 as a monthly magazine Soviet Russia in Pictures. In 1926, the German publisher Willi Münzenberg began to publish it biweekly. Its contributors ranged from George Grosz to Maxim Gorki, George Bernhard Shaw, Käthe Kollwitz, Erich Kästner, and Kurt Tucholsky. Between 1933 and 1938, the AIZ was published in Prague.

31 *Simplizius* (Simplicius): Satirical weekly magazine, founded in 1896 in Munich, by Albert Langen and Thomas Theodor Heine (Th. Th. Heine), whose caricatures during the Empire and Weimar Republic presented the sharpest social criticism in Germany. Contributors included Fritta, Haas, Thomas Mann, Rainer Maria Rilke, Hermann Hesse, among many others.

32 *Kč*: Koruna česká, Czech crown.

33 *Oscar*: Ilse's younger brother.

34 *Lizzie* (Gross): Friend of Ilse and a *Kränzchen* magazine sister. The *Kränzchen*, was a weekly girls' magazine which Ilse read. At the age of 13 she put an advertisement in this magazine looking for pen pals. Lilian von Löwenadler was among the responding girls.

35 *Bruno Ries*: Ilse's cousin; member of an inner group of her cultural circle, which she had gathered around her during her teenage years in Witkowitz.

36 *Schlesische Bühne*: Silesian Theater. MS

37 *[Now] everything, everything must change*: chorus line from "Faith in Spring," a poem by the romantic poet Ludwig Unland (1787–1862), and to which Schubert composed music. MS

38 *Elli* (Wendland): Ilse's school friend from Witkowitz and *Kränzchen*-sister.

39 *Neil*: Alexander Sutherland Neil (1883–1973), progressive educator, had his own school, first in Dresden-Hellerau, after 1927 in England, which became internationally famous as the Summerhill School. It specialized in problem children, who seemed difficult, lazy, sluggish or antisocial at other schools. Neil developed an upbringing free of pressure that strove to give the children a free emotional development through happiness, voluntary classes, and absence of moral and religious instruction. He was regarded in Germany as the founder of anti-authoritarian education, since the German translation of his works was wrongly published as "Theory and Practice of Antiauthoritarian Education." Neil himself followed Wilhelm Reich, and used the term "self-regulatory education."

40 *Treue (*Fidelity), by Otto Zarek (1898–1958): German Jewish playwright, director, writer, critic and journalist. Jewish and gay, he fled to Hungary and, in 1938, to England where, in 1940, he joined the British army. He returned to West Berlin in 1954, where he continued his journalistic and theatrical work. In 1942 and 1946, he published *German Kultur: The Proper Perspective*, in which he explained the contradiction of German culture and Nazi brutality as deriving from a Faustian ambivalence, a theme that was also central in Thomas Mann's *Doctor Faustus*. MS

41 *Terýho Chalet*: the highest mountain chalet in the High Tatras (2,015 meters high). MS

42 *Tatra*: High Tatras is a mountain chain along the border of northern Slovakia and southern Poland. They are the highest mountain range within the Carpathians. Since they originate in the Alpine orogeny, the landscape is quite similar to that of the Alps, yet significantly smaller. MS

43 *Silver Jubilee*: May 1935 was the 25th anniversary of King George's coronation.

44 *Žid peichlatý*: side-lock Jew, referring to the traditional long side locks or side curls (Payot) Orthodox Jews grow. MS

45 *Altvater* (Old father): the highest mountain of the Ash Mountains, a mountain range in the eastern Sudeten Mountains on the border of the Czech Republic and Poland. MS

46 *Já*: "I" in Czech. MS

47 *Karl Kraus* (1874–1936): Writer, journalist, language and culture critic and sharp critic of the press and the yellow press, or as he himself called it, *Journaille*. (French pun on "canaille," meaning scum. MS). From 1899 to 1936, he published his newspaper *Die Fackel* (The Torch), which featured mainly satirical aphorisms, epigrams, commentaries, essays and poems; the journal became Kraus' forum in his battle against

"the rack and ruin of language," as an expression of cultural decline. Ilse Weber was an admirer of Karl Kraus and read *Die Fackel* regularly.

48 *"Pfui Teufel"*: Pfui the devil!: Meaning Ugh, disgusting! MS

49 *Ostrauer*: born in Ostrava. MS

50 *Jo van Ammers-Küller* (1884–1966): Dutch novelist. Her novel, *Herren, Knechte, Frauen* was published in 1934 as *The House of Taverlinck*.

51 *Die Frauen der Coornvelts*: *The Rebel Generation*, 1925. MS

52 *Karel Čapek* (1890–1938): One of the most popular Czech writers, who above all has become known as a critic of civilization. In his science fiction play from 1920, "R.U.R" (i.e. Rossum's Universal Robots, the name of an American corporation in the play), he coined the term robot. (The word *robota*, drudgery in Czech, was introduced by his brother, Josef Čapek, born in 1887, and murdered in Bergen-Belsen in 1945.) Karel's novel *The Absolute at Large* appeared in 1922. Čapek was a strict anti-Fascist; above all in his play, *The White Disease*, from 1937, where he settled a score with Fascism. He died on December 25, 1938. Officially, his death was said to have been caused by a lung inflammation. But a few days before, he had gone on a hunger strike to protest against the Allies, who were about to "sell" Czechoslovakia to Hitler's Germany. Since he took a prominent stance not only against National Socialism but also against Communism, his work was hushed up in post war Czechoslovakia.

53 *Seltsames England*: *Letters from England*, (*Anglické listy*, 1924). MS

54 *Alice Berend*: Sister of the painter Charlotte Berend-Corinth. Born in 1875, Alice Berend published numerous novels mostly between 1909 and 1930. This German-Jewish author, whose 25 books sold in the hundred thousands, became first known with *Mr. Sebastian Wenzel's Travels*. Her reputation as a humorist was made with *Babette Bomberling's Bridegroom*. In 1933, the National Socialists put her books on the "List of damaging and unwanted literature." Persecuted as a Jew, Alice Berend immigrated via Switzerland to Italy, where she died in 1938, penniless and forgotten.

55 *Bruders Bekenntnisse*: Bruder's Confessions. MS

56 *National Holiday*: the anniversary for the founding of Czechoslovakia on October 28, 1918.

57 In German, a quarter eight (Viertel Acht), is seven fifteen in English. MS

58 *Coup*: a failed Nazi coup in Austria that culminated in the assassination of the Austrian Chancellor Engelbert Dollfuss. MS

59 *Erbrichterei*: Refers to the village judge's complex of property and rights that was hereditary (See, M.M. Postan Ed. *The Cambridge Economic History of Europe*, 1966, 2 ed. Vols. 1, Cambridge University Press, Cambridge, p. 471). Ilse's grandfather gave that name to the house where the Herlingers lived after it had become inheritable in the family. Compare footnotes 20 and 21 "Afterword."

60 *The Balfour Declaration*: On November 2, 1917, Britain declared its agreement to establish Palestine as national home for the Jewish People (whereby preserving the rights of the existing non-Jewish communities in Palestine). It was first formulated in the form of a letter from Arthur James Balfour, the British foreign minister at the time, sent to Lionel Walter Rothschild (2nd. Baron Rothschild), a prominent British Zionist.

61 *Jehuda Ehrenkranz*: physician and notable reciter and travelling lecturer.

62 *malheur*: misfortune in French. MS

63 *Irene Harand* (1900–1975): Austrian Catholic and resistance fighter. In autumn 1933, together with a Jewish attorney Moritz Zalman, she established the Weltorganisation gegen Rassenhass und Menschennot (World Organization Against Racial Hatred and Human Suffering), which became known as the Harand-Movement. She expressed her views in the weekly magazine *Gerechtigkeit* (Justice), which was directed against Hitler and the growing antisemitism. Irene Harand recognized at an early stage the dangers of National Socialism and in 1935 published her main work: *Sein Kampf. Antwort an Hitler* (*His Struggle: An Answer to Hitler*), which was translated into English and French and immediately banned in Germany. In 1937–1938, the Harand Movement protested against the antisemitic exhibition in Munich *Der ewige Jude* (The Eternal Jew), by plastering the walls and frames with images of notable Jews.

64 *Prager Tagblatt* (Prague Daily Paper): German language newspaper published in Prague from 1876. It was considered the most important and influential liberal-democratic German newspaper in Bohemia. It closed in 1939, with the German occupation of Czechoslovakia. It featured many prominent writers and journalists, such as Alfred Döblin, Max Brod and Joseph Roth. MS

65 *Dr. Spitzer*: belonged in the 1920s to Ilse's cultural club. See p.284.

66 *on the last day*: Ilse is referring to the last day of the Sukkot holiday. MS

67 *Jungfernstieg*: A promenade in Hamburg on an artificial lake (originally created as a water reservoir in 1190). The name originates from a past tradition, as families came to the promenade on Sunday to walk and introduce their unmarried daughters, "Jungfern." MS

68 *Ludwig Hardt*: Born 1886, Upper Silesia, Germany (today Poland)—died 1947, New York city. Jewish actor, famous reciter of modern and classic poetry. In 1938 he immigrated to Czechoslovakia and in 1939 to the USA. MS

69 *Henlein-Movement*: Konrad Henlein (1898–1945), founded in 1933 the Sudeten German Home Front (SHF), which as Sudeten-German party (SdP) became in 1935 the second largest party in Czechoslovakia. Henlein demanded, cooperating with the national socialist government in Germany, the annexation of Sudeten German areas to the German Reich. In 1938 he was appointed Reichskommissar and SS group leader,

and as of 1939 he was the party leader of the Sudetenland. During the last years of the first Czechoslovakian republic, the SdP was systematically extended by the National Socialist Party as the fifth column of the German National Socialist Reich.

70 *The coup in Austria*: On March 11, 1938, the Austrian Nazi party seized power with a well-planned coup and on March 12, 1938, Austria was annexed into the German Third Reich. MS

71 *Frau Ilka from Budapest*: Linking person between Oscar and the family. She was an acquaintance of Ilse's mother, Theresa. Since back then there was no connection between Palestine and Germany, the post passed through Hungary, from where Frau Ilka forwarded Oscar's letters from Palestine to his mother and family in Ostrava.

72 *Acki and Ocki*: The family nicknames for Lilian's two brothers, Carl-Axel and Oskar von Löwenadler. During the war Oskar was liaison officer in the Swedish army (with the *Wehrmacht*), facilitating the transit from Germany to Norway.

73 *Steninge*: a suburb in Halmstad Municipality on the Swedish coast, and where Lilian's mother, Gertrude, rented a summer cottage. MS

74 *Pontoppidan*: Henrik Pontoppidan (1857–1943), modern Danish writer, naturalist in style. In 1917 he received the Nobel Prize, which he shared with Karl Gjellerup.

75 *The Weavers*: refers to the German Ore Mountains region where weaving was one of the main traditional occupations. MS

76 *President Benesch's resignation*: The Munich agreement, September 29, 1938 (Annexation of the Sudetenland to the German Reich; the autonomy of Slovakia and Carpatho-Ukraine), the betrayal of the French-Soviet mutual assistance treaty, which was aimed against Germany and was supplemented by a mutual assistance treaty between the USSR and Czechoslovakia, and the weakness of The Little Entente (treaty between Romania, Yugoslavia and Czechoslovakia) all led to the Czech president's resignation.

77 *I am sitting on Your Bed*: a manuscript found later, from the time when Ilse Weber familiarized herself with the idea to send Hanuš to safety in England.

78 *Wellner*: Jossel Wellner, acquaintance of Lilian and Ilse, member of Ilse's cultural group.

79 *Zdenka* (Drapalova): Youth friend of Ilse and neighbor from Witkowitz. Before their deportation, Ilse and Willi had left a file with papers for safekeeping with her.

80 *Tausend Worte Englisch*: Thousand English Words. MS

81 *Die Weisse Krankheit*, *The White Disease* and *Die Mutter*, *The Mother*. MS

82 *Settler in Palestine*: Willi Weber worked as member of a Chalutz (pioneer) group for nine years in Palestine where he contracted malaria.

83 *The Baldwin Fund*: Following the November 9, 1938 pogrom in Germany, on November 15, a group of prominent leaders of the British Jewish community met with
the British Prime Minister, Neville Chamberlain, to request the entry of unaccompa-
nied Jewish child refugees from Europe for which they promised to take financial and
physical responsibility. On November 21, the British government announced it would
allow into Britain all of the refugee children whose maintenance could be guaranteed.
A significant amount was to be provided by the British Jewish community, and the rest
was to be raised through a non-sectarian charity, the Lord Baldwin Fund. MS

84 *Grünspan*: a pun that means both a Jewish surname and verdigris; a green or bluish
deposit naturally occurring on copper or brass. MS

85 *Hindu Song*: or the "Indian Guest" from Rimsky-Korsakov's *Sadko*. MS

86 *servus*: a salutation used in Central and Eastern Europe for greeting or parting.

87 *Hackenkreuze*: swastikas. MS

88 *Anschluss*: Connection. Hitler's definition for annexing Austria. MS

89 *Dummheiten*: stupid things. MS

90 *Frl.*: abbreviation for Fräuline (English: Miss).

91 *Affidavit*: A documented statement given under oath explaining a person's living circumstances, including a guarantee to cover the immigrant's living expenses until he or
she became able to support herself. An affidavit by friends and acquaintances outside
Germany or Czechoslovakia was required for emigration to England or the USA.

92 *Barbican-Mission*: The Barbican Mission was founded in England in the 19th century
by evangelical and interdenominational societies for the explicit purpose of convert-
ing Jews. In 1938, it offered Jewish children in Prague a ticket to freedom in exchange
for entering the Christian fold. The Mission rescued about 60 children from Prague.
MS

93 7:30. MS

94 Sic. MS

95 *Office*: Willi opened a small collection agency after he and Ilse married. MS

96 *Stürmer* (The Attacker): A weekly Nazi tabloid from 1923 to 1945. It formed a significant constituent of the Nazi propaganda and was fervently antisemitic. MS

97 *Gajda Party*: Czechoslovakian Fascist movement based on the Fascism of Benito Mus-
solini and led by Radola Gajda, a Czech-Serbian military commander and politician.
MS

98 Lp: Chilean Pesos. MS

99 *Mr. Winton*: Sir Nicholas George Winton (1909), British stockbroker. He organized

the rescue of more then 600 Czech children, mostly Jewish, during the months before the Second World War. The operation is known as the Czech Kindertransport. It was with the train of the Ostrava Kinderaktion that Hanuš arrived in England. In 1998, Winton was awarded, by President Václav Havel, the Masaryk Order, and in December 2002, he was knighted by Queen Elizabeth II for his service to humanity. In 2007, he was nominated for the Nobel Peace Prize by the initiative of thousands Czech school children. Further letters by Ilse with mention of Winton do not exist as they were probably confiscated by the censor. See pages 264-265 as well as footnotes 1 and 3 in Afterword.

100 *Zofiah*: Wife of Oscar Mareni, Ilse's brother. Hanuš received this letter from Oscar Mareni during a visit to Jerusalem.

101 *the truth prevails*: Hanuš adopted President Tomáš Garrigue Masaryk's motto: "Pravda vítězí!" Masaryk chose those words for the newly-established Czech Republic from Jan Hus (1370?–1415) and it also played a major role in his political biography.

102 *Nazdar*: Next to *ahoj* in Czech, a common oral greeting up to this day. In the 20s and 30s it was also prevalent as a form of greeting in letters.

103 *Ať tě husa kopne!*: The goose should kick you! A family saying of the Webers.

104 *Uncle Walter*: Walter Freed, husband of Willi's sister Selma.

105 *Babička*: grandmother in Czech. MS

106 *Vyšehrad*: A high fort south of the Prague Castle, on the opposite bank of the Vltava (Moldau) river. According to legend it was the seat of the first Czech rulers, above all the legendary ruler Libuše, ancestress of the Czech people. The Vyšehrad cemetery was established in the 1870s as a national burial ground. Among the buried are composer Antonín Dvořák, Bedřich Smetana, and the conductor Rafael Kubelík, as well as the poet and journalist, Jan Neruda.

107 *Božena Němcová* (1820–1862): Considered the most significant representative of 19th century Czech literature. Like George Sand, her model, she rebelled against the dictated restrictive roles for women. Her first published text in 1843 was a lyrical appeal "To the Czech Women." From 1845 she published stories as well as her own versions of Czech and Slovakian folktales. Her main work is the novel *Babička* (Grandmother) from 1855.

108 *Kočkenen*: cuddle.

109 *Kde domov můj*: Where is my home? A song written by the composer František Škroup and the playwright Josef Kajetán Tyl for a comic play first performed in 1834. In 1918, the first verse became the Czech part of the national anthem. MS

110 *Omama*: granny in German. MS

111 *Buchteln*: Bohemian sweet rolls made of yeast and filled with jam, poppy seeds or curd

and baked in a large pan so that they stick together. MS

112 *As many languages you know, as many times you're a mensch*: This sentence is a Masaryk-quotation which Hanuš Weber remembers from his childhood. The list of supposed originators is long. Most likely it leads back to a saying by Karl V. (1500–1558): "*Quot linguas calles, tot homines vales.*" In the Czech cultural context, the saying also leads back to Johann Amos Comenius (1592–1670).

113 *Manistana (Ma Nishtana)*: The four questions, part of the Haggadah that tells the story of the Exodus from Egypt on Seder evening of the Passover festival. Traditionally these questions are sung by the youngest at the table.

114 *Vineyards: Vinohrady*, an area that was home to the royal vineyards from the 14th century, later became a garden city and was incorporated into Prague in 1922. MS

115 *Ach, synku, synku* (Ach, my son, my son): Thomáš Masaryk's favorite song.

116 *Aunt Meller*: Grete Meller, a Sudeten German who was married to a Czech Jew and lived in Prague. They were friends with Ilse and her family. Her husband was deported to Theresienstadt. It was through her that the mail was sent from Sweden to the camp: letters and parcels from Gertrude and Hanuš to Ilse, Willi and Tommy in Theresienstadt.

117 *Čeladná*: a village in the Moravian-Silesian regions of the Czech Republic, at the foot of the Moravian–Silesian Beskids mountain range. MS

118 *Öre*: one Swedisch krona is divided into 100 öre. MS

119 "*My Little Boy*": *Mein Bübele* in the original. 'Bub' in German means boy, and 'Bubele' means in Yiddish sweetie or darling. MS

120 *farbror*: uncle in Swedish. MS

121 *tant*: *Tante* in German means aunt. MS

122 *Mladý hlasatel*: Young Announcer, was a Czech weekly magazine for youth with information from different disciplines. It was issued from June 1935 until May 1941, when it was closed by the Nazis. MS

123 *Bårarp*: small town south west of Stockholm. MS

124 *The Jews*: this poem was written around 1940 and discovered later.

125 *Frau Treen*: Lilian. MS

126 October 28. MS

127 *Carl Larsson* (1853–1919): Swedish painter, whose book about his family *The House in the Sun*, 1909, made him famous in the German-speaking world. Postcards prints of his paintings, representing Swedish nature and customs, were widely distributed, as well as prints of his painting the *Lucia* festival, celebrated in Sweden on December

13th, in previous centuries the day of winter solstice. *Lucia* is a young girl wearing white robes and a candle-lit wreath on her head.

128 *Budulinka*: a Czech fairytale. MS

129 *Billroth Batiste*: water-proof material named after Theodor Billroth, founding father of modern abdominal surgery. MS

130 *Thirty hellers*: approximately 1.25 US cents in 1941. MS

131 *Nana*: Had been Hanuš' nanny and regarded as part of the family. Hanuš visited her after the war and Willi aided her financially. MS

132 *Martha*: A friend of Ilse. She hid some of her letters, articles and pictures.

133 Aunt Haberfeld: not a family member according to Hanuš' memory. MS

134 *Sixty Hellers*: around 2.5 American cents in 1941. MS

135 *"eternal light"*: an ironic hint to the "Ner Tamid," the eternal light that hangs above the ark in any synagogue. MS

136 *"Gaudeamus"*: "So Let Us Rejoice," a popular academic festive song in many European countries. MS

137 *Barmizwah*: Bar Mitzvah, which literally, in Hebrew, means "son of commandments." When a boy reaches his thirteenth year he is recognized by Jewish tradition as having the same rights and religious duties as an adult.

138 *Mormor*: grandmother in Swedish. MS

139 *songbook*: Ilse sent Hanuš a songbook *Deutsches Lautenlied*. It contains around 600 German folk and art songs.

140 *Your Lilli*: probably Ilse didn't sign her name here because she took a risk in writing a longer letter than permitted.

141 *T.G*: Thank God. MS

POEMS

1 See: Ulrike Migdal, Afterword, pp.275-76.

2 *The Way to Theresienstadt*: The "new-comers" had to get off at the Bauschowitz (Bohušovice) train station and walk, goaded by guards and with their luggage, the more than two kilometers to Theresienstadt. From June 1943, a connecting track (built by inmates) reached into the core of the camp, concealing arrivals and deportations from the outside world.

3 *seventy centimeters*: 27 inches. MS

4 *A Satchel Speaks*: The arriving inmates tried hard to keep most of their luggage with

them. They were allowed to take 50 kilograms, and carried it themselves to Theresienstadt. The big luggage pieces that had been taken from them at the train station were
brought to the "Sluice Barrack" (see footnote 24) and most of the contents were sent
to the Reich as "winter help." Whatever was not sent was brought to the yard, where
each searched for whatever was left from his possessions.

5 *Picture*: Traditional hearses from the disbanded Jewish communities in Bohemia were
brought to Theresienstadt and served there as transportation for everything, from
bread to corpses. They were pulled by men, women and children.

6 *bed*: Due to shortage of beds some children had to sleep on the floor (in the camp
dialect this space was called *Notbelag*, i.e. "emergency billet"). As a result, those who
had to relieve themselves at night stumbled over them.

7 *ward*: *Marodka* in the camp dialect.

8 *Ukolébavka*: Lullaby in the original Czech, followed by translation from German.

9 *Little Lullaby*: also titled "Lullaby for Hanička."

10 *To Go Home*: Behind the big fair building in Prague there were primitive shanties
that in the summer were used for displaying radios, washing machines etc. Those
who were listed for a transport had to assemble there, were registered, and most of
their belongings were taken again. Waiting for the transport, the people often had to
sleep on the bare floor for many days with no heating or any food; in winter the water
hydrant was mostly frozen and there were no amenities.

11 *Eldertransport*: Elder Transport, term for a transport deporting people older than sixty
five. There is another version of this poem, with slight variations.

12 "*Oh Fallada . . .* ": The poem draws on the "Goose Girl," a German fairy tale published by the Brothers Grimm. It tells the story of a betrayed princess whose loyal
magical horse was killed, but its talking head hung under the doorway where the
princess, who became a plain servant, passed every morning. Ilse quotes probably
from the 1857 version of this legend. Quotation in English: Lang Andrew ed. "Goose
Girl." *The Blue Fairy Book*. New York: Dover, 1965. (Originally published 1889.) MS

13 *The Seven*: On February 26, 1942, seven young men and, shortly afterward an additional nine members of the so called "construction crew," were hanged. Their "crime":
sending home forbidden letters. Jiří Lauscher, who witnessed the events and after the
war interviewed numerous witnesses from Theresienstadt, recalls that one of the condemned, shortly before the execution, sang: "Until millions of us will march against the
wind . . . " Silent prayers were held in the ghetto that evening. (The original version
of this poem is lost. It was translated from Czech into German by Hans Gärtner.)

14 *The Sheep from Lidice*: On June 10, 1942, Reiner Heydrich, head of the RSHA (Reich
Main Security Office) and the Nazi overseer of the Bohemia and Moravia Protectorate, was assassinated. In retaliation, the occupying forces destroyed the Czech village

of Lidice. The men were shot, the women and children deported to concentration camps, and the livestock delivered to Theresienstadt. Although historically the sheep in Theresienstadt at the time were not from Lidice, the poem symbolizes the tragic fate of so many. See Tomas Fedorovic, "Sheep from Lidice in Terezin—Fact or Myth?" In: Památník Terezin. Newsletter. *Educational and informative bulletin of the Terezín Memorial.* Newsletter 4/2013. MS

15 *Dawn*: many children died from typhus. No cure was available.

16 *Lute*: although it was illegal, Ilse managed to find a guitar which she called her "lute." MS

17 *A Stranger's Cradle*: Ilse Weber wrote this poem for a "poetic competition" organized by Philipp Manes, the founder of a series of lectures in Theresienstadt. From 200 contributions, Ilse's was awarded first place along with a lecture by Gertrude Spies. Philipp Manes, who in Autumn 1944 went to Auschwitz with the last transport, wrote a comprehensive report about the cultural activities in Theresienstadt. See: Philipp Manes. *Als Ob's ein Leben wär. Tatsachenbericht Theresienstadt 1942–1944*, Berlin: 2005 Ullstein Verlag, Hers. Ben Markov/Klaus Leist. Published in English as: *As If It Were Life: A WWII Diary from the Theresienstadt Ghetto*, Trans. Janet Foster, Ben Barkow and Klaus Leist, UK: Palgrave Macmillan, 2009.

18 *Modlitba*: prayer, in the original Czech.

19 *Slovenly Peter*: *Struwwelpeter*, was the subject and name of well-known children's book vividly showing consequences of forbidden behavior. It was written and illustrated by Heinrich Hoffmann and translated from German into many languages. It was translated into English in 1891 by Mark Twain but, because of copyright issues, his "Slovenly Peter" was not published until 1935. MS

20 *a seventy-five centimeter space*: Twenty-nine inches wide. These beds were called in Theresienstadt dialect *Kavalett*, a term in Austrian soldiers' language for bed frame. Each bed frame was 180 cm long and 75 cm wide. Some of the women slept in beds that were arranged in double-or triple-decker tiers.

21 *Hearse*: In the evening, after the arrival of a transport, hearses collected deportees who had collapsed or died on the route (see footnote 5). The inmates that pulled the hearses (sent from Jewish cemeteries in the "protectorate,") were known as "the rolling cart team."

22 *Bauschowitz*: see footnote 2.

23 *O.D*: *Ordnungsdienst*, security service; a subordinate Jewish police group that, until the summer of 1942, served in the isolated barracks. It later was deployed merely to keep order. The group included women.

24 *Schleuse, Schleuse*: Sluice, Sluice. Collection place for the arriving or departing deportees,

where their luggage was searched for objects one was not allowed to take: money, musical instruments, articles of value, tobacco etc. The so called "contraband" was confiscated. The looting of the newcomers' luggage was called "*Schleusen/ Schleusen*," "sluice/sluice." These words acquired the meaning of stealing. To "sluice" was to steal. One "sluiced/sluiced" a piece of bread, potatoes, or coals.

25 *Ration Card*: Points Card in the camp's dialect. With the help of ration coupons one could buy at (pseudo) "businesses" clothes, underwear, plates, cutlery and other commodities that the SS had robbed from the inmates earlier. However, "purchasing" was possible only when in possession of ghetto money.

26 *Prominent Figures*: A group of people marked by the SS as "prominent" and with certain privileges. The group included former military officers with high military decorations (or their widows), scientists and figures with international reputations. At times they arrived with their own "directive" or could, for instance, apply for better conditions. They received better accommodations, exemptions from forced labor, or easier work, and protection from deportation which, as it turned out, was limited. In the camp dialect the word "prominent" was used for any preferential treatment.

27 *Construction Crew*: AK in the camp dialect. AKI (arrival on 14.2.1941) and AKII (arrival on 4.12. 1941) were the names of two transports with young Jewish men from Prague, economists, administrators, engineers, physicians, craftsmen and workers, who built the ghetto, i.e. prepared the garrison town for its function as "gathering and transition camp" for the planned mass transportations. The AK, mostly young Jewish men, received an elevated status with some "privileges" like protection from deportation (which was removed in 1944—only few AK people survived).

28 *Evening*: As collective punishment for breaking regulations, of which inmates were never precisely informed, electricity was turned off. As a result, tens of thousands people in attics, washrooms and latrines groped in the dark.

29 *Ration*: *Menage* in the camp's dialect, a term for cooked meals. The term originated in Austrian and Czech military parlance.

30 *The Engineer's Barracks*: *Ženijní* in Czech. A building once used as headquarters of military engineering troops. (*Genietruppen:* engineer troops in Austrian German, or pioneer troops); the Engineer's barracks served until summer 1942 as a police residence. After that it housed old and sick people.

31 *Transport to Poland*: "Transport" in camp dialect refers to the mass deportation to the extermination camps in Poland. The Council of Elders and the camp's administration decided who would be deported. "Announced" (Austragen) in camp dialect, refers to the distribution of the deportees' names.

32 *Council of Elders* (Jewish Elders): Jewish administrative directors of the barracks.

33 *Ahasuerus*: King of Persia in the Purim story (Book of Esther). Known to the Greeks

as Xerxes. His successor, Cyrus, restored Jerusalem to the Jewish exiles in Babylon. In some versions of the legend of the 'Wandering Jew,' his name is Ahasuerus. This is also the name by which Emmanuel Kant referred to the 'Wandering Jew' in his work *The Only Possible Argument in Support of a Demonstration of the Existence of God*. MS

34 *A Transport is Called Up*: a slightly different version of this poem circulated in the camp with the title: "Five Thousand are Leaving Tomorrow."

35 *Barren of Earthly Possessions*: another version of this poem deviates slightly from this, which is probably the original one.

36 *Emigrant Song*: Some copies have alternate titles: "Everything Will Be All Right," "Swallow Your Tears" and "Do Not Despair."

37 *Wiegala*: Ilse Weber and her compositions, some with piano accompaniment, appear on a list of Theresienstadt's established composers in Joža Karas' work: *Music in Terezin*, (New York, 1985).

AFTERWORD

1 *Nicholas George Winton*: was the son of Jewish emigrants (which is the reason he was never awarded the title "Righteous Among the Nations") and was awarded knighthood for his deeds. See also footnote 99 in the Letters as well as footnote 3 below. MS

2 *Robert Maxwell* (1923–1991): Czechoslovakian born British media proprietor and Member of Parliament. Born in Czechoslovakia, he escaped the Nazis and joined the British army, where he was decorated. MS

3 Winton's operation has been the subject of three films by Slovak filmmaker Matej Mináč: the drama *All My Beloved Ones* (1999), the documentary *The Power of Good* (2002), which won an Emmy Award, and the documentary drama *Nicky's Family* (2011). MS

4 "*At home . . .* " English in the Original.

5 "*Month . . .* " English in the original.

6 "*Received . . .* " English in the original.

7 *several drawings*: Among the papers that Willi hid in the Theresienstadt "grave" were also six drawings by Malva Schalek, who in the prewar years was a court draughtswoman and worked with Egon Erwin Kisch: portraits of Ilse and Willi, the drawing printed in the book of *Ilse with a guitar*, a representation *Ilse at the door of the infirmary* as well as two drawings of the Theresienstadt barracks. In addition, the children's drawings "Earth" and "For Aunt Ilse Heaven" that are reproduced here.

8 "*Svoboda-Army*": Ludvík Svoboda (1895–1979): Following the annexation of the

Sudetenland by the German Reich 1938 and the call for a Slovakian autonomy, he took part in setting up the resistance organization Obrana národa. In the summer of 1939 he fled from the National Socialists to Poland where he became the head of the Czechoslovakian military unit abroad, which he took to the Soviet Union after Poland's defeat in September 1939. After Nazi Germany's invasion of the USSR in June 1941, he became commander of the first Czechoslovakian independent battalion and, in March 1943, took part at the front as brigade general. The battalion gradually grew to a 60,000 soldier army corps. From October 1944 until 1945 the "Svoboda-Army" under their commander, fought next to the Red Army and liberated the areas of Moravia and Slovakia. Until 1950 Svoboda was defence minister of the communist Czechoslovakian government under the leadership of Klement Gottwald, and the army supreme commander; 1949–52 and 1968–76 member of the Central Committee of the Czechoslovakian Communist Party. In March 1968, when the reformers of the "Prague Spring" elected him state president, he initially resisted the Soviet intervention. He resigned in May 1975 and was replaced by Gustáv Husák.

9 See footnote 14 p.330. MS

10 The sheep became a metaphor for the residents of the Theresiensadt Ghetto. MS

11 *Freizeitgestaltung*: "Administration for Leisure Activities"; initially, cultural activities at concentration camps were illegal and underground. However in 1941, as Theresienstadt became a "model Jewish city," the SS tolerated any activity that could be defined cultural, for propaganda purposes, in order to mislead the Allies and the Red Cross. MS

12 *Socialist Youth Organization*: Československý svaz mládeže.

13 Hanuš kept a diary, gave radio and TV interviews and was interviewed by Ulrika Migdal. MS

14 *ČSSR*: Czechoslovak Socialist Republic. MS

15 Officially, he was an employee of the Prague Radio, but he received permission from the foreign ministry to work for the Swedish media as a so-called registered correspondent, however without accreditation. MS

16 *Expressen*: one of the two nationwide evening tabloids in Sweden, founded in 1944. MS

17 *Oscar Mareni* . . . the Herlinger family chronicle (The Judicial Heritage and Its Children 1870–1939): No Year. The Yad Vashem Archives, Jerusalem, file nos. 0.64/72.

18 Information is taken from Oscar (Abner) Mareni's autobiography; "Die Erbrichterei und ihre Kinder 1870–1939." MS

19 *Das Kränzchen*: Literally Kränzchen is a small garland, but it also means coffee-party as well as friendship-circle. See footnote 34 in Ilse's Letters. MS

20 *Erbrichterei*: see footnote 59 in Ilse's Letters as well as footnote 21 below. MS

21 *Fojtství*: A Fojt was in old-Slavic a sort of a judge or a mayor, elected by the local villagers, who managed the village's administration. He also ruled on quarrels between the village's people. The word "Fojt" or "Fojta" is rarely used in Czech today; instead, these officials are called "Starosta." "Fojtství" was the Czech name for the "Erbrichterei." Ilse's grandfather had bought from the Viennese Bank Rothschild the rights for the house in 1870 and gave the building this name, which was mounted on the house's facade in German and Czech. After the invasion of the Wehrmacht it became "The Brown House," the headquarters of the Germans. It later became "Stalin-House," headquarters of the Communists, and, finally in 1950, after an accommodating renovation, the "Hornický Dům," the "Miners' House."

22 *Kapp-Putsch*: A coup attempt led by Wolfgang Kapp and General Walther von Lüttwitz on March 1920 (triggered off by the order to dissolve the Ehrhardt Brigade). The German government was forced to flee from Berlin, but the coup failed after a few days as a result of a general strike.

23 *G.I.F.T*: German acronym for Geist, Intelligenz, Freundschaft, Treue. The group, which existed until the late 1920s, chose an arrow as its sign, which, according to Ilse, was crafted from brass by a tinsmith. Its interior was hollow and the so-called "honor scroll" which contained the circle's laws and a list of its members was kept in it. Some 40 cm long, it closed on one end with a valve and the other end was pointed. During debates, the chairperson could grant the floor to a member by rolling the arrow aiming its pointed end at a specific person. The inner circle of the G.I.F.T met for a while every day; its members agreed about the program and on who could join the core. The meetings of the outer circle took place once a week.

24 *Die Fackel* (The Torch): see footnote 47 in Ilse's Letters. MS

25 *Die Rote Fahne* (The Red Flag): Created on November 9, 1918 by Karl Liebknecht and Rosa Luxemburg in Berlin, first as a left wing revolutionary newspaper, and in 1919 with the founding of the German Communist Party, it became the central publication of German communism. MS

26 Oscar Mareni died in 2011. MS

27 *Die Wahrheit* (The Truth): A Jewish weekly paper that appeared in Vienna between 1885 and 1938; it was banned in Germany when the Nazi party assumed power in 1933, and in Austria in 1938, when Nazi Germany annexed Austria. MS

28 *Jüdische Zeitung* (Jewish Newspaper): there were two Jewish newspapers in Breslau, Germany: *Jewish National Paper*, 1895–1937, and *The Breslau Jewish Community Paper*, 1924–1938. MS.

29 *Mährisch-Ostrauer Morgenzeitung:* Mährisch-Ostrau Morning Paper, a liberal newspaper that had seven issues per week. It appeared from 1913 until 1938. MS

30 *Selbstwehr* (Self Defense): A Jewish-Zionist weekly paper in German language that appeared in Prague from 1907 until end of 1938. From 1919 to 1938, the paper was edited by the philosopher Felix Weltsch, a close friend of Franz Kafka and Max Brod, who were contributors and avid readers of the paper. MS

31 *"Who . . . abode"*: from a hymn by Joachim Magdeburg, (1525–1587) German Lutheran theologian and Church poet and composer. MS

32 *Paul Keller*: 1873–1932, popular German writer and publicist. MS

33 *"Das Letzte Märchen"* (The Last Tale): a story about a journalist who arrives in a fairy-tale realm below the ground to establish a newspaper and blunders into the intrigues of the royal household. MS

34 *"Die Glocke"*: Most likely refers to Friedrich Schiller's poem published in 1798 "Das Lied von der Glocke," or "The Song of the Bell," often translated as "The Lay of the Bell." It is one of the most famous poems of German literature, and with its 430 lines, one of the longest. *"Frau Sorge"*: "Dame Care," (1887) is the poem that opens a novel with the same title by Hermann Sudermann (1857–1928), German author and playwright. MS

35 *Pustevna*: mountain huts and resort in the Beskids.

36 *being evacuated these days*: Ilse, Willi and Tommy were deported to Theresienstadt on February 6, 1942.

37 *T.G*: Thank God.

38 Jewish youth center: was opened daily, as most of the attending children had no place to go to during the day. MS

39 *Houses with numbers*: Only with the preparation for the "embellishments" of the camp did the streets receive names. Until then L stood for longitudinal streets and C for crossroads (*Langestrasse* and *Querstrasse*). The streets were all straight and intersected at a right angle; they were numbered in order; L204 for instance meant house number 4 in the second lengthways street.

40 *Dear Oscar*: Undated letter from Willi Weber to Oscar Mareni. The original letter is stored in the Yad Vashem Archives, Jerusalem, file nos. 0.64/73 and 0.64/72.

41 *P.O: Palestine Office*. MS

42 *Jankef Edelstein*: Jacob Edelstein (1903–1944), a Zionist, from 1933 director of the Palestine Office in Prague. On December 4, 1941 he was deported to Theresienstadt (with the first construction commando), and became the first president of the Jewish Council of Elders i.e. leader of the Jewish "self-administration" of the camp. On December 1943 he was deported to Auschwitz and shot on June 20, 1944.

43 Ruth Elias: *Die Hoffnung erhielt mich am Leben—Mein Weg von Theresienstadt und Auschwitz nach Israel*. Piper Verlag, München, 1988, translated by Margo Bettauer

as: *Triumph of Hope. From Theresienstadt and Auschwitz to Israel*. John Wiley & Sons, United States, in association with the United States Holocaust memorial Museum 1999.

44 *k.u.k.*: The German phrase kaiserlich und königlich (Imperial and Royal). It is a reference to the Austro-Hungarian Empire. MS

45 *Ostrava Special Action*: refers to the early deportations in connection with the Nisko-Plan, organized by Adolf Eichmann. MS

46 See footnote 31 in The Letters.

47 *counterfeiting team*: counterfeiting currency was a part of "Operation Bernhard," a scheme to crash the Allied economies. MS

48 *Erik Jan Hanussen*: Born Hermann Schneider (1889 Vienna–1933 Berlin), was an Austrian Jewish publicist, charlatan and clairvoyant. He was active during the Weimar Republic and subject to numerous scandals and court cases. In 1930 he started a monthly occult magazine which drew the attention of the rising Nazi elite. Hanussen's associations with Nazis and later Hitler have titled him as "Hitler's Nostradamus" and the "prophet of the Third Reich." He was assassinated in 1933 in Berlin. MS

ABOUT THE TYPE

This book was set in Adobe Garamond. Garamond is a group of many old-style serif typefaces, originally those designed by Claude Garamond and other 16th century French designers, and now many modern revivals. Though his name was written as 'Garamont' in his lifetime, the typefaces are invariably spelled 'Garamond'. Garamond typefaces are popular and often used, particularly for printing body text and books.